LIVERPOOL
THE FIRST 1,000 YEARS

written by

Arabella McIntyre-Brown

photographs by

Guy Woodland

garlic
PRESS

Liverpool
the first 1,000 years

Written by **Arabella McIntyre-Brown**
Photography by **Guy Woodland**

Proofreader: Judy Tasker
Extra research: Fiona Shaw
Production: Ken Ashcroft, Angela Hurren
Cover design: Ken Ashcroft

Supplementary photography:
p30 Liverpool Empire Theatre
p44 Liverpool Football Club
p162 and p214 (*two ladies*) David Travis, Simon Travis,
Martin Murphy of the Disability Equality Project
p173 Chris Brown

ISBN 1-904099-00-9

First published in November 2001
Reprinted January 2002
Garlic Press
PO Box 72
Lark Lane
Liverpool L17 9YX

www.garlicpress.co.uk

Printed and bound in Spain by Bookprint, S.L.

Authors' note

AMB: Stuffing 1,000 years of Liverpool into 240 pages is impossible. It's been fun trying, but I'm all too well aware that some readers will be aghast at my leaving out this story, that fact or those people. To do this city justice would need at least 1,000 pages and I'm not sure even that would be enough. As I have researched each chapter subjects have been crying out for entire books all to themselves; many have already been written by erudite and enthusiastic Liverpool experts, and many more are waiting to be written. Some readers may find it bizarre that I have kept football, the Beatles and one or two other enormous subjects to a page or two, given their impact on the city – but this book is an attempt to show how much more there is to Liverpool than the clichés.

I have made every attempt to ensure that the words are accurate and fair; I have had a lot of help to do so, and any errors are mine alone.

I would welcome any suggestions for inclusion in future editions – do please write to me, or get in touch through the Garlic Press website.

GW: Everyone has their favourite views of Liverpool and sees things in their own way; I have tried to be impartial in photographing the city for this book, and hope that the images show Liverpool as a city rich in history and magnificent in stature.

The process of photographing over the last six months has added to my archive of Liverpool images built up over the last 15 years: a collection which inevitably reflects my personal interests and the projects I have worked on. This physical book is an end result but also the start of something else. The words cover Liverpool's past as well as its present, but the images are all contemporary and will become a social document of Liverpool in 2001.

We cannot know what will become valuable in the future, as the city evolves; look back on photographs from the past and it is often the mundane or unconsidered details that become precious in time to come. Who knows which images in this book will become important in 10 or 100 years time?

Guy Woodland
0151 608 7006
71 Prenton Road West Prenton Bhead Merseyside
CH 42 9PZ

Acknowledgements

Our thanks go to everyone at the University of Liverpool who helped us get the book from an idea to this glossy publication – and for the University's generous support which made the project feasible.

Special thanks, though, to Ray Buss and David Bamber, without whose enthusiasm, support and expert advice this book would have remained a nice idea.

The team has done us proud – Ken, Judy, Fiona; Bill Moore, David Ridley – have all worked their customary magic to make us look cleverer than we deserve, for which we are endlessly grateful. Special thanks to Angela Hurren for a very long weekend's work.

For their expert advice and support, our thanks to Lew Baxter, Jon Flinn, Daniel Harris, David Nicholls, Jackie Humphreys, Joe Riley, Mike Storey.

And to all those who have given Arabella their time and the benefit of their considerable knowledge – including Adrian Allen, Annette Butler, Peter Rowlands, and Bob Williams – my grateful thanks.

Guy would like to thank Jenny Douglas at Liverpool Vision; Colette Gill at Ropewalks; Ian Archer at the RLPO, Tom Miller at LCC, the Owen Ellis Partnership, Intercity / Corporate Culture, LIPA, Erik Lynch, the Park Rangers, the Anglican Cathedral, Aintree Race Course, Life Long Learning, Villages, and all those at Liverpool City Council. Thanks to Tricia Duncan who gave me my first professional commission when she worked with MEB.

Special thanks from Guy to a very patient partner – Debbie Woodland – and from Arabella to a forgiving family.

THE UNIVERSITY
of LIVERPOOL

07968742165

Liverpool
the first 1,000 years

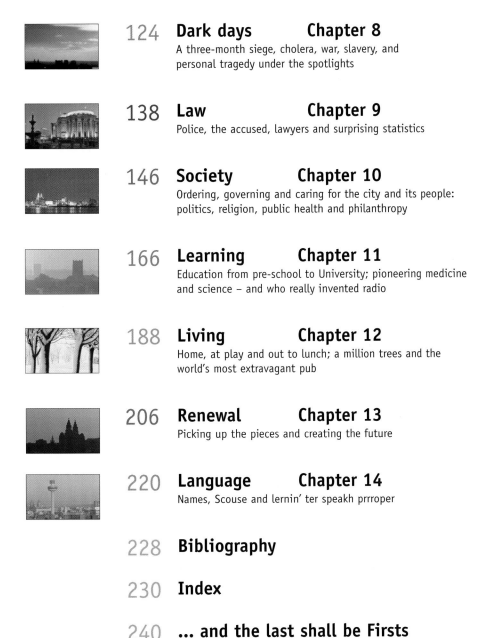

ver the years, many books have been written about our great city, its people, its architecture, its history, its sporting achievements, its humour, its successes and its failures. This book has all of these elements and more, but it is the first of its kind, combining the story of Liverpool's past with wonderful images of Liverpool today and an enthusiastic look at the excellent prospects for Liverpool's future. I was born in Aberdeen and spent most of my life in Scotland but, having lived and worked here in Liverpool for the best part of 10 years, I am proud to describe myself as an adopted Liverpudlian.

My 10 years here represent just 1% of the first 1,000 years of Liverpool which this book describes, but I am a great enthusiast for the city and fully committed to its regeneration, especially as we approach the 800th anniversary of the granting of the city's Royal Charter in 2007 and, I hope, its designation as European Capital of Culture in 2008.

I know that both of the authors of this attractive book are as dedicated to Liverpool as I am, even though they too are relative newcomers. Arabella McIntyre-Brown, who wrote the text, was born in West Sussex and came to Liverpool in 1988. Guy Woodland, who took the photographs, was born in Karachi and came here in 1979. Both are passionate about their adopted city.

Such passion is common amongst Liverpool's citizens, whether they be born and bred here or recent converts like myself. It is a testimony to the qualities and strengths of Liverpool that it has such a positive effect on so many people, including a large proportion of the many thousands of students who come to the city to study each year. Some of that attractiveness is down to the complex and rich history of Liverpool, but much is due to the friendliness of its people, the excellence of its cultural and sporting activities and, of course, the beauty of its architecture and open spaces. All of these are captured in some way in this book.

Many institutions and companies are also committed to Liverpool, especially those which have their origins in the city. Typical of these is the University of Liverpool, created by the citizens of Liverpool in the 19th century 'for advancement of learning and ennoblement of life'. The University today is proud of its roots and of its role as a key player in the heart of Liverpool. As a research-led university with excellent teaching, we are also working hard with a whole range of partners from business and industry to help bring wealth back to the city and help to restore Liverpool to its former glory.

As the University looks forward to celebrating the centenary of the granting of its own Royal Charter in 2003, I am delighted that we are able to sponsor the publication of this new book, which I am sure will be welcomed by all the many fans of Liverpool, wherever they may be living today. If you are not already a fan, then I am sure that you will catch more than a sense of what Liverpool was, is and will be, as you leaf through the pages that follow.

Professor Philip N Love CBE DL
Vice Chancellor, University of Liverpool

Very few cities in the world are famous enough to need no further address. No-one needs to ask where New York is, or San Francisco, Beijing, Paris, London, Sydney, Moscow, Hong Kong, Athens, Rome ... or Liverpool. No matter where you go in the world (outside Britain), say you come from Liverpool and people's faces light up with big smiles. It's almost certainly going to be one of two things that people associate with Liverpool: football or music. In the USA, it's music; in Brazil it's football; Japan – music; Greece – football.

But whatever foreigners think of when they hear the word 'Liverpool', it is positive. In Britain, the image is rather different. You'd think that Liverpool sprang into being 30 years ago, fully formed as a depressed northern city populated by work-shy, bolshie trouble makers, comedians and criminals. As for industry, or culture, or learning – tsk! Everyone knows the docks are dead, the city is a hideous blot, Scousers are stupid and aggressive, and they wouldn't know culture if they fell over it. Everyone knows that.

When I first came to this city taxi drivers – having established that I wasn't from round here – would commiserate with me at having to move to Liverpool. 'It's not so bad, love. Why do you come 'ere, anyway?' They'd be pleased when I ticked off a dozen reasons why I'd left London and moved up here, and told them that it had taken me half a day, on my first visit, to decide that this was the city for me. I had gone back, put my flat on the market, sold up and escaped north without a backwards glance.

It's not just that Liverpool people are friendly, or that I could afford to buy a house here. It's not only that Liverpool is warmed by the Gulf Stream or that the air is cleaner here than most other cities, or that it has 2,500 listed buildings and as many acres of park and woodland. It's the kindness of strangers, the human scale of the city, the lightness of heart, the battling spirit, the imagination, the passion and the expression.

When southern friends and family heard I was moving here, they said: 'You're mad!' or 'How brave!'. They all changed their minds when they came up here to visit. I felt instantly welcome here; I'm proud to call Liverpool home, and can't imagine living in another city.

As Liverpool reaches the end of its first thousand years, it can look back on a story that has been turbulent, thrilling, pioneering, desperate, joyful, ruthless, shaming, wealthy, powerful, depressing, glorious, hopeless, and hopeful. Like any city, Liverpool has its problems. Half a million people living in a small space will create dramas, tragedies and comedies; in this city the dramas are more exciting, the comedies funnier and the tragedies as tragic as anywhere else.

In the 1960s Liverpool was one of the coolest cities on the planet; by the 1980s it was the pariah city of Britain. How quickly people forget – within living memory Liverpool has been one of the world's most powerful trading cities and the main link between the Old and New Worlds. But it's not the first-ever radio broadcast that people remember, or the beginnings of the railways and the canals; not the world's largest Anglican cathedral or the start of the NSPCC and the RSPCA. The name Toxteth doesn't remind people of the Domesday Book and King John's hunting park. Liverpool is more famous for an ordinary road in a pleasant suburb (Penny Lane) than for a sporting event watched by over a billion people each spring.

Writing this book has given me a new perspective on Liverpool: looking at 1,000 years of the city's life, the shape of its growth and the turning points in its story, how its strengths in one century became its weaknesses in another, the heights of its power, the speed of its decline and the guts with which it is regenerating itself.

Geographically English, Liverpool is not an English city. From its earliest days Liverpool has attracted people from other places, people with an appetite for the new and the different – people with the courage to travel and explore, people with ideas, and people with the vision to back them. Risk takers, pioneers, entrepreneurs, inventors, reformers – this is not a place for quiet contemplation, but for doing, changing, trying.

God knows Liverpool has got a long way to go. But this is an extraordinary city, with a world-leading past and a world-class future; how exciting to be in at the start of its renaissance and the first of its next 1,000 years.

Arabella McIntyre-Brown

Here are two dozen of the city's many Liver Birds... but do you know where they are?

chapter 1
timeline

In his geography of 150 AD Ptolemy – the geographer of Alexandria – mentions Liverpool as Portus Segantiorum, but makes no mention of the Mersey estuary at all.

Some of the markings on the Calder Stones are extremely rare

The Norsemen who settled all over the Merseyside area, were forced out by the fierce resistance of Princess Elfleda, daughter of Alfred the Great, who in 916 AD built Runcorn Castle and a large fleet to repel the invaders.

Hard to imagine, perhaps, but 100, even 50 years ago Liverpool looked very different to the city we know today. One of the world's most famous waterfronts was only built in the first dozen years of the 20th century, after all, and the May Blitz destroyed so much of the city centre that photos of Liverpool in the 1930s are often hard to recognise as today's city. But go back in time some 4,000 years and there wasn't even the River Mersey. In the Neolithic period, about 2000 BC, this area was marshland and forest stretching miles alongside a big lake that extended about 30 miles from Warrington to Bootle (as we know them now). A primeval forest of oak, pine and birch stretched from Freshfield south-west across the top of the Wirral; some ancient oak tree stumps have been uncovered – a piece of oak from Leasowe has been carbon-dated to about 1740 BC.

The great 19th-century engineers Stephenson and Telford reckoned that it must have been an earthquake that created the Mersey estuary in Roman times, somewhere around 400 AD.

The earliest evidence we have of a settlement is the Calder Stones, now in the park named after them to the south of the city centre. The very rare megalithic tomb, older than Stonehenge, was composed of a dozen or more sandstone blocks that made up the burial chamber at the heart of a sand tumulus. Some of the stones were carved with cup and spiral markings – the only examples in England. The tops of the stones were visible in the mid-16th century, and in 1765 a local farmer dug into the tumulus for building materials and uncovered several urns. Forty years later, most of the burial mound was used to build houses, and one workman said he took several wheelbarrow loads of the burnt bone and ash from the burial chamber to use as fertiliser.

In 1840 the stones themselves were moved when the road was widened, and lay in a local farmer's field acting as cattle rubs till Joseph Walker set six of them in a circle in front of his house. Only in 1954 did the Liverpool Corporation move the stones into a greenhouse within Calderstones Park, where they remain.

American visitors can't understand how such a rare and important site can be so undervalued – isn't it time that the Calder Stones are given the respect and attention they deserve? How many people born in the city even know they exist?

Bronze Age Liverpool, between 1800 BC and 550 BC, saw the gradual switch to using bronze tools rather than stone and flint; bronze axes and arrowheads have been found in Knotty Ash, Woolton, Walton and Speke. But the biggest find from this period was in Wavertree, discovered in 1868 when a house was being built in North Drive. While digging the foundations the builders uncovered eight urns, one of which contained the bones of a child. The urns were close to their funeral pyres, and close by was a line of 14 upright stones 18 inches high and standing edge to edge.

Archaeological finds from the Iron Age (550 BC to 43 AD) are thin on Liverpool ground – a Celtic torque was found in Liverpool, and a 1st-century AD sandstone head was dug up in Mossley Hill. This was the time when Celts, Gauls and Phoenicians came to Britain, bringing the first coinage, metalworking skills and trading in tin, gold, slaves and dogs.

The Iron Age overlapped with the Roman invasion of Britain, when for several centuries life outside the main settlements continued much as it had since Neolithic times, the northern Celts resisting the influence of their Roman invaders and rulers.

Romans never settled in Liverpool itself, but built a fort at Chester (which they called Deva) in about 73 AD for the legions forced to stay in the North to try to keep some kind of control over the bolshie Brigantes (the Celtic tribe that lived in the north of England – no coincidence that their name is much same as the word 'brigand'). The XXth Legion, based at Deva from about 90 AD, could move easily between Deva and settlements in Wilderspool, Wigan, Manchester and north to the Ribble.

The most important Roman site in the Merseyside area is Wilderspool, near Warrington, but there was a camp in Woolton, and a Roman road found in Grassendale between Aigburth and Garston, south of the city centre. The Grassendale pavement, unearthed in 1858, was found only seven inches below the Victorian road, running south. Another section of the same road was found at Otterspool.

Once the Romans had gone, the northern Europeans moved in. The Saxons and Angles colonised Britain very successfully, and have left their mark on Liverpool with a handful of churches such as St Chad's in Kirkby and place names such as Bootle (from an Anglo-Saxon word for village: *botl*) and Aigburth (grove of oaks). Christianity began to take a hold, with holy men and women coming from all directions to convert the farming and fishing folk on the north-west coast.

Later still the Vikings arrived and settled (having been raiding for several centuries) in areas like Crosby, Kirkdale and Kirkby. Crosby (Old Norse for village of the cross) was named in 900 AD by Norsemen coming from the Isle of Man and Ireland; a hoard of coins found in Crosby included some from the reign of Saxon King Alfred, and Danil Gulfrith, King of Northumbria in 883.

St Patrick, on his way to Ireland, is said to have preached in Liverpool before setting sail. It was not an easy trip across the Irish Sea – he was shipwrecked off the Isle of Man (or was he captured by pirates and sold as a slave in Ireland?). The place where the saint preached is roughly where the Holy Cross Church is now, at the corner of Tithebarn Street and Marybone.

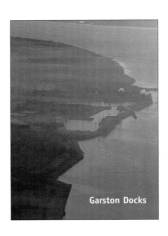

Garston Docks

The Pool was an inlet of the Mersey; the creek ran from what is now the Mersey Tunnel entrance by Old Haymarket, down to what is now Canning Place, where it joined the river.

Stochestede (Toxteth) is in the Domesday Book with a rent of four shillings; Esmedune (Smithdown) was worth 32 pennies to landlord Aethelmund.

The earliest record of the term charwoman is in Liverpool's Common Council records of 1596.

West Derby Castle was built around 1050 in the reign of Edward the Confessor; there are traces of it (not visible) between Croxteth Hall and Derby Chapel.

King John acquired Esmedune in 1204 to be part of his hunting park of Toxteth. As compensation, he gave the Thingwall estate to Esmedune's Saxon landlord Richard, son of Thurstan.

t is not Liverpool that gets the first mention in records, but Halewood – part of the little village of Hale to the south of Liverpool; the Wood of Hale appears on the map in 1001 AD according to the Domesday Book. Next on the roll comes the River Mersey, mentioned in a document of 1004 during the reign of Ethelread II. In the Domesday Book (1086) there is still no mention of Liverpool itself, although Smithdown, Toxteth and West Derby are named. The very first mention of Liverpool is in a deed signed by Prince John in 1190 (while his brother Richard I was off crusading): 'Know ye that we have granted, and this by our deed confirmed, to Henry Fitzwarine, son of Warine of Lancaster, the lands which King Henry our father gave to Warine his father, that is Ravensmeols, Ainsdale, Litherland, Liverpool and French Lea.'

Land 'between the Mersey and the Ribble' had originally been given by William the Conqueror to one Roger de Poictiers but, when he later betrayed the King, Poictiers forfeited his lands to the Crown. So it was, in 1165, that Henry II gave these lands to Warine of Lancaster as a fee for his services as a falconer.

In 1207, now King, John bought Liverpool back, and on 28th August 1207 signed the royal charter founding the town of Liverpool: 'John, by the grace of God King of England, to all his faithful people who have desired to have burgages at the township of Liverpul, greeting. Know ye that we have granted to all who have taken burgages at Liverpul that they shall have all liberties and free customs in the town of Liverpul which any free borough on the sea has in our land ....' The original charter, in Latin, signed by the King and witnessed by Simon de Pateshill, is still in the city archives.

There were a number of charters granted by various monarchs down the years. Henry III confirmed Town and Corporation for the sum of ten marks; Charles II's charter, however, took some privileges away from the town, presumably peeved at Liverpool's Roundhead leanings in the Civil War. In 1880 Queen Victoria made Liverpool a city, with the right to have a Lord Mayor granted in 1893.

King John's interest in Liverpool was as a point of departure to Ireland, for which he built Liverpool Castle (completed in 1237, long after his death). In 1272 there were 168 burgages (tenancies) and 840 inhabitants in the town; over the next six centuries the population would grow by almost 1,000 times.

In 1226 Liverpool's rents were worth just £9; when Edmund, Earl of Lancaster, died in 1298, his lands around Liverpool were assessed as worth £25 6s 10d for rents, the ferry, the mills, tolls and court dues; by 1327 the herbage of Toxteth Park alone was worth £11.

Liverpool, like most towns, was beset by plagues throughout its history; the Black Death of 1360 saw victims buried in the chapel yard (now St Nicholas's churchyard), but the plagues in 1548 and 1558 each wiped out 250 inhabitants – a fair proportion of Liverpool's population. This put the brakes on Liverpool's development and led the inhabitants to beg Elizabeth I for help as Liverpool was 'a decayed town', with a smaller population than 300 years earlier. The Queen's secretary Walsingham remarked upon 'the great number that be retailers and the small number or none at all here that be mere merchants.'

In 1561 there were 690 people living in 138 cottages in the town's seven inhabited streets: Chapel Street, Castle Street, Dale Street, Bancke (now Water) Street, Moor (now Tithebarn) Street, Juggler (now High) Street, and Peppard (now Old Hall) Street. Liverpool as yet was not attracting much maritime trade anyway – and this wasn't helped by the destruction of the haven by the great storm of 1560.

The Childe of Hale, John Midleton (1578-1623), was an astonishing 9ft 3in tall, his hand was 18 inches long. Originally a farm labourer, he was hired by Sir Gilbert Ireland – Lord of the Manor of Hale – as his personal bodyguard. The King, James I, sent for him and set him to wrestle the King's Champion. Midleton won, taking the 20 guinea gold prize. There is a lifesize wooden statue of Midleton in Hale village, and a painting of him in Brasenose College, Oxford.

The Tower, built about 1252 by Sir John Stanley, was on the shore where Tower Buildings now stand. Embattled in 1404, the Tower was used as a house, a fortress, a banqueting hall, and was finally bought in 1737 by the Corporation to use as a gaol. Napoleonic French prisoners of war were among those confined. The Tower was completely demolished by 1821.

Enterprising Queen Elizabeth I kick-started Liverpool's expansion as a wealth-generating port when she granted letters of marque and privateer status to Liverpool sailors such as Humphrey Brooke. Privateer status was little more than licensed piracy, and the prizes won on the High Seas began to bring juicy profits into Liverpool. But, although the Mersey estuary was a deep natural harbour, there was still nowhere for ships to dock and unload – at low tide ships would keel over onto their sides because there was no deep water anchorage. In 1635 a bridge was made over the Pool, and a quay and harbour built 'for the succour of shipping', and – a key point in Liverpool's development – in 1647 Liverpool was made a free and independent port, no longer subject to the Port of Chester.

Liverpool's shipowners had been deeply unhappy about Charles I's treatment: in 1628 the King sold his rights in Liverpool to the City of London, and in 1634 and 1636 had illegally exacted ship money of £25 from Liverpool. Little wonder, then, that Liverpudlians favoured the Parliamentarians in the Civil War, even though Liverpool officially declared for the Royalists. The town went through two sieges in 1644, ending up a Roundhead town – for which it was punished by Charles II after the Restoration.

The 1660s saw the swift expansion of trade with America and, in 1709, Liverpool saw the return of Richard Norris's ship *The Blessing* from a hugely profitable trip. The first slave ship from here was the *Liverpool Merchant* – her cargo of 220 Africans was sold in Barbados in the 1740s; the last slave ship (the *Kitty Amelia*) sailed in 1807. An estimated two million slaves were taken from West Africa, of whom fewer than half survived the horrific conditions on board ship, and the brutality and disease they suffered afterwards.

Only 25% of Liverpool's ships were slavers; the rest found more honourable ways to make a profit – although life on board was not exactly a genteel way of earning a living. Sailors on merchant ships were often treated brutally, and the Royal Navy used press gangs to 'raise' men for service which, in plain English, was kidnapping. Any man could be hoicked out of his house or off the street and thrown on board a Navy ship to serve King and country.

As the 18th century turned into the 19th, Liverpool saw an explosion of economic and social growth as Liverpool moved into its position as second port of the Empire. There were serious ups and downs in the city's fortunes – the disruption to trade first of the American Revolution and then the American Civil War was disastrous, given the enormous volume of goods being shunted back and forth across the Atlantic on Liverpool ships – particularly cotton, which had become the key commodity for Liverpool and the hundreds of cotton mills in Lancashire.

Influential local families were making their mark on Liverpool – the Holts, Bibbys, Rathbones, Billingtons; and the town was beginning to attract entrepreneurs and scholars from elsewhere – Scots names like Laird and Gladstone, Welsh like Lewis and Owen, Italians, French, Dutch, Germans, Scandinavians ... and Americans.

Alongside the enormous wealth generated by maritime trade went indescribable poverty and overcrowding. The mid-1800s saw a sizable proportion of the Irish population becoming refugees from poverty and famine: between 1831 and 1841, Liverpool's population rose by 43%. In 1847 alone, 300,000 Irish refugees came to Liverpool to leave the famine behind. Passage on the 'coffin ships' across the Irish Sea was sixpence, but the Irish often found nothing better in Liverpool.

In one ward, Vauxhall, there were 142,000 people per square mile, with an average life expectancy of 17 years. Back-to-back housing and the notorious courts were one thing – cellar dwellings were something else. Densely overcrowded, with no sanitation, infested with insects and parasites, often flooded, the cellars were ripe for epidemic; no wonder this was declared the unhealthiest port in Europe. Cholera arrived in 1832, and although typhus and other diseases killed far more people, cholera was terrifying in its speed and spread.

In 1855 there was a serious riot, when most of the bread and flour shops were plundered by a mob several thousand strong; trade in Liverpool was brought to a standstill. The great and good realised this was not the lower orders being difficult – this was desperation; there was a tremendous fundraising effort to help the poverty-stricken.

The 18th and 19th centuries saw a flowering of philanthropic activity driving and financing public health, learning, arts, architecture and Liverpool's ring of public parks. From Bryan Blundell's foundation of the Bluecoat School in 1709 to the foundation of the University in 1881; hospitals, orphanages and asylums were born – including the first school for the blind and the origins of the NSPCC; art, music and literature flowered; libraries opened across the town (including the world's first public circulating library); Anglican and Roman Catholic churches were built in great numbers. In one year alone, the philanthropists of Liverpool made charitable bequests totalling £4 million.

And then there were the canals, and the railway. Liverpool played a central role in the development of both these revolutionary modes of transport. The world's first true canal, the Sankey, was cut in 1755, inspiring a 50-year boom in canal building across the country. As for the railways – from the Rainhill Trials to find the best locomotive (*Rocket* won) to the world's first passenger line (to Manchester), Liverpool has a string of world firsts.

It is said that the coming of the age of steam has been one of a handful of key developments in western civilisation – the beginning of globalisation. Certainly for Liverpool the transformation was radical – after all, it was only in 1760 that the first stagecoaches linked Liverpool and London; 60 years later the trains made Liverpool a gateway between old and new worlds. The speed of change had made a quantum leap.

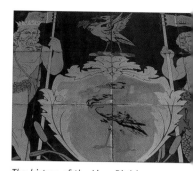

The history of the Liver Bird is as clear as Mersey mud. Liverpool's coat of arms was granted in 1787, but the town's common seal had carried an image of a bird with a twig in its beak since much earlier days. The original bird is thought to be the eagle of St John the Divine, carrying a sprig of broom (planta genista), the emblem of the Plantagenets. When the original seal was lost in the siege of 1644, and a new one made, it was made by someone who was badly briefed, and who either couldn't draw, knew nothing about birds – or both. What they ended up with was a cormorant-like creature with a bit of seaweed (or laver) in its beak. The heraldic description is: 'Argent a Cormorant in the beak a branch of seaweed called Laver all proper, and for the Crest, on a wreath of colours a Cormorant, the wings elevated, in the beak a branch of Laver proper.' Around the device are the words: 'Sigillum Commune Burgenium Leverp'. Supporters were granted ten years later, with Neptune and Triton to either side. Neptune has a trident in one hand and a banner carrying the Liverpool arms in the other; Triton holds a banner with a ship under sail.

Liverpool's population reached its highest point in 1931: the census showed 855,000 people living in the city – more than 1,000 times the population in 1272. The 2001 census figures show a drop of just on 50% from the 1930s – a reflection of Liverpool's economic decline from then to the nadir of the early 1980s.

Emigrants, sailors and merchants took Liverpool with them around the world: there are at least 12 other Liverpools, in New South Wales (Australia), Nova Scotia (Canada), Liverpool Land (Greenland), on the River St Paul in Liberia, and on the Rio Pongas in Guinea. In the US there are Liverpools in Illinois, Louisiana, New York state, Pennsylvania, Texas, West Virginia, and in Ohio, East Liverpool.

As Victoria's reign came to its end, Liverpool was riding high as the second port of the Empire, and one of the world's great cities. In 1850 the town's trade had been double that of London, and more than half that of the entire nation. Despite the building of The Ditch (the Manchester Ship Canal) to give Manchester a commercial leg-up, Liverpool was the world marketplace for cotton and grain, it led the world in insurance, it was dominant in several manufacturing sectors and, between 1830 and 1930, Liverpool was the gateway to the New World for nine million emigrants, flooding through the port from Britain, Ireland and Europe.

The end of the 19th and the early years of the 20th century saw another enormous expansion of housing, with vast tracts of land given over to solidly-built terraced streets all round the city centre to cope with the inexorable rise in population. There were also the private estates of huge villas built for wealthy families, estates such as Fulwood Park, stretching from Aigburth Road down to the river.

The elegance of comfortable living was evident, but below Liverpool's genteel and prosperous surface was a fermenting vat of troubles. Despite the enormous charitable and philanthropic efforts of the last 150 years, Liverpool had not recovered from the impact of the tidal wave of humanity that swamped the town. Along with all the good that came of the learning, enterprise, energy and fresh blood that washed through Liverpool came the inevitable stink of crime, poverty and ill-health. No city on earth has yet found a way to solve the complex problems of a small area of land teeming with human beings.

Possibly one of the clearest contrasts between top and bottom of the heap came in 1911: the building that has come to be the symbol of Liverpool – the great Liver Building – went up in this year but, as the building progressed, there were strikes and riots in the streets; the Riot Act was read to railway strikers and, in August, over 100 were injured when the police tried to disperse a mass meeting on St George's Plateau.

From its high point in the 1930s after 200 years of rapid growth, Liverpool was to dive to disaster in a couple of decades after the war. The seismic shifts which knocked Liverpool off the top of the tree were the shift in freight movement to containers – and to the air; and the radical changes in manufacturing and the shape of business in the 1960s and 1970s. The enormous loss of jobs, the gradual flight of so many people to find work elsewhere, and the move out of the inner city to suburban estates in Runcorn, Skelmersdale and the like, saw Liverpool depopulated, depressed and ready for a fight.

Meanwhile the artistic life of the city was flourishing. From the late 1950s through the 1960s, Merseybeat kept time for the world. The Beatles were the biggest single influence on pop culture at the time, but a whole slew of musicians, artists and writers made Liverpool the coolest city on earth before San Francisco got a look in.

And then there is sport. Or to be specific, football. There are other sports in Liverpool – world class, too – but football is the lifeblood here – red and blue.

The 1970s saw strikes all over Britain – but Liverpool's strikers were more articulate than most and the media fed on endless images of strife and gloom. This skewed image of Liverpool persists today for anyone who hasn't visited the city in 30 years. Militant's political rise and fall did the city no favours; in 2001 it is a very different story.

Now that the first 1,000 years of recorded history are complete, Liverpool is already steaming full ahead into its second millennium. With such an extraordinary history behind it, what must Liverpool's future hold?

Toxteth is one of Liverpool's best secrets. The press would have it that this is the epitome of inner city deprivation; but journalists who persist in allying the name of Toxteth with the inner city are ill-informed. The name acquired a whole new image after three days of strife in July 1981, but it might surprise those who associate the name Toxteth with the word 'riots' that Toxteth (and not Liverpool) is mentioned in the Domesday Book of 1086, and covers a hefty chunk of south Liverpool – including Granby, where the riots took place.

The name is written *Stochestede* in the Domesday Book and might mean either Toki's landing-place or homestead, or might be a Norse name for a wooded shore.

For most of its thousand-year history, Toxteth was a park covering many square miles, created by King John as a hunting park under forest law (forest, in this context, does not mean woodland, but refers to the Norman forest law which protected deer habitats for royal hunting). The park had been part of a huge forest, but in 1190 King John "disafforested" everything but Toxteth and Croxteth.

Edward I, at the end of the 13th century, decided to turn Toxteth into an enclosed deer park, turfing out everyone who lived there and making the park a forbidden area, which is how it stayed for about 300 years.

Toxteth Park was sold in 1592 by the King to the Earl of Derby who, having purged the park of deer and split the land up into farms, sold it on to Richard Molyneux (later Earl of Sefton) 12 years later.

The park's history meant that it was outside parish boundaries, and therefore an ideal refuge for religious nonconformists to live unmolested by canon law. In the early 1600s Toxteth attracted Puritans, who settled around Otterspool (first mentioned in records of 1228) and the Dingle. At Otterspool, the stream running from what is now Sefton Park to the Mersey was dubbed Little Jordan, and the settlement itself, Jericho.

(Jericho dairy farm was demolished in the 1960s to make way for a small housing estate. The Hogg brothers, who retired only in 1989, remember driving their small dairy herd back and forth between Jericho and the dairy in Alwyn Street.)

The Ancient Chapel of Toxteth, built in 1618, was the centre of nonconformist worship until 1811, when the Unitarians began to meet in a chapel in Renshaw Street (in 1896 they built a magnificent church in Ullet Road). At the corner of Park

Road and Dingle Lane, the Ancient Chapel was unlicensed until 1672, when after Charles II's Declaration of Indulgence, a licence was signed by Thomas Blood (a reformed adventurer who, the previous year, had tried to steal the crown jewels, but was visited by the King in the Tower of London and pardoned).

The Chapel's first minister was Richard Mather who, suspended for nonconformist practices, became one of the first emigrants to the Puritan settlements of New England.

The surviving pieces of King John's deer park are Sefton and Prince's Parks; although there are still plenty of green spaces, woodlands and gardens around the leafy avenues, Victorian villas and elegant Georgian terraces of Toxteth.

chapter 2
performance

Liverpool's Somali community has a strong poetic tradition – in fact poetry is at the heart of Somali life. A nomadic people, Somalis have an oral tradition and do not write poetry (they had no formal written language in 1972). Each clan has an official poet who has a strong voice in the community and influences clan politics – his poems can be an emollient to soothe warring factions, or be as powerful as a physical assault.

The poet Felicia Hemans lived in Duke Street; her name is mostly forgotten, but her most famous poem is Casabianca. *Still no wiser? The first lines are: 'The boy stood on the burning deck/ Whence all but he had fled.' Another of her poems (The Homes of England) was skitted by Noel Coward: 'The stately homes of England/ How beautiful they stand/ To prove the upper classes/ Still have the upper hand'. Hemans' line was also borrowed by the much-lamented Quentin Crisp, who famously declared himself one of 'the stately homos of England'.*

Scouse wit is the stuff of legend: an innate sense of timing, of the music of words, the contrast of economy and the lyrical, the dark humour and the lightness of spirit. Liverpool's particular mix of the exotic and the stolid, in the gateway where the wide world meets old Lancashire, has produced a distinctive sound and rhythm, with music or without. The whimsy and imagery of the Irish, the melancholy of the Welsh, the sharpness of the Scots, the dry irony of the English and the spicy notes of the foreigner are an unbeatable set of ingredients matched, perhaps, only by New York – which has much the same ingredients. Anyone who loves words only has to go into a Liverpool pub, hop on a bus, or simply hang about and keep their ears open, with pen and notebook in hand to jot down all the bons Scouse mots.

Liverpool is home to all sorts of writers: poets, dramatists, novelists, comedians, lyricists, and some who can claim the whole lot.

Willy Russell, for instance, who may be best known for plays (and later films) such as *Shirley Valentine* and *Educating Rita*, but also wrote book, lyrics and music for his long-running hit *Blood Brothers* and is now squirming under the weight of outrageously good reviews for his first novel *The Wrong Boy*.

Russell left school at 15; he worked as a ladies' hairdresser for six years, stacked stockings at Bear Brand and cleaned girders at Ford. He was a songwriter first, playwright second. 'There is something absolutely particular about Liverpool because of the nature of the idiom here,' he says. 'It is a wonderful language for someone who works in the spoken form.'

Two of the many ecstatic reviews for his novel sum up Russell's work: 'Unusual, funny, unsettling and rich with sadness [it] manages to work on a multitude of levels. It also showcases Russell's gift for sinking deep into the minds and motivations of his characters, offering a voice to the dispossessed .... Once again he has proved himself to be a multi-faceted Renaissance man.' (*The Times*). And according to *The Mirror*: '... he's still got that magic touch. Hilariously miserable ... big-hearted, wonderfully funny and engrossing ... with a deadpan delivery Alan Bennett would be proud of ....'

A night cherished by those who witnessed it was the performance of *Shirley Valentine* (a one-woman show) when the star fell ill. Russell climbed up on stage and did it himself.

> 6 *Encouraging goodwill and motivation towards thinking of others, about change, with an altruistic attitude: this I can proudly say I achieve every day.* 9

Tony 'Chestnut' Brown, the People's Poet of Liverpool

Poets flourish in Liverpool – well, mostly. Matthew Arnold (*The Scholar Gypsy, Thyrsis, Dover Beach*) used to come often to Liverpool to stay with his brother-in-law; but running for a tramcar one day, he had a heart attack and died. By and large, though, Liverpool is a healthy poetic environment. Too healthy, perhaps, since while Liverpool prospered, the educated wealthy were too comfortable to write poetry, and those with something to write about didn't have the education.

Arthur Hugh Clough was an exception. Born in 1819 at 74 Rodney Street, he only lived to the age of 42. Clough's most quoted line is 'Say not, the struggle nought availeth', but his line in comic cynicism is probably more to modern tastes. *The Latest Decalogue* is a swipe at the ten commandments; *How Pleasant It Is To Have Money* has a pop at the careless rich, and *There Is No God* holds as true today as it did then.

ASJ Tessimond is a Liverpool poet who deserves a better hearing, too. With great bad timing, Tessimond died in 1962, just as the Liverpool Poets were gearing themselves up for the great creative explosion that rained Liverpool's youth all over the world in the 1960s. Roger McGough (*pictured right*), Adrian Henri and Brian Patten led the charge for the poets; McGough and Patten are still charging, but Henri died in great style in 2000.

McGough, possibly because of his stint with pop group The Scaffold, has been tagged with a 'light' label as a poet and not given credit for being a bit of a genius. (The Scaffold – McGough, John Gorman and Mike McGear – were funny, charming, ever so slightly subversive and quite a lot silly.) McGough is vexed by the snobbery of the poetry establishment which says that anything that might be categorised as light or funny is not regarded as 'proper' poetry. 'We were seen as interesting sociologically, but nothing to do with English literature,' he says. So how come McGough sells piles of books and pulls droves of cheering fans? McGough has published eight collections of poetry for adults, six of children's poetry, six story and picture books. His poetry is brilliantly accessible (which is a Bad Thing in some poetic circles, for a start) no matter how deep and dark he goes, and it achieves what so much poetry fails to do: it works, on the page and in performance.

Brian Patten, the youngest of the three, said Liverpool taught him that poetry was not the property of an elite, but the stuff of daily life. 'Among the rubbish in the demolished alleyways, there were lilac bushes and campion flowers. To me, that proved beauty could exist anywhere.'

All three Liverpool Poets were made Freemen of the City of Liverpool in 2001 (Adrian Henri was told of the plans just before his death the previous December). McGough said he valued his Freedom even more than his OBE: 'There is no bigger honour than being recognised by your own people,' he said.

The first anthology by McGough, Henri and Patten (The Mersey Sound, 1968) is still the world's million-selling number one poetry book of all time.

Jimmy McGovern, writer of Cracker, Priest, The Lakes *and others, came out of the first Liverpool writers' workshop, set up in the 1970s in Scotland Road. A warehouseman then, McGovern started writing scripts for* Brookside *before he made his name with* Cracker.

Liverpool-born novelists include as radically different a trio of writers as Beryl Bainbridge, Edwina Currie and Helen Forrester.

Liverpool screenwriters include Linda la Plante, Frank Clark, Carla Lane, Jim Hitchmough, Alun Owen, Jimmy McGovern, Terence Davies, Alex Cox and Frank Cottrell Boyce.

For Alan Bleasdale, the beauty was harder to find in the bleak urban landscape of the late 1970s and early 1980s, when unemployment was running at impossible levels and the city was breaking apart. Bleasdale, born here in 1946, taught for a while (including three years in the Gilbert & Ellice Islands), then became resident playwright at the Liverpool Playhouse in 1975. Since then he has written more than a dozen stage plays and some of television's most remarkable drama – and has won a series of awards, just to push the point home.

TV drama such as *Scully*, *The Monocled Mutineer* and the extraordinary *GBH* all made their mark, but Bleasdale's masterpiece (to date) was *Boys From The Blackstuff*, a series of five BBC2 dramas in 1982 repeated nine weeks later on prime time BBC1 (unprecedented, and unequalled) and won the Bafta award.

Showing the experience of unemployment from the point of view of the unemployed, it was 'an absurd, mad, black farce', according to Bleasdale. All five plays were acclaimed, but it was *Yosser's Story* that created a legend. Bernard Hill's colossal performance as the manic, self-destructive Yosser Hughes, incoherent, pathetic, savage and desperate, trailing his brood of children round after him as he pleads for work: 'I can do that. Gizza job.' The phrase went into the language.

Lines spoken by Julie Walters as Angie, one of the wives, summed up the series, and the feeling in Liverpool at the time: 'It's not funny, it's not friggin' funny. I've had enough of that 'if you don't laugh you'll cry'. I've heard it for years. This stupid soddin' city's full of it. Why don't you fight back, you bastard. Fight back.'

Bleasdale's view of Liverpool's situation may have been bleak, but there is hope and strength and dignity and love in his characters. He hates sentimentality, but makes the distinction between that and sentiment, referring to the aftermath of Hillsborough. '"Sentimentality," the intellectuals wrote. "Sickly," they sniggered. They were wrong. Our actions weren't sentimental, but they were full to overflowing with sentiment, with love and respect and sorrow and understanding.'

Brandon Thomas was born in
1856 at 101 Mount Pleasant;
he worked in the shipyards before
turning to journalism, then
drama. His farce Charlie's Aunt
has never fallen out of favour
with audiences.

Among writers influenced by their
time in Liverpool were Charles
Dickens, John Masefield, Gerard
Manley Hopkins, Hugh Walpole,
Washington Irving, Nathaniel
Hawthorne and Daniel Defoe.

Nicholas Monsarrat was the son
of a surgeon, born at 11 Rodney
Street in 1910. His 1951 novel
The Cruel Sea described his own
experiences in a corvette in the
North Atlantic.

Harry Potter was not the first children's book series to sell in barrowloads, despite what the media might suggest; Brian Jacques's *Redwall* series have been best-sellers since 1986; the 15th book was published early in 2001, and his website gets almost four million hits a year from fans in 126 countries. Jacques is a local radio broadcaster as well as a writer, and in his time has been a merchant seaman, railway fireman, longshoreman, long-distance truck driver, bus driver, boxer, policeman, postmaster and stand-up comedian.

No wonder he says he doesn't have to worry about coming up with ideas. The Redwall books are centred on the medieval setting of Redwall Abbey, and the heroes are peace-loving mice, moles, shrews, squirrels. They face the dark side of the animal world – rats, weasels, stoats, foxes and their allies – in the day-to-day struggle of good and evil. 'Mice are my heroes because, like children, mice are little and have to learn to be courageous and use their wits,' says Jacques. In 2000 he set up the Brian Jacques Literary Awards for primary schoolchildren in years five and six, wanting to encourage children of his city 'which has contributed so much to the richness of my life'.

Unlike Jacques, horror writer Clive Barker – born in south Liverpool – says that far from giving him inspiration, his childhood environment wasn't anything special. 'I had a perfectly sane upbringing; I remember seeing the Beatles go by in a car, but it didn't have a great deal of romance at the time – it was where I lived.'

Barker is author of best-selling novels such as *Weaveworld, Imajica,* and *Cold Heart Canyon*; he also directed the *Hellraiser* film series, *Candyman* and *Nightbreed,* and was executive producer of the Oscar-winning *Gods and Monsters.*

A childhood in Anfield as the son of communist party members gave Alexei Sayle (*pictured left*) a suitably unorthodox springboard, first into performance (stand-up, then roles from the *Young Ones* to movies), and now into full-time writing. 'Writing is terribly important. You only reach a miniscule audience compared to films and TV, but I don't care.' Sayle wants to be taken seriously, and reckons he has a better chance as an author. His first book *Barcelona Plates*, is followed by the second, *The Dog Catcher*, published in July 2001.

Liverpool's crime novelists
Margaret Murphy, Martin Edwards
and Ron Ellis all set their books
in the city. Ron Ellis's key
character is DJ and private eye
Johnny Ace; Martin Edwards –
a leading employment lawyer –
has created seedy solicitor Harry
Devlin ('based on no-one I know,'
Edwards insists) who has an
alarming tendency to get mixed
up in murder. It's a wonder
Devlin has any friends at all –
not a man to spend much time
with if one wants to survive ...

Rogues and vagabonds – that's how actors and theatricals were regarded in the 17th century, and deportation was a distinct possibility. However, the first mention of theatre in Liverpool was a playhouse at the bottom of James Street, in 1649; not quite the theatre as we would recognise it – this would probably be a little less civilised. In the 17th and early 18th centuries actors would perform in old cockpits, assembly rooms or the inns on Dale Street and Water Street. Then, in 1759, a theatre was opened in Drury Lane, on the corner of Brunswick Street; the first performance was the tragedy of *The Orphan*.

Thirteen years later, in 1772, the Theatre Royal was opened in Williamson Square, and all the great actors of the day played there, including the Kembles (John Philip Kemble, later a great actor-manager, was born here while his father was on stage). Charles James Matthews, another of the great actor-managers, was also born during a theatrical tour – in Basnett Street in 1803. By contrast, John Palmer, an untrustworthy character known as Plausible Jack, dropped dead on stage during a performance of *The Stranger* in 1798.

A number of famous theatrical names played in Liverpool en route to America: Sarah Bernhardt, Beerbohm Tree, Lily Langtry, Grimaldi, General Tom Thumb, and John Julius Booth. Booth, a popular actor in Liverpool, emigrated to America, where his sons were born; one – Edwin – became a famous actor, the other – John Wilkes – also became famous, as President Lincoln's assassin.

Liverpool launched the careers of others: Noel Coward and Gertrude Lawrence appeared here as children, Mrs Patrick Campbell, Macready, Richard Burton (at the Royal Court in 1943), Michael Redgrave, Cecil Parker, Clive Brook, C Aubrey Smith, Diana Wynard – all made their debut in Liverpool. Morecambe and Wise made their debut at the Liverpool Empire as a double act, and Henry Irving made his last appearance here, in 1904.

Quintessential Englishmen John Gregson and Rex Harrison (real name Reg Carey) were born here, as was Oswald Stoll, who would go on to own and manage several West End theatres and found the Stoll Moss empire. Ellen Terry spent her childhood in Liverpool.

A couple of theatrical firsts: the Sans Pareil theatre in Manchester Street was the first in Britain to run twice-nightly performances. And in 1895 at the old Royal Court the demand for tickets was so great that the management insisted that the pushing, shoving crowd form an orderly line – nicknamed a queue, after the sailors' pigtail. From then on the British have queued politely for everything, to the bewilderment of most of the rest of the world.

The Playhouse repertory company was established in 1910 by Professor Charles Reilly and a group of fellow enthusiasts, including Ronald Jeans of the Daily Post; the company performed for a while at Kelly's Theatre before taking an option on the old Star Music Hall, which they renamed the Playhouse. Ramsey Muir wrote: 'There was a real vitality, fizz and go … and the city was wealthy.' But it was not universally popular. Muir wrote: 'Opponents thought a repertory theatre would be a cranky affair of problem plays and advanced women. Surely Liverpool didn't want to encourage that sort of thing?'

Liverpool now has the Playhouse, the Everyman (started in the 1960s with a stunning reputation as a nursery for top-class talent and new writing), the Empire (the big touring venue) and an excellent group of smaller venues led by the Unity and the Neptune. The 1938 Deco Royal Court has been shamefully neglected for years, serving as a shabby gig venue for touring rock bands, but is now refurbished, with a broader theatrical programme. After a dodgy couple of decades, Liverpool's theatrical life looks set for a renaissance.

Some Scouse actors & comedians:
Arthur Askey
Ann Bell
Mitch Benn
Judy Bennett (Shula Archer)
Craig Charles
George Costigan
Les Dennis
Ken Dodd
Fred Emney
Kenny Everett
Tom Georgeson
John Gregson
Derek Guyler
Tommy Handley
Rex Harrison
Margaret Kelly (Miss Bluebell)
Bill Kenwright
Joe/Mark/Paul/Stephen McGann
Andrée Melly
Derek Nimmo
Tom O'Connor
Ted Ray
Leonard Rossiter
Lily Savage
Andrew Schofield
Freddy Starr
Alison Steadman
Jimmy Tarbuck
Ricky Tomlinson
Christine Tremarco
Rita Tushingham

The magnificent green and gold extravaganza of a concert organ in St George's Hall was the largest organ in Europe when it was installed; it was overtaken by the huge instrument in the Anglican Cathedral, which at its installation in 1926 was the biggest in the world with 10,690 pipes. Even now it is the biggest cathedral organ in the world.

The Liverpool Mozart Orchestra was formed in the 1950s, and has been associated with famous names such as Zubin Mehta, Sir Charles Groves, Carl Davis and the orchestra's current president, Sir Simon Rattle.

The mighty Wurlitzer organ was invented by Birkenhead man Robert Hope Jones, but he lost the rights to his design after going to see the Wurlitzer Corporation in America.

A city that can claim to be the pop capital of the world might not be blessed with a classical tradition as well, but Liverpool boasts a track record of world-class musicians and music-making over several centuries; the town's first purpose-built concert hall (on the corner of Concert Street and Bold Street – now Waterstones bookshop) was opened in 1715. The original scheme for St George's Hall was a new concert hall – £30,000 had been set aside for its building in 1839, but in the end it became an all-purpose civic palace, including assize courts, police cells, the small concert room and the great hall with its fabulous concert organ. The acoustics in the great hall are lousy, which is rather unfortunate for a music venue, so the Philharmonic Hall (which was opened in 1849, 10 years before St George's was completed) became the principal music venue for the city.

Liverpool has produced a slew of world-leading musicians, from conductors Adrian Boult and Simon Rattle and jazzman George Melly to the Beatles; from soprano Rita Hunter and heldentenor Alberto Remedios to folk group the Spinners. The world's most successful musician – Paul McCartney – brought the two halves of Liverpool's music together with the premiere performance and recording of his *Liverpool Oratorio*, premiered at Liverpool Cathedral in 1991, with a cast topped by Kiri te Kanawa, Willard White, Sally Burgess and Jerry Hadley, with the RLPO conducted by Carl Davis.

Liverpool Cathedral's amazing organ is rare in having a concert console at ground level, so that audiences can watch organist Ian Tracey play; with five manuals and the pedals, it is quite a show. The console was given to the cathedral in 1989 by Vic Hutson CBE, a long-time benefactor of Liverpool music.

No surprise, in Music City, that Liverpool University has a thriving music scene, with its own jazz band, brass band, chamber orchestra, renaissance music group, wind orchestra, university choir, university singers, and the Liverpool University Symphony Orchestra.

t's official – Liverpool is the world's number one city for pop music, according to Guinness World Records. From 1953 to summer 2001 there have been 53 No1 chart hits by 23 different bands and soloists, from Lita Roza to Atomic Kitten. Every chart hit is recorded on Mathew Street's Wall of Fame (just yards from the Cavern) opened in March 2001 by Lita Roza and the Lord Mayor.

The chart is taken from the Record Retailer (now Music Week) which began in 1952, and apart from Liverpool's No1 status, the top three spots for individuals go to Paul McCartney (21 No1 singles), John Lennon (20) and George Harrison (18). Fourth was Elvis Presley with 17, and fifth came Cliff Richard with 14. McCartney, by the way, has reached No1 on his own, in a duo, a trio, a quartet and a quintet, and has also had six No2 hits.

A Liverpool name missing from the Wall is Billy Fury: although he had 29 hits (19 in the top 20) and spent 281 weeks in the charts, he never reached No1. The highest he got was No2 with *Jealousy* and No3 with *Halfway to Paradise*.

Frankie Vaughan – Liverpool's most popular entertainer before the Beatles – had his first No1 with *Garden of Eden*, although he is probably best remembered for *Give Me the Moonlight*. Born Frank Abelson in 1928, the singer decided he needed a better showbiz name, and rang his mother for advice. 'My grandma, god rest her soul, said in the background: "Vatever he picks, he'll alvays be my number von." I was her number one grandchild, so Vaughan it was.'

Two of Gerry Marsden's hits have become Liverpool anthems: *You'll Never Walk Alone* and *Ferry 'cross the Mersey*. Gerry & the Pacemakers were the first band to get to No1 with their first three singles, not equalled until Frankie Goes to Hollywood in 1984 and not surpassed until the Spice Girls (including Scouser Melanie C) in the 1990s.

Remarkably, half the singles on the Wall of Fame were produced by the brilliant George Martin, who should probably be made an honorary Scouser, bearing in mind how much he has done for the city's music-makers.

Liverpool's No1 hit artists:
1953 Lita Roza
1957 Frankie Vaughan
1958 Michael Holliday
1960 Michael Holliday
1961 Frankie Vaughan
1963 Gerry & the Pacemakers (3)
1963 The Beatles (3)
1963 The Searchers (2)
1963 Billy J Kramer
1964 The Searchers
1964 Cilla Black
1964 Billy J Kramer
1964 The Beatles (3)
1965 The Beatles (3)
1965 Ken Dodd
1966 The Beatles (2)
1967 The Beatles (2)
1968 The Beatles (2)
1968 The Scaffold
1969 The Beatles (2)
1971 George Harrison
1976 The Real Thing
1977 Wings
1980 John Lennon (3)
1982 McCartney/Stevie Wonder
1984 Paul McCartney
1984 Frankie Goes to Hollywood (3)
1985 Dead or Alive
1989 The Christians/Holly Johnson/McCartney/Marsden
1989 Sonia
1996 The Lightning Seeds
1998 The Lightning Seeds/David Baddiel/Frank Skinner
2000 Melanie C (2)
2001 Atomic Kitten

Hit singles about Liverpool:
Long Haired Lover from Liverpool (Jimmy Osmond)
Ferry 'cross the Mersey (Gerry & the Pacemakers)
Penny Lane/Strawberry Fields (The Beatles)
Anfield Rap (Liverpool FC)
Liverpool Lou (The Scaffold)
In Liverpool (Suzanne Vega)
Going Down to Liverpool (Bangles)

During the Beatles' first US tour in 1964, the fans' reaction was beyond anything seen before: screaming, sobbing girls besieged the Fab Four at all turns. Ice cream-maker Baskin-Robbins created a new flavour called Beatle Nut.

Richard Starkey born 7.7.1940
John Lennon born 9.10.1940
Paul McCartney born 18.6.1942
George Harrison born 25.2.1943.

John Lennon died 8.12.1980.
George Harrison died 29.11.2001.

The Beatles' record label Apple discovered James Taylor, Mary Hopkin, Badfinger and the classical composer John Tavener.

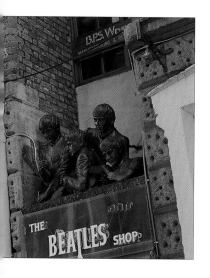

The melody of Lady Madonna *was compared to the 1956 jazz hit* Bad Penny Blues *by Humphrey Lyttleton, but Humph said: 'You can't copyright a rhythm, and a rhythm was all they'd used. Actually, we'd borrowed it from Dan Burley.'*

Amongst the 300 or so bands performing in and around Liverpool at the end of the 1950s, there were probably a dozen who could claim to be part of the original Mersey sound. Names like Freddy Starr and the Midnighters, Kingsize Taylor and the Dominoes, Rory Storm and the Hurricanes, Cass and the Casanovas, Faron and the Flamingos. And the Beatles. The Four Lads who were about to shake the world were then doing gigs at the Jacaranda for five shillings apiece, but in a few years the boys would be millionaires and the biggest pop group the world has ever seen.

It began with the Quarrymen – a skiffle band formed in 1957 by John Lennon and his mate Pete Shotton, who were both pupils at Quarry Bank School. Another friend, Ivan Vaughan, introduced John to Paul McCartney, who was at the Liverpool Institute and later that year, Paul brought in another Liverpool Institute boy, the 13-year-old George Harrison.

Buddy Holly, who wrote and played his own songs, showed Lennon and McCartney that writing their own material was possible, and the world's greatest songwriting partnership was born. The iconic name was inspired by the Crickets, Buddy Holly's band, and was suggested by Stuart Sutcliffe, an art student friend of John's (who by this time was at Liverpool Art School). Sutcliffe was playing bass, and Pete Best was the drummer with the Beatles when they went to Hamburg in 1960 for four months to play first at the Indra, and later at the Kaiserkeller. The band had been forged in the rowdy fires of Hamburg; their playing style had come together, and they had learned how to hold an audience.

The band made their Cavern debut in 1961 for the princely sum of £1 5s each, and then went back to Hamburg for a few months, at which point Stu Sutcliffe left the band and the others came home to Liverpool. Sutcliffe died nine months later of a brain haemorrhage.

Now regulars at the Cavern, the band acquired a new fan – Brian Epstein, manager of a record shop called Nems in Whitechapel. He had been curious to see the band, as customers were asking for their record *My Bonnie*. Epstein offered to manage the Beatles – who had been under the aegis of Alan Williams – and the deal was done. EMI's Parlophone label signed them up in 1962 and put them in the charge of producer George Martin. It was at this point that Pete Best was replaced by Ringo Starr, who the lads had met in Hamburg when he was drumming for Rory Storm. The sacking of Best was not popular with the fans, but Ringo settled in, and the famous line-up was complete.

Girls were already screaming – Beatlemania had begun, but parents approved of them: they were four nice-looking boys, squeaky clean, beautifully groomed and in sharp suits. They were to get several nasty shocks in future years ....

The Beatles' first Parlophone single was released in October 1962, and scraped into the charts at No48 (Brian Epstein had bought 10,000 copies). *Love Me Do* reached No17 in December, and the Beatles were off and running. Beatlemania infected the world, and the 1964 US tour was so wildly successful that British prime minister Alec Douglas-Home declared that the Beatles were 'my secret weapon'.

As for the rest, you'd have had to come from Mars not to know. Twenty-seven No1 singles, the films, the drugs, the Maharishi, Linda, Yoko, Apple, Sgt Pepper .... The last official gig (the first ending) was in San Francisco, at Candlestick Park. The impromptu gig on the roof of the Apple building in London in 1970 (the second ending). The band was no more, but the dream was shattered in December 1980 when John Lennon was shot dead in New York.

Millions come to Liverpool each year on their Beatles pilgrimage, and in 2000 the Beatles album *One* shot to No1 on both sides of the Atlantic.

Of the four Beatles, Paul McCartney has maintained the strongest links with his home town

MMDA – the Merseyside Music Development Agency – backs local talent and brings music into the city. One of MMDA's key projects is to raise the profile and the economic impact of black music and musicians in the city.

As befits Music City, Liverpool has the full spectrum of musical styles from salsa to folk, African to renaissance – and venues to cater for them. Jazz and soul, for instance, pull large audiences at venues like Zanzibar, Heebiejeebees and Cafe Jaz bar.

George Melly is one of Liverpool's treasures. The Mellys are one of the city's great Unitarian families, although there's nothing very Puritan about George. Writer, art expert, painter, and jazzman supreme, Melly first performed with the Feetwarmers at a gig in Picton Library.

Willard White

Senegalese musician Mamadou Diaw says: 'If you are popular in Liverpool you can play anywhere in Europe. Liverpool has such a good music scene – I wouldn't want to be anywhere else in England.'

Popular music didn't start with the Mersey Sound in the 1950s – the ballad-singers and bards go back as far as you like, but without the benefit of records, of course. And this being a port, sailors would bring their sea-shanties and songs from all over the world. Song-sheets from the 19th century show the use of song as social and political satire and protest, and cheeky Scousers wouldn't have hesitated to immortalise their tormentors, rivals, employers and enemies in irreverent, scathing or comic song.

The *New Song on the Turn-out* from around 1870, begins by urging men to rise against the master builders, and the last verse goes: 'So to conclude and make an end/ Success attend each loyal friend/ That will a hand to freedom lend/ To crush Monopoly;/ Be firm, undaunted, loyal and true/ The Master Builders you'll subdue/ They are beginning to look blue/ The tyrannizing creatures.'

In the 20th century, though, with other means of getting the message across, music veered more to entertainment – although there was no shortage of political lyrics. For some, music offered a way out of the daily grind. The mix of tuneful Welsh and lyrical Irish in the Scouse gene pool has made this Music City over the last 50 years, and there are no signs of the trend changing direction. Names from the Merseybeat days – the Swinging Blue Jeans, the Mojos, the Undertakers, the Chessmen, Rory Storm, Billy Fury, PJ Proby, Billy J Kramer, the Big Three, Cilla Black – were followed in the 1970s and 1980s by the likes of Wah!, Echo and the Bunnymen, the Icicle Works, Sonia ... then in the 1990s by the Las, River City People, Seed, Cast, Space and now Atomic Kitten and Mel C. Of the bands making news in 2001, how many will last? Which, of names such as BBMak, Junk Culture, Gloss, Chiver, will be more than a distant memory by the end of the decade?

Alongside the musicians and singers has emerged another phenomenon – the star DJ. Disc jockeys used either to be genial intermediaries like Tony Blackburn and Mike Read, or experts like John Peel (a dyed-in-the-wool Scouser) and Bob Harris. Now they're the main attraction in the massive club culture of the 1990s onwards. Cream – Liverpool's superclub which pulled punters from all over Europe – and Voodoo are worldwide brands, and Liverpool DJs like Adam Maddox, Lil John, Ste Cocky and Ste Robinson are making waves.

Festival is an over-used word these days, attached to feeble events gathered under a convenient umbrella. Not in Liverpool! The summer in this city seems to be one long party, whether or not the climate condescends to be helpful. Rain or shine, Scousers, visitors, adopted Scousers, their friends and relations fill the streets with colour and noise, often as much from the audience as the performers. Music, theatre, visual art, sport, hot air balloons, boats, and things which defy description, bring out all but the most cantankerous anti-social misanthropes. Even misers come out to play, because so much is free (except the beer).

Liverpool has the UK's only African music festival – Africa Oye; the award-winning Brouhaha street theatre festival, which began in the late 1980s with troupes from Russia and Eastern Europe, and continues with a great spread of international theatre. There's the Merseyside Caribbean Festival and Liverpool Now music festival.

The monster hit, though, is the International Beatles Week at the end of August, with the Mathew Street Festival as its climax. Squillions of Beatles fans descend on the city to hear live bands, watch films, buy vast amounts of memorabilia, drink the city dry and have a good time. Nine years ago, the first MSF pulled a crowd of about 4,000 to hear a line-up of Beatles tribute bands in a car park next to the Cavern. Now it is one of the biggest musical showcases in the world. The geographical term 'Mathew Street' is no longer entirely accurate during the three-day festival, as the street itself is short and narrow: 300,000 people spill out around the music stages scattered all over the city centre.

On a sunny weekend in June, the River Mersey becomes the stage for Liverpool's River Festival, the banks either side lined with thousands coming to see ships and boats and planes and people doing their remarkable thing; the river is also the setting for Guy Fawkes fireworks. But ... oh for a proper fireworks festival in this country! Liverpool, take note.

At Creamfields on August bank holiday 2001, some 45,000 clubbers flocked to eight different arenas on the old airfield at Speke to dance themselves to a standstill. Non-stop music from Saturday afternoon through to 6am on Sunday could be heard as far away as Ellesmere Port.

The Summer Pops began as the Royal Liverpool Philharmonic Orchestra's programme of light classics in the Big Top on King's Dock. Under the aegis of conductor Carl Davies, the Summer Pops became the biggest summer event in Britain, pulling vast audiences. In 2001 the emphasis switched to big name gigs, with Bob Dylan, Elton John, Little Richard, Chuck Berry, Jerry Lee Lewis, George Benson, Tom Jones, Ray Charles, Shirley Bassey, Lionel Ritchie, and Ladysmith Black Mombazo.

LIVERPOOL FIRSTS – ROYAL LIVERPOOL PHILHARMONIC SOCIETY

William Sudlow, a Liverpool stockbroker and amateur organist, used to meet friends to rehearse and perform choral music in St Martin's Church throughout the 1830s. The group decided, in January 1840, to found the Liverpool Philharmonic Society – the fifth oldest concert-giving organisation in the world – and nine years later they built the Society a fabulous new concert hall in Hope Street, designed by architect John Cunningham, and blessed with superb acoustics.

A fire in 1933 reduced the hall to ashes, but the Society commissioned Herbert Rowse (architect of the Mersey Tunnel and Martin's Bank building in Water Street) to build a new hall. The stark brick Deco exterior of the new hall must have prompted a few gasps of shock at its opening in 1939, but the lush interior and the near-perfect acoustics would have been reassuring.

The Philharmonic Hall was the first concert venue in the world owned by its society and orchestra and remained so until the 1990s – and is still the only one with its own hall, orchestra choir and youth orchestra. The Phil, in fact, now has a community choir (formed in 1991), gospel choir (1994) and chamber group Ensemble 10:10 to add to its tally of music-makers.

The RLPO's principal conductors make a distinguished list: Max Bruch, Sir Charles Hallé, Sir Henry Wood, Sir Malcolm Sargent, Sir Charles Groves, Walter Weller, Marek Janowski, Libor Pesek and Petr Altrichter.

Succeeding Altrichter in September 2001 was Gerard Schwarz, who came from a successful tenure with the Seattle Symphony Orchestra. Schwarz, a 54-year-old New Yorker, was hailed as the 'new Bernstein' when he began conducting at the age of 30; until then he had been a trumpet player, beginning with Leonard Bernstein's New York Philharmonic (which was founded, incidentally, a year after the Liverpool Phil). Liverpool audiences will be treated to performances of pieces by America's forgotten generation of composers from the 1930s, 1940s and 1950s – names such as David Diamond, Howard Hanson, William Schuman – the 'American Sibelians'.

Soloists over the Society's 160 years have included a long roll-call of famous names, from Jenny Lind (the Swedish Nightingale), the piano virtuoso Busoni to Rachmaninov, Casals and Menuhin. The roll-call of guest conductors includes William Walton, Michael Tippett, Aaron Copland, and Vladimir Ashkenazy – who in the early 1970s announced his defection to the West at the Adelphi Hotel in Liverpool.

The Phil, which was given its 'Royal' prefix in 1957, has seen the premieres of some famous works. Ben Britten's *Young Person's Guide to the Orchestra*, Elgar's *Pomp & Circumstance March No1*, Bartok's *Piano Concerto*, and the first appearance of Sibelius in an English concert; the 12 minute piece *Liverpool* by Alfred Schnittke was commissioned by the Phil, and Paul McCartney's *Liverpool Oratorio* was premiered by the RLPO, although at Liverpool Cathedral, not at the Philharmonic Hall.

Two local lads who became great conductors were Adrian Boult and Simon Rattle. Boult, born in 1889, was the son of a Liverpool import merchant and became the Phil's youngest conductor in 1916. Simon Rattle, who went to the Bluecoat and joined the Merseyside Youth Orchestra, was Liverpool's loss when he went to Birmingham and did wonders with the CBSO.

The RLPO has some great innovations to its credit, such as the post-war Industrial Concerts; it needs to come up with some more radical ideas if audience numbers are to revive and the Society's finances to improve. Such a great orchestra, with such a stunning concert venue must discover a whole new – young – audience for the classics, which despite the big-name visitors from jazz, rock, folk and world music, is still the essence of the RLPO.

chapter 3
sporting life

RACING
SPECIALIST
263
1116
SCHWALBE
1998/99
JOIN OUR CHRISTMAS CLUB NOW!
CAN MATCH
OUR DEALS!
LIVERPOOL'S LONGEST ESTABLISHED BIKES
BEST DEALS GUARANTEE
STAFF EXPERIENCE SECOND TO NONE
LIVERPOOL'S LONGEST ESTABLISHED BIKE SHOP
IF WE
'EM, NO-ONE CAN
Merry Christmas and Happy New Year
SCHWALBE SALESPOINT
HOPE TECHNOLOGY
Pete Matthews
matthews
Rockport

On 10th July 1827 Liverpool man Dr Bedale and Mr Matthew Vipond from Manchester made a wager on a race. They swam from the Queen's Dock to Runcorn. The doctor won by about half a mile, in three hours 35 minutes.

Weightlifter Julian Creus was the only British competitor to get a world record in the 1948 Olympics.

Lottie Dodd was a remarkable sportswoman. At the age of 15, in 1886, she won her first Wimbledon tennis title – she won six in all. She won the British Women's Golf Championship in 1904, played hockey for England, and won the silver medal in archery at the Olympics in 1908. As she comes from Bebington on the Wirral, she can't be claimed for Liverpool, but deserves an honourable mention.

port in this city means two things: Liverpool or Everton. Football is genetic here, in the blood, whether it's red or blue. But beyond the all-pervasive roar of the footie crowd, there is a whole lot of other sport going on, whether to local, national or international standards – or at street level. For heaven's sake – the world's single biggest sporting event, watched by over one billion people all over the planet in 2001, is staged in Liverpool each spring. If it's not immediately obvious, read on. It's not the Derby which, despite being run at Epsom these days, is named after its founder the Earl of Derby (as in West Derby, Liverpool), owner of Leasowe Castle, who first ran the race in 1780 over the Leasowes. Racing had been going on for much longer: there was horse-racing over Kirkdale sands to celebrate Elizabeth I's ascension to the throne in 1558, and in 1577 Mr Torbock donated a silver bell for the winner of a race each year on Ascension Day.

Before either Everton or Liverpool Football Clubs were even thought of, Liverpool Rugby Club was going strong; the oldest rugby club in the world, it was founded in 1857; three of the England team in the first ever rugby international match (1871) were Liverpool players, and in 1914 the captains of England, Scotland and Ireland were all Liverpool members. Waterloo RC, incidentally, has produced five England captains.

Smaller, cleaner and more colourful than footballs, snooker balls are made at Clare's in St Anne Street, and the firm has the world's only snooker museum. Exhibits include an eight-sided table, and cues used by cavalry officers on India's North-west Frontier in the 1870s – where snooker was invented. Liverpool lad John Parrott shot to fame when in 1991 he beat 'the Tornado' Jimmy White to become world snooker champion.

On wheels, Liverpool has a long pedigree: the Liverpool Self-propelled Traffic Association organised a trial for self-propelled vehicles on Everton Brow in 1896. On two wheels, Liverpool Velocipedes was the first cycling club, and Pete Matthews Cycles in Lower Breck Road was established in the 1930s by cycling expert Jim Soens and bought by Matthews – also a top racer, in 1972. Matthews' customers come to the crowded little shop from all over Europe to have their bikes quite literally tailor-made for them, down to the last millimetre.

Boxing glory most recently came via John Conteh, world light-heavyweight champion in 1974, but Jem Mace (who died in 1910) had the longest boxing career of all time: 36 years.

Swimming is producing some strong contenders – Catherine Smith was in the first-ever relay team to swim the length of Loch Ness and back, in 26 hours 13 minutes; in the Sydney Olympics 2000, Stephen Parry came sixth in the 200m butterfly, and has his attention fixed on Athens for 2004.

And this being a maritime city, watersports are popular; the biennial Lyver Trophy, organised by the Liverpool and Royal Dee Yacht Clubs, is a 180-mile race from the Mersey and is now a qualifier for the Fastnet race. Sailors don't have to go into international waters for a thrill – in the first-ever Mersey Regatta (1828) there was a severe thunderstorm.

Although Liverpool hasn't produced a Scouse Tiger Woods yet, golf is an abiding passion here; there are 34 golf courses on Merseyside, including Royal Birkdale (where the 100th British Open was held,) and Royal Liverpool on the Wirral.

An ancient sport that has survived into the 21st century – hare-coursing – is centred on Altcar, where the Waterloo Cup is run each year, from 1836. These days it attracts hunt saboteurs and anti-blood sports protesters as well as the sport's followers.

More than 10,000 children in Liverpool have started playing tennis, through a ground-breaking scheme, the City Tennis Programme (CTP); the only CTP scheme outside the USA, and the third largest after New York and Washington, Liverpool's tennis-mad youth won on behalf of the city the award for local authority of the year 2000 from the Lawn Tennis Association.

Liverpool's CTP scheme is in its seventh year, and the results have been stunning. In its first year, the Liverpool team was the first British team to win the World Grassroots Championships, and 21 young players won free training internships at the John Newcombe Academy in Texas. Another Liverpool lad, Anthony Hardman (now 23) won a place at Murray State University in Kentucky and has now reached world-ranking standard.

The point of CTP is to get away from the image of tennis as an elitist middle-class sport; future champions are being lost because traditional tennis clubs can seem intimidating. Some tennis clubs can charge £30 an hour and only coach in the summer; Liverpool Tennis Centre charges £60 for an entire term (clinics in deprived areas are free) and coaches all year on its 14 courts, accepting children as young as four. However, the point of the CTP is not just to produce champions; a priority of the tennis scheme is to use the sport as a means of steering children away from crime and drug-related activities.

Given the success of the Liverpool CTP, the Lawn Tennis Association is following its example and rolling out a £500,000 programme in other British cities.

The tennis-watching world was on the edge of its collective seat in the summer of 2001, when local hero Barry Cowan (ranked 265th in the world) took top seed Pete Sampras – undefeated at Wimbledon since 1994 – to a nail-biting five sets before the champion aced two serves to win.

43

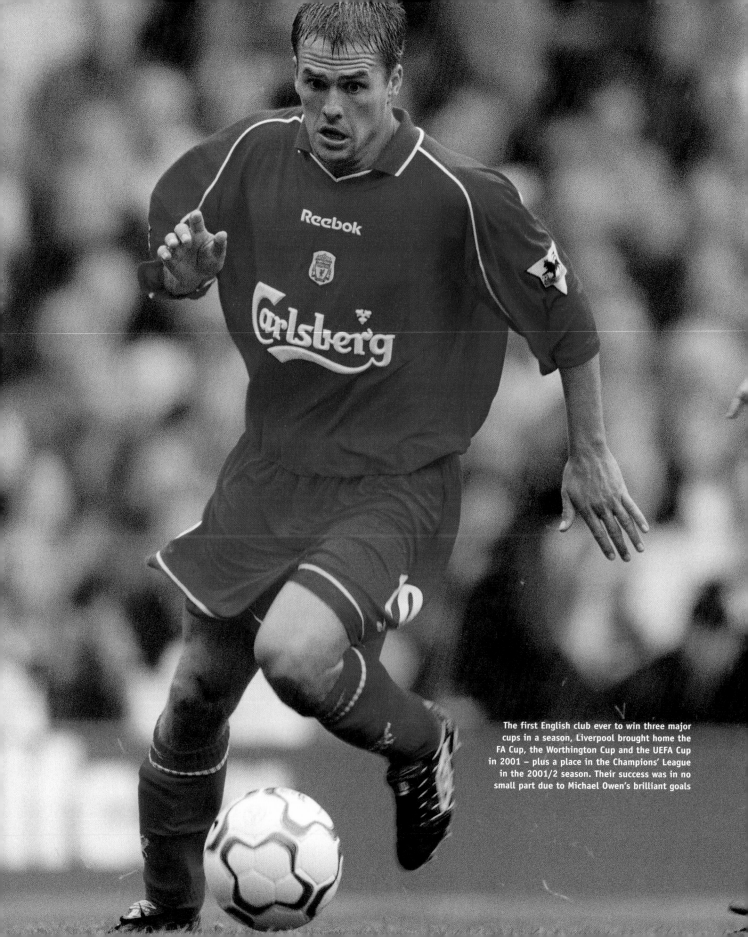

The first English club ever to win three major cups in a season, Liverpool brought home the FA Cup, the Worthington Cup and the UEFA Cup in 2001 – plus a place in the Champions' League in the 2001/2 season. Their success was in no small part due to Michael Owen's brilliant goals

Football – soccer, that is – boils down to two names in this part of the world: Everton and Liverpool. In the past team supporters divided along sectarian lines: Catholics for Everton (Blues), and Protestants for Liverpool (Reds). But in these more ecumenical and secular times there may still be a tendency for catholic families to support Everton, and protestants Liverpool, but the religious element has largely faded away, and although there is fierce rivalry between red and blue, it is friendly enough. The worst that gets hurled between fans these days is a hail of insults and some expressive gestures. It must have been galling for Evertonians to watch Liverpool fans dancing in the streets in May 2001 when the Reds brought home the treble, but odds are that there were a few generous Evertonians who raised a glass to them. For many, though, the red/blue rivalry is deep-dyed, and a true Blue would rather a trophy went to almost any other club than Liverpool FC.

Both Everton and Liverpool originated in 1878 from the youth club at St Domingo methodist church, which played in the newly laid-out Stanley Park. The club, which was known as Everton, was managed by local publican John Houlding (later Lord Mayor of Liverpool); Houlding was not universally loved, and in 1892 a group of anti-Houlding rebels decamped across the park and took over a derelict nursery garden, turning it into Goodison, and keeping the name Everton. Houlding created a new team at Anfield and called it Liverpool FC – a decision that incensed Liverpool Rugby Club which had then been in existence for almost 40 years.

Everton's first game (they won 4-2) was a friendly against Bolton; the next victory came three weeks later when they thrashed Newton Heath 6-0 (Newton Heath changed its name 10 years later to Manchester United). The first match against deadly rivals Liverpool didn't happen for two years, when Liverpool was beaten 3-0.

Liverpool didn't stay beaten for long. The club finished their very first season in the Lancashire League, and the next season went unbeaten in the Second Division. Then it was the First Division until the 1950s, when Liverpool lost their first Wembley cup final and were relegated in 1954. The legendary Bill Shankly's arrival as manager in 1959, followed by Bob Paisley and Joe Fagan, transformed Liverpool into champions. Between 1965 (FA Cup) and 1984 (their third European Cup) Liverpool were virtually unbeatable; when they lost, Everton won. (Joe Fagan, who died in 2001, steered Liverpool to a treble in his first season: League Championship, League Cup and European Cup.) In those days, remember, Liverpool was more successful than Manchester United has been recently.

Liverpool won trophies in the 1980s, but the disasters at Heysel and Hillsborough *(see chapter 8)* scarred the club for ever. A thin decade followed, with Graeme Souness and Roy Evans failing to recapture past glories. The appointment of Frenchman Gerard Houllier – who was introduced to Liverpool as a schoolmaster in the late 1960s and became a keen Koppite – has put Liverpool right back in the hot seat.

Everton have been nine times league winners (the last time in 1987) and five times the FA Cup winners, most recently in 1995. The Blues' striker Gary Lineker was top scorer in the Mexico World Cup in 1986 and scored 30 goals for Everton that season, when they were narrowly beaten to the League Championship and the FA Cup by Liverpool. Everton has retained Premier Division status since 1954 – sometimes by the skin of its teeth – but a change of ownership and a brand new stadium (possibly at King's Dock) for 2003/4 might give Everton the shot in its blue-sleeved arm that it needs.

In the 1920s the sports editor of the Echo, Bee Edwards, suggested that both teams came on to the pitch together in an Everton-Liverpool derby match, to avoid any hint of preference.

Liverpool was the first team to be televised, in 1965, and four years later Liverpool was the first club to be televised in colour.

Everton's greatest player was centre forward Ralph 'Dixie' Dean in the 1920s and 1930s; the first player to score 60 goals in a season, and still the only player to have scored 82 goals in a single season.

One of Liverpool's legends died in July 2001: Billy Liddell – the man who got Liverpool nicknamed 'Liddellpool'. A teetotal Scot, Liddell joined Liverpool in 1938 (when Matt Busby was in the team) and only hung up his boots in 1961. In a fantastic career, Liddell scored 229 goals in 537 games for the club. Liddell became bursar to Liverpool University's students' union, was a Justice of the Peace, and a lay preacher in 'retirement'.

Everton was the first club to put heating under the pitch to avoid the hazards of winter weather, and was the first club to issue programmes with team details.

Liverpool city engineer John A Brodie and his brother invented goal nets, in 1892; they were first used at Bolton Wanderers.

The youth team (below) set up by Howard Gayle in Granby has grown from a small group to a posse of boys who train five nights a week. Gayle, who was Liverpool FC's first black footballer, played with the club from 1977 to 1982; he retired from professional football in 1993.

Sport is not just for spectators. It's for dads having a kick-about with their kids in the park, or for the thousands of women who come to Liverpool for the women's 10k run each summer. Back in the 18th century one of the favourite sports was archery on the ground in Cazneau Street ('being quite in the country'). The middle class amused themselves with tennis, skittles, bowls and cricket; on the street cock-fighting, dog fights and bull-baiting were common. (Football was still a street game, played since the 12th century, but a lawless and often vicious sport until a system of rules was established in the 19th century.)

Today there is the chance to have a crack at almost any sport you care to name from rugby to gymnastics, from long distance running to ocean going yacht racing; whether you prefer solo challenges, one to one competition or team sports.

Liverpool's sports development programme is aimed not only at finding and developing potential champions, but at getting kids into the habit of sporting exercise (and adults out of the habit of not doing any). In 2000 Liverpool's tally of results showed how the programme is paying off. A junior Commonwealth champion; a junior Olympic champion; four Olympians, a junior Olympian and two Paralympians at Sydney; 23 national titles, 15 runners-up, 34 international call-ups. Nearly every single sportsperson who excelled at national and international standard came through the city's development programme – including swimmer Stephen Parry and hurdler Diane Allahgreen.

Names to watch for in future years are some of Liverpool's junior winners, like flyweight boxer Derry Matthews, cyclist Matt Brammeier and swimmer Michael Rock.

A 14-year-old wunderkind is Toni Walsh. Already British kickboxing champion, Toni went to Greece in June 2001 to compete in the world championships. Only 4'8" tall, she won the silver in Thai boxing, but lost out to a 33-year-old opponent in the kickboxing final, settling for a second silver medal in the 49kg category. Toni trains at Lea Manor sports centre in Netherley, where aged just 13 she became the only girl at the club to get a black belt.

Already with red belts, and aiming to get black belts within two years are young Muslim women taking karate classes in Liverpool. Happily confounding the stereotypes, the women had been looking for martial arts courses, but couldn't find a female instructor; now, through the Muslim women's karate group, these young women are learning self-defence techniques, increasing self-confidence.

Racing at Aintree began in 1828 under the aegis of Waterloo hotelier Bold McLynn. Lord 'Dashalong' Sefton got together a syndicate of friends to succeed McLynn; the first Grand Steeplechase was run on 1st March 1837, and has run every year since.

In 1870 there was an extra meeting, when local athlete Tom Scott jumped every fence on the course.

The race has been under threat once or twice, due either to lack of funding, or wobbly management; it was saved at one point by Seagram; that first year, with the luck of the gods, the winner was none other than the chestnut Seagram.

One of the most emotional races in living memory was the 1981 National, when Bob Champion brought Aldaniti home a winner. Champion had recovered from a long battle with cancer, and the 11-year-old Aldaniti had been written off the previous year with tendon and foot problems. Fairy tale stuff. The soundtrack from the film *Champions* has been played at the start of Grand National television coverage every year since.

The best-loved horse, though, is the extraordinary Red Rum. A local hero, Rummy

Red Rum's grave at the finishing post

was trained in Ginger McCain's yard at Southport, and was to be seen galloping along the sands and through the shallows. Red Rum won the Scottish Grand National, came second in two Aintree Grand Nationals, and won three times, in 1973, 1974 and 1977. More fairy tale stuff – his third victory broke all records. Rummy, who died in 1995 at the grand age of 30, is buried by the Aintree finishing post.

There were two extraordinary Nationals in the 1990s. In 1993 it was the National That Never Was: after a second false start half the field rode the entire two laps, not realising that the race had been stopped. Esha Ness romped home, only to be told that there was no race, there was no winner.

The race couldn't be re-run because so many horses would no longer be race fit.

In 1997 an IRA bomb scare meant postponing the National till the Monday, leaving thousands of racegoers stranded in Liverpool on Saturday night *(see chapter 6)*.

In 2001, thanks to global TV coverage, the Grand National was watched by over one billion people; the 100,000 who turned up to Aintree in the rain made enough noise to be heard in Hong Kong. A unique event, and one that is wholeheartedly Liverpudlian.

chapter 4
import/export

Eric Lynch (pictured above) is second-generation British; his father came to England from Barbados before the war.

Mean Sea Level – the standard against which every contour on the world map is measured – was first taken in 1844 from Liverpool's Victoria Dock.

Royal visitors to Liverpool included Tsar Nicholas (1816), the Duc d'Orleans (1833), the King of Portugal (1860), the Prince of Orange (1860), the Emperor of Brazil (1871), the King of Belgium (1873) and the Shah of Persia (1873).

Super Lamb Banana is a quirky reminder of the banana's introduction to Britain, through the enterprise of Sir Alfred Lewis Jones who first promoted the exotic fruit to the sceptical Brits. The Japanese sculptor, Taro Chiezo, said the piece 'reflects Liverpool's heritage of import and export and contains a visionary examination of genetic engineering'.

Riches can be counted a number of ways but, however value is calculated, Liverpool has been one of the world's wealthiest cities – and although in economic terms the city is no longer at the top of the tree, Liverpool can still count a long list of assets, from architecture to ideas. But the greatest value Liverpool has lies in its people. The city of Liverpool is a polyglot collection of travellers and traders – those who washed up here by design or by default. The English are in the minority – even assuming one can easily define 'English'. Even the Neolithic residents of Liverpool – the ones who left behind the Calder Stones – are thought to have been Boat People; so, from the dawn of human habitation, this has been a point of arrival and departure. The Roman legions turned up early, as did the Phoenician traders, to be followed by Saxons, Vikings, Normans, Celts and Hibernians; then the rest of the world.

Liverpool's culture is complex, like its gene pool. The city is said to be the capital of Wales, Scotland and Ireland; its ties with America are stronger than any other British city; its Chinese community is the oldest in Europe; its black population is one of the oldest in Britain; and there can be few countries in continental Europe without links to Liverpool.

The world has been exporting to Liverpool for centuries – it's only fair, then, that Liverpool should have given back so much. The city has spawned a catalogue of world-beaters. Apart from the screamingly obvious, Liverpool people and products have become famous around the globe. A long, long list of firsts – in science, business, medicine, social structure, public health, arts – has made a serious impact on the world, and Liverpool continues to come up with world-class thinkers, entrepreneurs, scientists, writers, artists and performers.

Who were the original Scousers? The Neolithic Boat People can probably claim the title in Liverpool's prehistory; on marsh and heathland they created scattered settlements of fishers and farmers. The Romans weren't impressed, although they did build a road through here, they stuck to Chester and other less boggy parts of the North West. (Chester's Roman name was Deva; our name for it derives from the Latin word *castra*, or camp: hence Man-, Rib-, Win-, Chi-, Dor-chester, etc.)

Saxons drifted in, building small settlements and churches; Vikings, who had been raiding the west coast sporadically for a while, eventually started to settle and built more churches. Place names and a few archaeological finds are all that's left of these early settlements.

The Normans, auditing their newly acquired kingdom in 1086, didn't bother to note down Liverpool in the Domesday Book. Toxteth, yes, and West Derby, but not Liverpool. It wasn't till King John (bad King John, Richard the Lionheart's naughty younger brother) twigged that Liverpool was a handy point of departure for Ireland that things started to move. For the next 300 years the population grew as soldiers were shipped in and out along the Mersey, traders started to scent a new market and moved in, and the town began to establish itself. Under the reigns of the Tudors and Stuarts, Liverpool stagnated; the Civil War and a string of plagues knocked the town for six.

From the late 1600s, though, Liverpool opened up to the world, and the world obliged by turning up to see what was going on. But while strangers from distant parts might have brought a little spice to the town, much of Liverpool's modern culture was imported from nearer neighbours – Wales, Scotland and Ireland.

The Welsh came to Liverpool in droves; the first Welsh chapel was built in Pall Mall in 1787; the Welsh population grew so large that Pall Mall became known as Little Wales, and in 1788 there was even a Liverpool Welsh penny minted. They may have been here a good deal earlier; place names like Walton and Wallasey (on the Wirral) suggest that Welsh Celts may have made their homes here in the first millennium AD. By 1813 one in ten of Liverpool's citizenry were Welsh and over the next 40 years the Welsh community grew from 8,000 to 40,000, many of whom spoke no English; in Everton and Kirkdale advertising hoardings and local newspapers were in Welsh. At the end of the 19th century, there were four National Eisteddfodau held in Liverpool – in 1840, 1855, 1884 and 1900.

On 28th May 1865 153 Welsh men, women and children left Liverpool in a tea-clipper, bound for Patagonia, on the southernmost tip of South America. Three years later there were 5,000 of them there, and Welsh is still spoken in Patagonia today, despite the best efforts of the Argentinian government to promote Spanish.

As for the Scots, they came to prosper. Medics, scholars, engineers and entrepreneurs saw opportunity in Liverpool – famous names such as Gladstone and Laird, for example. By 1837 there were enough Scots to support six congregations (the Scottish church of St Andrews, though ruined, is still in Rodney Street) and they prospered in ship-building, rope-making, engineering, and sugar-refining. The Scottish presence was less obvious than the Welsh or Irish because the community didn't live in definable areas; the independent Scots weaved themselves into the fabric of Liverpool life in more subtle patterns.

The Irish have made Liverpool their home for centuries (Freemen of Liverpool were Freemen of Waterford and Wexford too), brought here as labourers, fleeing here from famine or persecution and, later, passing through on their way to the new world. The Irish influence on Liverpool has been enormous, from the Scouse accent to politics, literature and music.

Sewills has been making time-pieces in Liverpool since 1800: clocks, watches, chronometers and barometers. In 1862 Napoleon III awarded Sewills a gold medal at the Paris Exhibition, and the firm was appointed maker to the Queen of Spain. Seven years later Sewills made a chronometer for the Cutty Sark to help it win the great Tea Races from China. After winning the Admiralty Trials twice, Sewills' chronometers were installed in many Royal Navy ships, including Ark Royal and HMS Belfast.

For Irish men, women and children fleeing from an Ireland devastated by famine and ruled by absentee landlords, Liverpool must have seemed like a safe haven – where the streets, if not paved with gold, at least offered a path to a decent life. The irony of flying from the cruelty of English landlords only to land up in the grip of urban sharks happy to chew up the new arrivals and spit them out into the gutter. Many were forced to sleep on stone floors in cramped cellars; if they could afford the shilling per day for the emigrants' boarding house in Moorfields, they still slept on bare boards. They were fleeced by passage brokers, touts, provisions merchants and the infamous runners (one lot was known as the Forty Thieves).

Even the crossing from Dublin to Liverpool could be tough. On board the so-called coffin ships, livestock were carried between decks, to arrive in fine fettle. The human passengers, on the other hand, were packed like sardines on deck, regardless of the weather; the journey across the treacherous Irish Sea could take up to three days in bad weather, and people died. The journey to America for those who couldn't afford 15-guinea staterooms and private saloons was an ordeal. For steerage passengers conditions weren't much better than on slave ships; slave ship captains had an incentive to keep slaves alive and in good condition; but as emigrants had already paid their way, if some had to be buried at sea, well ....

In 1847 some 17,500 emigrants (one in every six) who sailed for New England died en route; six years later about 40 of the emigrant ships were struck with cholera.

In all, two million Irish (a quarter of Ireland's population) came to Liverpool in a decade; many stayed, many more were among the nine million emigrants to America who sailed from the Mersey; at the height of the rush to New England, a thousand ships a year left Liverpool. How ironic that the potato blight that caused the famine originated in America.

lthough Europeans had been coming to Liverpool for centuries, it wasn't until the 19th century that specific communities began to grow. The exception was the Jewish community, who came to Liverpool from the early 1700s; one of the first groups came from Spain, and later from Germany, Poland and Russia; in the 20th century, of course, many Jews fled from persecution in Nazi Germany and Eastern Europe. It was Methodist John Wesley who, in 1775, referred to the Jewish community of about 100, mostly silversmiths and tradesmen; today there are about 3,000 Jews in Liverpool.

Among the founders of the Athenaeum (the first in Britain) in 1797 were four Liverpool Jews; within 15 years the Jewish community had set up a philanthropic society 'to give relief to their distressed brethren' – early days of a continuous charitable tradition.

An unwilling influx of Frenchmen came to Liverpool during the Napoleonic Wars – about 4,000 prisoners of war were incarcerated in the Tower of Liverpool. When the survivors were released (230 died in the Tower) most went home, but some stayed in Liverpool and settled.

The 19th century saw a great tide of Europeans coming to Liverpool to exploit the opportunities offered by such a rich and dynamic seaport; Scandinavians followed their Viking forebears – Danes, Swedes, Norwegians, Finns, Icelanders and Faroe Islanders; from the other side of the Baltic came Russians, Estonians, Lithuanians, Latvians; the Baltic Fleet pub, opposite Wapping Dock, flies the appropriate flag whenever a Baltic ship is in port.

A steady flow of Italians came to Liverpool between 1880 and 1912; they worked as organ-grinders, street entertainers, musicians, knife-sharpeners and hotel staff – and notably as ice cream makers. Incidentally Silkhouse Court (Tithebarn Street) was possibly Liverpool's first factory, run by Italian silk manufacturers. The streets around Scotland Road became Little Italy – by 1913 there were more than 400 Italian-born residents here, but in the slum clearances of the 1930s most of these little streets were razed and their residents rehoused.

One of Little Italy's celebrities was Dom Volante, born to Italian parents in Gerard Street, and later a world-class boxer who topped the bill at Madison Square Gardens in New York.

The Greek community, now about 3,000 strong, began in 1810 with shipowners and traders (in 1855 George Papayannis founded the Ellerman & Papayannis steamship line) and in 1871 there were about 300 Greeks here. At the start of the 1900s most of the wealthy Greeks left for Australia and America, and it wasn't until British soldiers brought Greek brides home after World War II, and the Cypriots came over in the 1960s, that the community began to revive and prosper. The Greek Orthodox Church, consecrated in 1870 by the Archbishop of Syra and Tinos, these days has a regular congregation of 150, and big attendances for Easter, Christmas and the important saints' days.

In June 1999 Liverpool welcomed 200 Kosovan refugees, airlifted out of the camps in Macedonia. Among them was the Hajdari family – Ekrem, Nazlie and their five children (pictured below). The eldest, Saranda, was ten. The only English she knew when she arrived was 'My name is Saranda'; two years later she is fluent, complete with Scouse accent. 'We all love being in Liverpool – everyone welcomed us, and kissed all the children,' says Saranda. 'When we arrived, we had nothing – all we wanted was somewhere to sleep. Before the camps in Macedonia we were in the mountains for a week when we escaped from Kosovo. My mum cried because she had nothing to give my baby sister.' Before the war, she says, it was very hard; Saranda's father Ekrem is a primary school teacher, and her mother Nazlie had a shop, 'but we had no freedom', says Saranda. The children all love school and work like fury – Saranda's head teacher said he wished all his pupils were as enthusiastic and keen to learn. Most of the Kosovar families had gone back by the summer of 2001, but the Hajdaris still hope to stay. Such a family would be an asset to the city.

The splendid Chinese Arch at the top of Nelson Street is the largest outside mainland China

Chinese sailors began to arrive in Liverpool around the middle of the 1800s, and moved into the area near the south docks – Cleveland Square and Pitt Street – amongst Scandinavian, Lascar and African seamen, European Jews and Irish immigrants. The origin of the Chinese community on Merseyside dates from 1834 when the East India Company's charter was amended and the China trade was thrown open to private enterprise. On 12th June 1834 the *Duchess of Clarence*, belonging to John Bibby & Co, became the first Liverpool ship homeward-bound from China to arrive in the River Mersey. Her cargo was tea and on board was a crew of Chinese sailors.

By 1918 there were 3,200 Chinese men on shore, most of whom were connected to seafaring. During the Second World War Liverpool was the home of the Chinese Merchant Seamen's Pool; there may have been as many as 20,000 Chinese men registered – most of whom came from the Chinese mainland, especially Shanghai – who were escaping political turmoil in China. Then in the early 1940s the Japanese occupied the Chinese treaty ports so that many Chinese men in Liverpool couldn't return home and were forced to stay here.

The decision to settle here meant, for most, marrying and having a family; as there were few Chinese women in Liverpool, the men tended to marry local girls – British-born women automatically lost their British citizenship when they married a Chinese man. For white women, Chinese men were preferable to local men because they were kinder, more considerate and gentle. In many poor white households, the men would get drunk and beat the women and children – the Chinese were horrified by such behaviour, and by contrast would often, if they saw a child barefoot in the street, go and buy them shoes.

Within the Chinese community, there was little racial or religious strife between the various nationalities and cultures living in the area; the local school was nicknamed the League of Nations. But the Chinese Liverpudlians came up against discrimination when they tried to get jobs in the city; they still do. The number of ethnic Chinese in today's private sector management or the professions wouldn't run into double figures. If bright young Chinese Liverpudlians want a good career, they go to London, or go abroad.

The English perception that the Chinese were stupid or illiterate was far from the truth – they may have had little knowledge of the English language and English ways, but they were educated; in China more respect is given to intellectuals than to the wealthy. But, despite a higher level of educational qualifications than their English counterparts, and a highly developed work ethic and entrepreneurial culture, the Chinese still struggle to get decent jobs outside their own community.

At the start of the 1990s, there was a concerted campaign in Liverpool to draw on historical trading links with Shanghai, and in 1999 the twinning ceremony between Liverpool and Shanghai cemented the two cities' relationship. As a most generous gift to celebrate the connection, the city of Shanghai gave Liverpool an archway – the biggest outside mainland China. A team of civil engineers and skilled workmen came over to Liverpool to put the hundreds of pieces of this splendid, spectacular structure in place – it took several months, and was officially opened in September 2000. If there was ever any doubt where Chinatown was in Liverpool, there can be no doubt now. With the arrival of new Chinese settlers – this time after the return of Hong Kong from British rule – Liverpool has another chance to make the most of an undervalued community that has contributed a good deal, taken very little and remained loyal to the city.

Apart from seafaring, the early Chinese in Liverpool had four main occupations: laundry work, running boarding houses, grocery shops and restaurants. Chinese settlers did not speak good English and would have very limited access to capital.

Tung Chee Hwa, governor of Hong Kong, is an engineering graduate of Liverpool University.

At Liverpool Museum is one of the world's finest collections of Chinese porcelain.

There are two monuments, erected by Chinese freemasons, to the Chinese who have died in Britain. One is in Anfield cemetery (1950), the other is in Everton cemetery (1972).

Kwok Fong (1882-1969) came from Canton to Liverpool in the early 1900s. He made a living as a provisions merchant, but for 50 years his main work was the welfare of Asian crewmen on Liverpool ships. He was Uncle Fong to scores of Chinese he helped over the years.

The goods in Liverpool's bonded warehouses on 30th September 1863 included: 1.3 million pounds of cocoa; 1.8 million pounds of coffee and 3.3 million pounds of tea; 5,130 tons of currants, 11,404 tons of molasses and 1.2 million pounds of pepper; 2.5 million gallons of foreign spirits, 1.2 million gallons of wine; 37,512 tons of sugar, 16.7 million pounds of tobacco and 178,007 pounds of cigars and tobacco products.

Mamadou Diaw is a master musician from Senegal; he was touring Europe with his band Libidor, and when he came to Liverpool in 1996, he liked the city so much he decided to stay. He liked the people as soon as he got here: 'Liverpool people are open; it's a big place but it's connected and people know each other – and it's a lot cheaper than London.' Mamadou plays all kinds of instruments and sings too, but is a master of traditional African drums and teaches drumming workshops at the Blackie Arts Centre as well as school lessons. He is a great advocate for Liverpool. 'Some people say this city is full of problems, but every place has problems. How you feel about a place depends on you, and how you deal with people.'

The city's black population is as diverse as its white European population, with people coming here from all over Africa as well as America and the West Indies.

Liverpool has one of the oldest black populations in the UK, the early settlers mostly seamen recruited from West Africa, America or the West Indies, or children of black traders sent to Liverpool to be educated. There were also freed slaves (as soon as a slave set foot in England after 1772 he was a free man), and servants of wealthy families with slave trade connections. Some freed slaves signed up as seamen on ships in the American Civil War and ended up in Liverpool that way.

Even at the height of the slave trade there were never many slaves brought to Liverpool – the abominable trade was outward, from West Africa to America, and the story that there were slaves chained to rings outside the Goree Warehouses or on the Pier Head is untrue.

There may have been no ships docking in Liverpool with cargoes of slaves, but there were some slaves sold here, auctioned in coffee houses, warehouses, shops and on the steps of the Custom House. There was an advertisement in the Liverpool Advertiser in 1766: 'To be sold at the Exchange Coffee House in Water Street, this day, the 12th of September, at 1 o'clock precisely, eleven negroes imported by the *Angola*.'

A number of black Americans would have been among the thousands that came through Liverpool en route to France in the First World War – they were billeted at a vast camp in Knotty Ash – and the huge numbers of army, navy and air force personnel either stationed here or en route to other bases or front lines in Europe.

Two distinct communities have grown up in Liverpool over many decades. The Somalis number about 4,000, mostly living in the Granby area of Toxteth. The first generation of Somali settlers were sailors working for the British Navy when the country, in the Horn of Africa, was British Somaliland. Then a wave of Somalis came to Liverpool in the early 1990s, after war broke out in famine-hit Somalia in 1991; around 50,000 people were killed and another 300,000 died of starvation.

A nomadic people, the Somalis are very independent and protective of their cultural identity. Reluctant to integrate for fear of losing their identity, many Somali families have felt very isolated in Liverpool; this has meant a lot of misunderstanding about Somali culture.

The level of educational achievement for young Liverpudlian Somalis has, till now, been relatively low, as has their self-confidence; unemployment levels are high. The community is eager to see a Somali academy linked to the universities to help the young achieve their ambitions and make stronger links within the city.

The Nigerians first came to Liverpool when Nigeria was a British Protectorate (1914-1960), as crew on Liverpool ships; many have since come here to study at university and to start their careers. Angus Chukwemeka, chair of the Nigerian Community Association, came to Liverpool in 1968 to study electrical engineering; of his five children, one son is a barrister, one a pharmacist, and his daughter has just qualified in law.

But again, subtly racist attitudes have made it difficult for Nigerians to prosper in the city. Despite being better qualified than many white Liverpudlians, Nigerians, like the Chinese, suffer far higher unemployment levels. There may not be overt racist hostility, but one Nigerian businessman, who is a JP, and has his own main contracting construction company, says: 'I have five A levels and two degrees, but it's impossible to open a bank account here as a black businessman.' All is politeness and consideration, but the answer is still no. And again, like the Chinese Liverpudlians, the number of black senior managers or professionals is negligible. For a city with such a cosmopolitan history, it is way beyond time to readjust the racist attitudes that waste talent and ambition on such a grand scale.

Scouse was an import from Scandinavia. The dish Lobscouse, or Labskause, was first mentioned in 1708, in Ned Ward's 'The Wooden World Dissected'. Scouse – a stew of mutton, onions and potatoes, served with pickled red cabbage or beetroot – is possibly not the greatest or most subtle example of world cuisine ever created, but it obviously did the trick for hungry sailors. It is not on every menu in Liverpool, but can be found if you're really keen.

Miss Bluebell – Margaret Kelly was brought up in West Derby, brought here from a Dublin orphanage. She made her stage debut aged 12 in Liverpool, and founded the Bluebell Girls in Paris aged 21. With her Jewish husband she stayed in Paris throughout the war and was a heroine to the French.

The Mersey Foundry produced cast-iron for export to Australia, New Zealand, India and Africa. Liverpool's cast-iron churches became the model for pre-fabricated cast-iron churches shipped all over the world.

Liverpool's commercial and industrial life has made quite a dent in world trade through names like Ferranti and ICI, which both began here. In science the work of physicist Oliver Lodge and 17th-century astronomer Jeremiah Horrox were catalysts for communications and space exploration. Sir James Chadwick's work on atomic physics was an integral part of the Manhattan Project.

Christopher Columbus's statue, which stands outside the Palm House in Sefton Park, bears the inscription: 'The discoverer of America was the maker of Liverpool'. By the end of the 18th century, trade with America was so great that an American Chamber of Commerce was set up in Liverpool in 1801 and operated for 100 years. America was nearly the undoing of Liverpool, too, when first the Revolution, then the Civil War stopped trade in and out of Liverpool; there were 500,000 cotton workers out of work and starving during the Lancashire cotton famine caused by the Civil War.

There are those who complain about the Americanisation of everything – the bastardisation of English, baseball caps, McDonalds, My Little Pony, Jerry Springer, chewing gum, gansta rap, and the Internet, for a start – but as Liverpool has built a vast proportion of its wealth upon trade with the Americas, and principally the United States, to complain that cultural influence is now being reversed after 400 years seems a little ungracious.

But it wasn't all bad. Some of the more civilised names coming to Liverpool from the US include Mark Twain, Frank Woolworth, Herman Melville, James Audubon, James Whistler and Washington Irving.

Herman Melville was following in his father's footsteps, but having tried to get into the Lyceum gentleman's club, was reputedly thrown out by the seat of his pants. He didn't take offence, and used his memories of Liverpool in his book *Redburn*.

Washington Irving was in Liverpool for four years, managing his brother's business at 1 Goree Warehouses; when the business went bust, Irving had a breakdown and, during his convalescence, wrote *Rip Van Winkle* and *The Legend of Sleepy Hollow*.

In the 1820s James Audubon came to Liverpool with several hundred drawings; his exhibition at the Royal Institution in Colquitt Street was a great success and, with financial backing from the Rathbones, he published his four-volume *Birds of America*. Three of Audubon's oils are in the University's art gallery in Abercromby Square.

Among other American writers to visit Liverpool were Mark Twain, who lectured at the Mechanics Institute, and Harriet Beecher Stowe (author of *Uncle Tom's Cabin*) who visited Speke Hall in 1853. Going west, Oscar Wilde sailed from Liverpool in the *Arizona* – the ship which had on an earlier voyage crashed at full speed into an iceberg, and survived. Wilde, on reaching New York and being quizzed by customs officers, uttered the humble words: 'I have nothing to declare but my genius.'

Speke Hall was also home to shipowner FR Leyland, the patron of American painter James McNeill Whistler, who often stayed at Speke Hall after moving to England in 1859.

An altogether livelier visitor to Liverpool was Colonel William F Cody – Buffalo Bill – who brought his *Wild West Show* (400 performers including Little Annie Oakley, Sioux, Araphoe and Cheyenne Indians); in 1891 they performed in Newsham Park; 15 years later they were back with a show at the Exhibition Ground in Edge Lane.

Permanent residents in Liverpool include several Americans buried in St James's cemetery by the Anglican Cathedral. The most illustrious of them is probably William Taylor Barry, Envoy Extraordinary and Minister Plenipotentiary to the Court of Spain, who died in Liverpool in August 1835.

It wasn't all one-way. American architect John Root was deeply influenced by the work of Peter Ellis, 16 Cook Street. Root went back to the US after the Civil War, and as a founder of Chicago firm Burnham & Root designed many landmarks, including the Monadnock Building, one of the world's first skyscrapers.

Columbus is a controversial figure: the quincentenary celebrations of his landing in the New World were tempered by the knowledge of what that discovery led to – the appalling treatment of Native Americans and, later, the slave trade and its long aftermath.

The poet Felicia Hemans, who was born at 118 Duke Street in 1793 and later lived at 17 Wavertree High Street, is most famous for two poems. Casabianca and The Landing of the Pilgrim Fathers, traditionally recited in American homes at Thanksgiving.

John Julius Booth was a popular actor in Liverpool, but he fancied his chances in the US and emigrated in 1821. His sons Edwin and John were both actors, but John Wilkes Booth, born in 1839, was rather better known for assassinating Abraham Lincoln at Ford's Theatre in Washington. Booth was killed two weeks later, while on the run.

Hollywood cowboy Roy Rogers came to Liverpool in 1954 and stayed at the Adelphi Hotel. He rode his horse Trigger up the steps of the hotel, and later Trigger appeared at a first floor window to greet the crowd below.

Comic actor Mike Myers (Wayne's World, Austin Powers) was born in Canada a couple of years after his parents emigrated from Liverpool. His father was a carpet salesman in Aigburth.

Baron Rio Branco – one of Brazil's greatest statesmen, lived in the Adelphi Hotel as Consul General from 1877-1892. Brazil's first overseas consulate after independence from Portugal in 1822, it marked vital trading links going back to the 1500s.

The first recorded cargo from America to land in Liverpool was in 1648. The first cargo of cotton was traded in Liverpool in 1709.

The Liverpool Merchant, the first Liverpool slaver, sold a cargo of 220 slaves in Barbados in 1700.

Crosswords were invented by Arthur Wynne, a Liverpool emigrant. The first 'word-cross' appeared in a New York paper on 21st December 1913.

Once the Pilgrim Fathers had sailed off to the New World to found the colony of New England, there followed a steady stream of migrants. The peak of emigration was from the mid-19th to the early 20th century when, between 1830 and 1930, nine million people sailed from Liverpool to find a new life in America. Not all those nine million survived the journey, and some of the survivors thought better of it and came back. This is excluding the forcible migration of perhaps ten million West Africans sold into slavery, the majority of whom were taken to America in Liverpool-owned ships. (One of them, the forebear of 1975 Wimbledon tennis champion Arthur Ashe, was transported with 166 others in the square-rigger Doddington.)

Liverpool's first gift to America (although it didn't know at the time) was one Richard Mather, who sailed from Liverpool in 1635 in the wake of the Pilgrim Fathers. Mather was a Puritan preacher, the first minister of the Ancient Chapel of Toxteth (he preached his first sermon in 1618). Continually under fire for his nonconformity and eventually silenced by the Archbishop of York, Mather gave up on merrie old England and went to New England, where he settled in Dorchester and became the leader of Congregationalism in Massachusetts. His son, Increase Mather, became president of Harvard, and Increase's son Cotton Mather was possibly the most famous of the lot, first for his part in the Salem Witch Trials of 1692, then as President of Yale, then as the man who set up a school to educate slaves, and introduced inoculation to a smallpox-ridden Boston.

A century after Mather sailed from Liverpool, Robert Morris was born on 20th January 1735 to a poor family living in Chorley Court (the site of Blackburn Chambers) off Dale Street. To escape poverty, Morris left Liverpool when he was 13 and headed to New England; within seven years he had got himself a partnership in a New York mercantile company.

Morris was the financial brains behind the War of Independence – the key deal-maker for the Revolution – and was one of the signatories to the Declaration of Independence in 1776. Afterwards, once Congress was established, Morris was virtually its financial director. He later founded the Bank of North America in Philadelphia – the oldest financial institution in the USA. But, despite owning millions of acres of the eastern seaboard at one time or another, Morris lost everything through speculative land deals, and died in a debtors' prison.

A Quaker family from Shropshire called Cunard sailed to Philadelphia in the 1600s, then moved to Halifax, Nova Scotia, where Samuel Cunard was born in 1787. The Cunard line was founded as the British & North American Royal Mail Steam Packet Company, when Samuel Cunard won the contract from the British Admiralty to carry the mail across the Atlantic.

From 1830 to 1930 Liverpool was the point of departure for nine million emigrants to America. By the mid-19th century there was an insatiable demand in America for labour; wages were about five times higher than in Europe, and almost 1,000 ships a year were taking emigrants from Liverpool. It was no picnic: the crossing could take anything from a month to 14 weeks. In steerage a berth for four people could be as little as six-foot square; below decks it was cramped, badly lit, smelly and stuffy. Food was poor and water was revolting. Disease (including cholera), fire, shipwreck and seasickness killed many; even when they reached America there was no guarantee of a better life. In 1854 and 1855 unemployment in America was so bad that 30,000 immigrants sailed back to Liverpool.

1852 was the peak of emigration from Liverpool: 299,099 people sailed that year, more than double the number for 1847. Of the 131,121 emigrants leaving Liverpool in 1848, 190 went to the West Indies, 298 to Australia, 14 to Hong Kong and 12 to the Falkland Islands.

In 1851 more than 85,000 Mormons sailed from Liverpool to America, including the father and grandfather of Butch Cassidy (outlaw partner of the Sundance Kid). As a tribute to Liverpool on the 150th anniversary of their emigration, the Mormon Church gave a statue to the city.

Richard Peter, once Liverpool's Town Clerk, founded the University of Philadelphia with Benjamin Franklin.

The Beatles first landed at JFK Airport in February 1964 to be met by screaming hysteria; 73 million watched their US broadcast on the Ed Sullivan Show. The group's last gig, in 1966, was at Candlestick Park in San Francisco.

A female crack shot and scalp hunter ... Ann Dennis, born in Liverpool in 1742, was kidnapped at the age of 19, taken to Virginia and sold into bondage as an indentured servant. She married a soldier called Bailey, who was killed by Indians at the battle of Point Pleasant. Ann's thirst for revenge drove her to become a scout and messenger on the Virginian frontier. In 1791, when Fort Lee in Charleston was under siege, Ann rode 120 miles, on her black horse Liverpool, to another fort to get ammunition and soldiers to save Fort Lee. Mad Ann's Ridge in Alleghany, New York, is named after her, and she is remembered in song and with monuments.

Liverpool's relationship with America faltered a couple of times after trade began, but ties were strong enough to survive the bad times. A conflict of interests arose in the War of Independence (this side of the Pond, known as the years when the Americans were revolting), although it only became obvious with hindsight. While the Scouser Robert Morris was funding the colonials' rebellion against his King, George III, another Scouser was trying his level best to keep the status quo. Banastre Tarleton, born in Water Street (about 100 yards from Morris's birthplace) in 1754, was only 22 when he went to America to fight for King and country against the rebels. In five years, he captured General Charles Lee from behind enemy lines and played a leading role in the taking of Philadelphia and Charleston, before being captured by George Washington at the surrender of York Town in 1781. He was a national hero in England, but his boast that he had laid more women and slaughtered more men than anyone else in the army earned him the nickname of The Butcher. He was painted a very ugly character in Mel Gibson's 2000 Hollywood movie *The Patriot* (not praised for its historical accuracy). The movie had Tarleton dying in America; in fact he came back to England as Major General Tarleton.

Seven years after the British acknowledged America's independence, George Washington appointed James Maury as American Consul in Liverpool. Maury – who had been at school with future president Thomas Jefferson – sailed to Liverpool with fellow diplomats John Adams and John Jay, who then travelled on to London and Paris respectively. It may only be by a matter of days, but Liverpool had the world's first American consulate.

James Maury lived in Liverpool for 40 years, from 1790 to 1829; his house was at 4 Rodney Street, and his office was in Paradise Street, by the Pool. Not all his consulate roles were glamorous – almost his first and last jobs were to bail out American sailors who had been chucked into the Tower of Liverpool for brawling or similar offences committed after getting pie-eyed in one of Liverpool's 2,300 drinking dens.

One of Maury's successors was Nathaniel Hawthorne, US Consul in Liverpool and author of books such as *The Scarlet Letter* and *Tanglewood Tales*. Hawthorne didn't enjoy Liverpool much: 'what with brutal ships' masters, drunken sailors, vagrant Yankees, mad people, sick people and dead people'. Not a sociable man, in four years: 'I have received and been civil to at least 10,000 visitors ... and I never wish to be civil to anybody again.' Still, there were compensations. One of the consul's jobs was to certify invoices for exports: at $2 per autograph, and up to 25 invoices a day, it was a significant extra income for the poor man.

Princes Dock, from where millions of Europeans left for the New World. The sheds are now gone

Having shrugged off British rule, the Americans then fought amongst themselves. The Civil War ran from 1861 to 1865, and Liverpool was at the start and the end of it. The first shot of the war was fired from a cannon made in Duke Street by Fawcett & Preston ('Fosset' guns were used on both sides in the Civil War).

Confederate president Jefferson Davis packed off a naval lieutenant, James Bulloch, to Liverpool with a brief to get arms and commission ships to use in the fight against the Union. Liverpool had, after all, strong commercial ties with the Southern states, much to the rage of the Yankee Union. Bulloch signed contracts with local shipbuilders for the first two cruisers – *Alabama* and *Florida*; there followed another 33 blockade-runners built on Merseyside for the Confederate cause. *Florida* sank 36 Union ships; under Captain Raphael Semmes and with a largely Liverpudlian crew, *Alabama* – in the space of two years – sank or captured 68 Union ships. The day *Alabama* was bested, by Federal cruiser *Kearsage* off Cherbourg, Semmes was rescued by another Mersey-built ship, the *Deerhound*. It caused serious ructions between the Federal and British governments, and after the war a tribunal in Geneva awarded the United States $15.5 million for the damage caused by the *Alabama* and other Confederate ships built on Merseyside. (James Bulloch stayed in Liverpool after the war, where he was visited by his nephew Teddy Roosevelt. Bulloch died in 1898 and is buried in Toxteth cemetery; the Daughters of the Confederacy put up a tombstone for him in 1968.)

Foreign bankers to the Confederacy, Fraser Trenholm & Co also had their offices at 10 Rumford Place. Up in Abercromby Square, No19 was built for CK Prioleau, a Confederate agent (whose wife was supposed to have been the most beautiful woman in Liverpool) working for Bulloch. Over the front door fanlight is the Bonnie Blue star of South Carolina; there are more on the entrance columns, while painted on the ceiling inside the door is the palmetto, the South Carolina state tree.

The last act of the Civil War was played out in Liverpool, too, when the Confederate ship *Shenandoah* sailed to Liverpool, where her captain Lt Cdr James Waddell surrendered her to Liverpool's mayor at the Town Hall on 6th November 1865, 211 days after Robert E Lee surrendered to Grant. Waddell and his crew of 130 were arrested, but were then immediately liberated.

In a reversal of the massive migrations of the 19th century, the World Wars saw a massive influx of American armed forces into Liverpool. In World War I Liverpool's temporary home for US soldiers was the huge army camp at Knotty Ash; there was also an American military hospital at Mossley Hill.

America's entry into World War II came after November 1941, when the Japanese bombed Pearl Habour; it wasn't long before troop ships were steaming across the Atlantic. Nearly 1,300 convoys, some of more than 60 ships, docked in Liverpool during the war (during the first half of 1944 alone some 750,000 men and two million tons of war supplies were unloaded at Liverpool). Ships would be queuing in the Mersey to dock, and troop trains were running incessantly from Riverside. With the huge US air base at Burtonwood, about 20 miles inland, USAF personnel, not to mention thousands of aircraft, were shipped through Liverpool.

In 1945, of course, the process was reversed, with hundreds of thousands of Americans going home, to be followed by 70,000 GI brides – many of whom left from Liverpool.

Colonel Harold Duffie, the US army's port commander, was awarded the Legion of Merit that year – the highest decoration awarded to a US army officer for non-combatant service.

Did Lloyd Grossman's forebears emigrate to Boston through Liverpool?

American horse Rubio won the Grand National in 1908.

The 2,118-ton square rigger Wavertree, built in Liverpool in 1885, is in New York's South Street Seaport Museum.

In 1807 Moses Liverpool, with a group of other freed slaves built the first school for black children in the District of Columbia.

In 1936 American aviators Dick Merrill and Harry Richman took off from Southport beach and flew to Musgrove Harbour, near St John's Newfoundland, in a record 17 hours and 47 minutes. The following year Merrill flew from Southport to New York, in 24 hours 22 minutes.

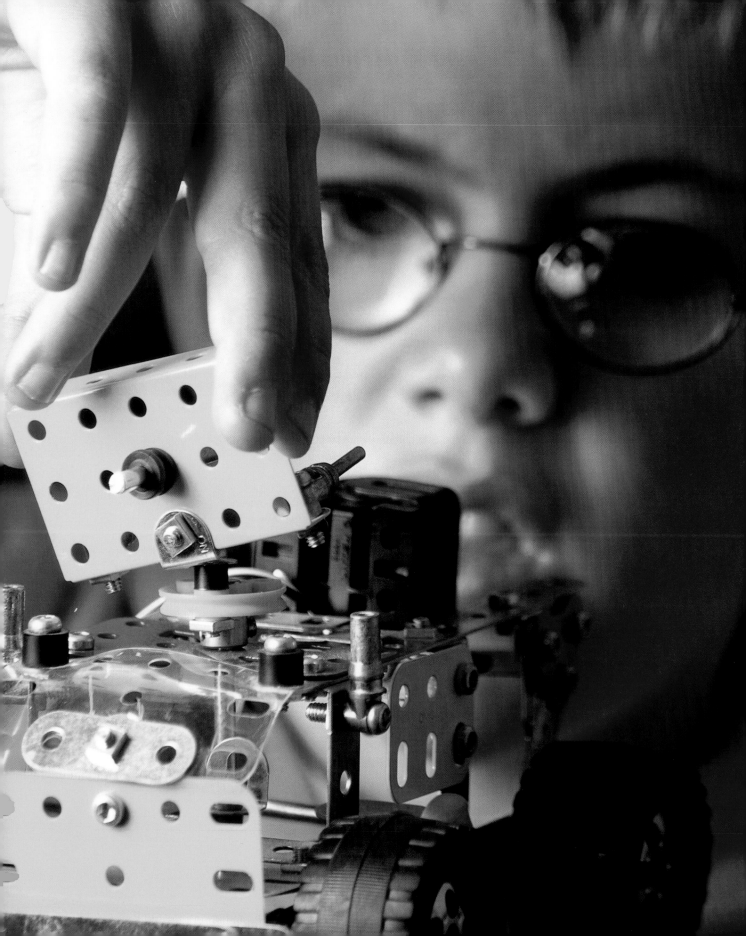

Frank Hornby is one of Liverpool's greats: a bookkeeper for a meat importer on Liverpool Docks, Hornby was to become one of the great names of childhood in the 20th century. The names of his great inventions? Hornby Dublo, and Meccano – the toys that fathers bought for sons because the fathers wanted to play with the toys. (Other Hornby toys included Aero, Motor Car, Kemex (chemistry), Elektron (electrical) and later Dinky Toys.)

Hornby was born in 1863 and worked for his father, a wholesale grocer. Frank married Clara Godefroy when he was 24, and had two sons, Roland and Douglas. It was to entertain his children that Hornby began to invent toys for them in his workshop at home. In 1900 he came up with a construction toy with interchangeable parts; the basic system had half-inch wide perforated metal strips, with nuts and bolts, wheels, axles and screws. The parts were virtually unbreakable, and needed no special tools to put them together: he called the toy Mechanics Made Easy, and patented it in 1901.

Hornby's employer, the meat importer David Elliot, backed him: he helped Hornby to lease premises, and gave him valuable introductions. Over the next three years, Hornby developed three sets of different sizes, including cranks, keys, hooks, gears and other components, and on 14th September 1907 he registered the Meccano name. Seven years on, and Hornby had a purpose-built factory in Binns Road (Wavertree); Meccano sets soon included clockwork motors and then electric motors.

In 1912 Hornby started production in Paris, and soon he opened an American factory in New Jersey. The Meccano magazine began in 1916, and Meccano clubs were formed into a Meccano Guild. Every member got a badge, and a member's certificate signed by Hornby himself.

By the time Hornby died in 1937 his own name, and that of Meccano, were two of the best known to children in Europe and America.

The Hornby Dublo train, incidentally, first appeared in 1920 – a vertical steam engine, it was made of nickel and powered by clockwork. In time, any child lucky enough to have a train-mad parent could create a layout covering hundreds of square feet, with landscaping (urban and rural), complex junctions and points to switch trains across dozens of tracks, sidings, stations, bridges and tunnels – scope for

a lifetime of running Hornby's beautifully detailed and stunningly engineered famous-name locomotives, carriages and freight wagons. Scope, too, for crashes of catastrophic magnitude, followed by in-depth analysis of the causes of each disaster and a lot of finger-pointing across the layout.

Meccano was bought in the 1950s by Lines Brothers (makers of Tri-ang), and the Liverpool factory closed in 1979. Meccano changed hands several times before being bought in 1989 by French company Dominique Duvauchelle; interest in Meccano has recently revived, boosted by interest in the great toy's centenary in 2001. A luxurious Centenary Set was made in a limited edition, which sold out long before the end of 2000.

Meccano is not just a toy – chemist Sir Harry Kroto (born in 1940) credits Meccano for helping him win his 1996 Nobel prize for mapping the structure of the C60 cage molecule. 'Meccano gave one the idea that there was an engineering explanation that could make the molecule so strong,' said Kroto. 'I imagined building molecules as if they were bits of Meccano.'

Kroto played with Meccano from early childhood. 'With Meccano, you learn how structures stay together. You make shapes and some are rigid and some aren't. Meccano gives you a feel for materials; you tighten a screw enough to stop things falling apart but not so tightly that you destroy the thread.' The great British scientist mourns the decline of Meccano as a disaster for British engineering; Kroto suggested that a graph of Meccano's decline would match the fall in Britain's young engineers and scientists.

chapter 5
moving

Until the mid 1700s the roads to Liverpool were impassable to anything but riders and packhorses. Until 1760 the nearest a coach could get to Liverpool was Warrington – then passengers had to find other means of travelling on to the port. Packhorses carried goods between the port and inland towns, along muddy lanes and moorland tracks. It was a slow, cumbersome and expensive process – no wonder that Liverpool didn't really start to develop as a port until overland transport improved. After much badgering from frustrated merchants, Parliament finally gave permission to local councils to build roads and collect tolls, and the network of turnpike roads grew.

The first in this area was from Liverpool to Prescot, opened in 1725; it was more than 25 years before the road was extended to Warrington to join the road network. Turnpike committees were corrupt, tolls were high and the state of the roads still poor. As late as 1788 a train of 70 packhorses set out daily from Dale Street to Manchester, trailing along Edge Lane, over Old Swan Hill, through Oak Vale and over Broad Green Moor.

It must have been an exciting moment when, on 1st September 1760, the first stage coach – the *Flying Machine* – left the Golden Fleece in Dale Street. Then it took four days to get to London but before long the competition drove down the journey time, and by 1785 coaching inns were advertising Liverpool to London trips in 26 hours.

The first mail coach service was run that year, on 25th July, leaving for London from the Golden Lion at 4am. The advertisement said: 'To go in 30 hours: fare £3 13s 6d.' Mail coaches carried only four passengers, the coachmen and an armed guard to fend off highwaymen.

The first omnibuses to run in Liverpool, in 1833, were horse-drawn; the first route was from Knotty Ash to the Town Hall. Motor buses didn't appear until 1884. Before that, trams had been introduced; the first trams in Europe ran in Birkenhead in 1860, but eight years later Liverpool was the first British town to have a comprehensive tram service.

The country's first street refuges for pedestrians were made in 1862, by John Hastings, a saddler. He had witnessed his friend John Walmsley being killed trying to cross Lord Street and built the first of several refuges in an effort to stop further accidents.

Horses continued to provide the horsepower for Liverpool's business community right up to 1968 when shipping turned to containerisation. The great Shires, Suffolks, Percherons and Clydesdales served the port for over 250 years; up to 1935 Liverpool had the second largest number of working horses outside London – almost 5,000 carthorses and ponies. Manufacturers such as Bibby's and Tate & Lyle relied completely on their carthorses, and the *Echo* ponies used to be a familiar sight, delivering papers around the city.

In the Second World War these gentle giants kept the port going when fuel became scarce and vehicles were requisitioned for the war effort. Even during the Blitz, when the docks were bombed day and night and conditions for the horses were terrible, they kept going: the forgotten heroes of the war (across the country about 286,000 horses were killed in the bombings). The Liverpool Carters' Association has commissioned the sculptor Judy Boyt to design a life-size bronze statue of a shire horse, to be installed at the Albert Dock as a monument to these magnificent animals. These days the only time they are seen on Liverpool's streets is in May for the horse parade, which winds from St George's Hall to Sefton Park in a great caravan of colourful carriages, gleaming tack and bright livery.

The first motorised charabanc trip was in 1906, organised by Graham Reece of J Blake & Co. Eighteen members of the club motored out to Llangollen, but the charabanc broke down on the way home and the passengers had to catch the train back.

As the 20th century came in, the internal combustion engine began to make its mark. Joe Blake, who had founded his coach building business in 1871 at premises in Mount Pleasant, went into motors as soon as he could. He was a Wolseley dealer in 1904, and in 1906 got the contract to carry mail between Liverpool, Southport, Manchester and Ireland. In 1910 he became a Ford dealer, and the firm grew to a substantial size selling Ford cars and trucks until the 1990s, when the company went into receivership.

Even before motor vehicles took over the roads, the first haulage company in Liverpool was using steam wagons. In 1902 Sharpnell Smith's Road Carrying Company hauled cotton and bulk products to and from the docks in 25 horsepower wagons, doing nightly runs from Liverpool to Blackburn. A six ton load (the wagons themselves were another four tons) took 12 hours to cover the 40 mile route.

It didn't take long for the motor vehicle to catch people's imagination, and by the early 1920s the leader of the City Council, Sir Archibald Salvidge, was worried about the growing queues of cars and lorries waiting for a ferry; he got up a committee to think about alternative ways of crossing the river. Marc and Isambard Brunel, the engineering geniuses, had actually proposed a tunnel under the Mersey 100 years earlier, but the idea was dismissed as preposterous.

Salvidge's committee looked at a bridge, but it was too expensive to build, let alone maintain. A tunnel, however, would be half the cost to build and much easier to keep up to scratch. (Or so they thought.) Winston Churchill, then at the Treasury, agreed to a capital contribution of £2.5 million with tolls over 20 years to repay it. The final cost was £7.7 million, and tolls were set for 40 years. But by then the interest on the debt had mounted so high that tolls had to continue. Every few years there is a row over the tunnel debt between local and central government, and motorists cough up ever-increasing tolls.

Liverpool and Birkenhead undertook the project, although Wallasey and Bootle were originally in on the discussions. The week before Christmas 1925, work began on the pilot tunnel from the Liverpool side; they began digging from Birkenhead the following March. It took three years to dig through – on 3rd April 1928 Salvidge and the Lord Mayor of Liverpool Margaret Beavan went underground and watched as workmen broke through the last thin wall of rock. Waiting on the other side was Alderman Naylor, Mayor of Birkenhead.

The engineers – JA Brodie and Sir Basil Mott – could give themselves a pat on the back: the two tunnels met in the middle to within an inch. Not that the tunnel was even straight: the opposition from the ferry operators and the railway (the train tunnel had opened in 1889) was so fierce that the council agreed to make the tunnel longer and windier than necessary to put people off driving through. So the Birkenhead tunnel is 2.13 miles long, whereas the later (straight) Wallasey tunnel is only 1.5 miles long. The first tunnel, with its entrances and ventilation shafts designed in elegant art deco style by Herbert Rowse, was opened in 1934 by George V, who named it Queensway in honour of Queen Mary.

By 1958 traffic was getting too much for the tunnel, so the decision was made to build another, from Liverpool to Wallasey. The councils didn't raise the cash for 10 years, by which time over 60,000 vehicles a day were trundling through. The tunnel was bored by the Mangla Mole (which had been used to build the Mangla Dam in Pakistan), the biggest machine of its kind in the world, with a 35ft diameter drill bit. The Wallasey Tunnel was finally opened in 1971 by the Queen, and named Kingsway.

Speke was the first regional airport in the country, with flights to Croydon in 1930, although it wasn't officially opened until 1933. The Marquess of Salisbury came to do the honours, and 100,000 spectators saw the biggest air show outside London. The first airport building was an old farmhouse with a big 'C' stuck on top of the dormer window to indicate the control tower. The splendid art deco air terminal and two hangars were built in 1936 and are now listed Grade II.

That year saw the first transatlantic flights by the dashing American aviator Dick Merrill, who with his chum Harry Richman took off from Southport beach and reached the coast of Newfoundland in just under 18 hours.

A local man had made the first powered flight from Liverpool more than two decades earlier, in 1910. In a Bleriot machine, Henry Melly took off from Waterloo Sands for a jaunt over the river; he then started a flying school on the beach at Waterloo, and crowds would gather to watch aircraft being tested. In 1913 Melly flew over the Mersey and circled the docks on 11th July – the day King George came to open Gladstone Dock. The King was said to have watched this swashbuckling flying achievement with fascination.

The earliest recorded flight from Liverpool was in 1785; Vincent Lunardi made a balloon ascent from the riverside fort (the site of Princes Dock) on 20th July, and another from Aintree a month later. In 1819 Mr Livingstone and Mr Sadler ascended in a balloon from Liverpool and in three hours, with a stiff wind behind them, got across to Stockton on Tees, where they landed safely. Poor Mr Sadler didn't survive an ascent in October 1824, when he was thrown out of his balloon over Blackburn.

Liverpool's first airfield was not Speke but Aintree racecourse. At the start of the Great War in 1914, aircraft parts were shipped in to Liverpool, assembled at Aintree and flown out to France to engage with the likes of the Red Baron. In the Second World War Speke's great hangars (one of which was, ironically, roofed by German engineering firm Fokker) were used to assemble hundreds of Douglas bombers and Lockheed fighters, shipped here in pieces from the US and Canada. Melba Haigh and Vera White were in their early 20s when they were amongst 12 girls working on the aircraft on night shift: 'Although we could laugh we realised it was serious business. It was hard work assembling the planes, but hard work never hurt anyone.' Both ladies were guests of honour at the reopening of the old air terminal as the new Marriott Hotel, suitably fitted out in distinctive 1930's style.

In 1966 Prince Philip came to open Speke's new runway; at 8,200 feet long, it was the longest provincial runway in the country and could take the biggest long-haul aircraft – even Concorde can visit Liverpool. The old airport closed in the 1980s, and the 'new' airport is now getting a complete overhaul with massive investment from owners Peel Holdings.

In 2001 Yoko Ono came to launch the renamed Liverpool John Lennon Airport, with Lennon's little self-portrait as a logo, and the slogan 'above us only sky'.

Liverpool Airport's fortunes took a massive boost when Stelios Haji-Iannou based easyJet here and in Luton. The low-cost airline took off, so to speak, and has grown hugely, with destinations all over Europe from Amsterdam to Nice and Madrid. When are we going to get the Athens route from Liverpool, Stelio?

Liverpool is the fastest growing regional airport in the UK, with passenger numbers increasing by 62% in 2000 to almost two million. The new £32 million terminal, scheduled to open in 2002, should see three million passengers in a year.

The following was written in response to Henry Booth's call for investment in railways. (The great speed referred to here was about 14mph.) 'As to those persons who speculate on making railways generally throughout the kingdom, and superseding all the canals, all the wagons, mails and stage coaches, post-chaises and, in short, every other mode of conveyance, by land and by water, we deem them and their visionary schemes unworthy of notice. The gross exaggerations of the powers of the locomotive steam-engine (or, to speak in plain English, the steam-carriage), may delude for a time but must end in the mortification of those concerned. We should as soon expect the people to suffer themselves to be fired off upon one of Congreve's richochet rockets, as trust themselves to the mercy of such a machine, going at such a rate!'
The Quarterly Review

Henry Booth was an engineer and part of one of Liverpool's big merchant families; he had no doubt by 1824 that the railway was the future. It was exactly 100 years earlier that Liverpool got its first turnpike road; stage coaches had only had access to the town for 60 years, and the Leeds-Liverpool canal had only been completed for eight years. Now these speed-merchants were pushing for machines to propel human beings at great speeds of 10 miles an hour or even more. Madness!

Opposition to the railway was fierce, even vicious – surveyors planning a rail route to Manchester had to be protected from the angry locals by hired bruisers, and Liverpool's pro-railway lobby was mugged at every turn by influential canal owners, road trustees and landowners. A declaration was signed by 150 Liverpool men – including a Rathbone, a Gladstone, and a Ewart, that 'new means of communication were indispensable'.

Henry Booth wrote the first ever English railway prospectus, issued on 29th October 1824: 'In the present state of trade and of commercial enterprise, despatch is no less essential than economy. Merchandise is frequently brought across the Atlantic from New York to Liverpool in 21 days; while, owing to the various causes of delay above enumerated, goods have in some instances been longer on their passage from Liverpool to Manchester. But this reproach must not be perpetual. The advancement in mechanical science renders it unnecessary; the good sense of the community makes it impossible.'

Outlining the benefits to all concerned, Booth went on: 'Moreover, as a cheap and expeditious means of conveyance for travellers, the railway holds out the fair prospect of a public accommodation the magnitude and importance of which cannot immediately be ascertained.'

Booth's foresight was remarkable, but even he was probably astonished at the speed and spread of the radical changes in society that the railway age was to bring.

After much political wrangling and tough commercial negotiating, the Liverpool railway lobby got an Act through Parliament in 1826 and set George Stephenson to work immediately to build the railway to Manchester. It was all so new that Stephenson and Booth had to invent special tools for the construction. (Booth also invented ball and screw railway couplings, the steam whistle and the method of greasing axles – still used; and he made the special multi-tubular boiler for *Rocket*.) There were 63 bridges to be built, plus viaducts, cuttings, embankments, a tunnel, stations and warehouses, engines, carriages and wagons, and the railway tracks themselves. They also had to find a way of crossing the treacherous Chat Moss.

One critic wrote: 'The making of an embankment out of this pulpy wet moss is no easy task. Who but Mr Stephenson would have thought of entering into Chat Moss, carrying it out almost like wet dung? It is ignorance almost inconceivable. It is perfect madness.'

Madness or not, the whole thing was completed in four years and on 15th September 1830 the Liverpool & Manchester Railway opened with seven of Stephenson's locomotives, led, of course, by *Rocket*. (*Rocket* had won the Rainhill Trials in 1829 – a competition to find a locomotive to carry passengers and freight. *Rocket* pulled a load of three times its own weight at 12.5 mph, and hauled a coach filled with passengers at 24 mph.)

The opening was hugely successful but marred by the awful death of William Huskisson, the cabinet minister who had done so much to push Liverpool's railway bill through Parliament. The following day the business of the railway began. The *Northumbrian* drew a train of 130 passengers to Manchester in an hour and 50 minutes, and by the end of the week there were six trains running daily. Of the 30 stagecoaches that had plied between the two towns, now there was only one left; but passenger numbers had more than trebled to 1,600. In February 1831 the *Samson* drew 164 tons of freight from Liverpool to Manchester in two and a half hours – a load that would have needed 70 horses to draw, over many hours.

How ironic that 170 years later the country's trains were travelling at speeds little faster than *Rocket* and *Samson* could manage. After the Hatfield crash in October 2000, Britain's high speed rail network was reduced to chaos when the cracks in the system widened to gaping chasms. And Henry Booth's excitement over 'cheap' travel would prompt hollow laughter from commuters on Virgin's West Coast line.

Still, back in the 1830s Liverpool's trains were marvels, and the list of innovations was long and illustrious. The Liverpool-Manchester Railway was the first passenger railway in the world; Edge Hill station was the first passenger station in the world (the original building is still used today); Crown Street in Liverpool was the world's first train shed; the line carried the first letters by rail (1830), etc etc: the engineering innovations are too many to list here.

The first Lime Street station was built in 1836 and was the first to have iron arcades and covered tracks; the current station is the third, built in 1879, and was then the largest engine shed in the world. The north barrel roof cost £15,000 to build in 1850; the 2000 renovation of both glass roofs, as well as a spruce-up for the whole station, cost £20 million.

A mention for Thomas Brassey, the world's greatest railway contractor, who started in Liverpool and built most of the railways in France as well as in Canada, Australia and India. And a word for Señor Joas Caffareas, Brazilian vice-consul in Liverpool, who on Christmas Eve 1873 was killed by a train on the level crossing at Broad Green station.

By the way, Freightliner trains were pioneered in Liverpool, from the terminus at Garston Docks, sending daily trains to Europe carrying bulk cargoes in containers.

William Huskisson, MP for Liverpool and Home Secretary, was with Prime Minister Robert Peel, the Duke of Wellington and 750 others on the railway's opening day. After a halt, Huskisson crossed the down-line to get back into his carriage, but was knocked flying by the door and fell into the path of the Rocket, which crushed his legs. Rocket's engine driver James Kennedy drove flat out (33 mph) to get Huskisson to a doctor, but the MP died that night. 15,000 mourners came to his funeral.

73

The Liverpool Overhead Railway – the Docker's Umbrella, as it was known – opened in 1893 and ran from Herculaneum Dock in the south to Alexandra Dock to the north. It was extended north to Seaforth Sands in 1894 and south through a tunnel to Dingle in 1896 – a total of seven miles. The journey then took under 25 minutes, compared to over 75 minutes by bus. It was the only elevated railway in the UK, and the first electric elevated railway in the world. It was the first railway to use automatic signalling, and the first with all-electric signalling using coloured lights. At Seaforth Sands station the first escalator was built in 1921: a narrow conveyor belt with slats to stand on. At its peak in 1919, the Overhead Railway carried 18 million passengers a year. By the 1950s the structure had become badly corroded by the effect of the smoke from dock engines mixed with salty wind and rainwater. The railway closed on 30th December 1956 and the dockers were deprived of their 'umbrella'.

George Stephenson lived at Otterspool during the building of the Liverpool-Manchester railway. He made a model of his railway in the dry bed of the River Jordan.

A locomotive was used to build the new promenade at Otterspool, but in April 1931 it crashed through the block at the end of its line and fell 15 feet into the Mersey, killing the driver.

Liverpool is the only city in England outside London to have an underground rail network. The only other in Britain is in Glasgow. After 1830 the railways developed fast on both sides of the Mersey: railway companies included the Lancashire & Yorkshire, the East Lancashire, the Liverpool Southport & Crosby, and the original passenger line, the Liverpool & Manchester Railway Company.

By the late 1800s it had become imperative to build a rail link between Birkenhead and Liverpool, and given the Mersey was enormously wide at this point, a tunnel was the only answer. Work began in 1881 and the first passenger service began in 1886, running between James Street (Liverpool) and Green Lane (Birkenhead) stations. This was the first underwater railway in the world.

Its main drawback was that being steam trains, the carriages were filled with filthy, choking smoke when they went through the tunnel. Even so, the railway carried 10 million passengers in 1890.

In 1903 the Mersey Railway Company electrified the line – the first in the world to change completely to electric traction. The project was done by British Westinghouse with a fair amount of financial support from George Westinghouse himself.

After post-war nationalisation, the Mersey Railway was folded into British Railways, and in 1962 the rail network was proposed, with a loop beneath the city centre to connect all four existing routes, a new link from Southport and Ormskirk into the city centre, and extensions southwards to Garston; the building work started in 1971 and opened in 1977. Merseyrail now has three lines – Northern, City and Wirral – stretching out east to Wigan, south to Hunts Cross, north to Southport, and west to Hooton (halfway to Chester). Through 72 stations and along 89 miles of track Merseyrail carries about 45 million passengers a year; bus deregulation in 1986 pushed Merseyrail passenger numbers up by 12.5%.

What next for Liverpool's railways? With such a track record (the puns are too easy), nothing less than a brilliant innovation will do. Locals have been pestering for a replacement to the Overhead Railway ever since the original was dismantled – and they might just get their wish. Final year students at John Moores University's School of the Built Environment have designed a solution to the city's traffic congestion, as part of a long-term project to solve engineering problems for Britain's next generation of trains.

The team, lead by Professor Lewis Lesley, has come up with a 21st century Overhead Railway which could take passengers from Kings Dock to Manchester Airport in 20 minutes, and to London in 90 minutes or less.

'The new railway will follow part of the original route,' said Lesley, 'and will be about 25 feet off the ground, giving great views of the docks just like the old system.' The main station would be at Kings Dock with access to Albert Dock and the city centre. The next station south would be Liverpool Airport, then Warrington and Manchester Airport, joining a new high speed railway to London and Scotland.

North of the city centre the line would skim across Collingwood Dock before climbing and arching over the Mersey on a new bridge 140 feet high at the centre. 'The views from the new Mersey bridge will be breathtaking, like approaching Liverpool in a low-flying aircraft,' said Professor Lesley.

British Waterways Board, however, are proposing a high-level viaduct to replace the old overhead railway so that instead of trains rattling past, people on the Strand could watch narrowboats chugging past at a leisurely four knots, high above the road traffic.

The 2,000-acre Port of Liverpool is busier now than ever, and one of the fastest-growing in Europe. Liverpool is the largest UK importer of grain, the largest exporter of scrap metal, and the leading timber port since about 1283 (when timber from Gill Moss forest was taken to Wales by pyckard boat to build Caernarvon Castle). The Freeport is the largest of the UK's six; Liverpool is the major port for trade with the eastern seaboard of North America, the major port for trade with Ireland and one of Northern Europe's top 10 container ports. Reports of Liverpool's death as a port are somewhat premature.

And that is only one of Liverpool's ports – the other is upriver at Garston, belonging to Associated British Ports and doing good business in short sea cargoes, mainly bulk materials for industry and agri-business, with great plans for the next stage of the port's development.

400 years ago, however, there was only the Pool – no harbour wall, no quayside, and no decent transport to and from the town – although there was a water bailiff as early as 1551 to stop congestion on the waterside.

The Mersey was once described as a 'wild raging beast of a river'. It is not an ideal waterway, with a six-knot ebb-tide and constantly shifting sandbanks. It had a naturally deep harbour, but ships with cargoes to unload had either to anchor in the Pool in the lee of Liverpool Castle, or out in mid-river. In the Pool, ships would keel over at low tide unless propped up; anchored in mid-river they had to ferry loads back and forth from ship to shore. Eventually the town grew big enough to build a bridge over the Pool and make a quay and harbour in 1635. Sixty years on, the mayor and local MP Sir Thomas Johnston (after whom Sir Thomas Street is named) pushed through the first Dock Act (1708) for the town. He got the channel dredged and appointed Dutchman Thomas Steers to buoy the Rock Channel and build the town's first enclosed wet dock. Construction started in 1710 and the first ships berthed in 1715. Steers became Liverpool's first dock master and water bailiff in 1717, and went on to build Salthouse Dock in 1737, followed by the first Canning Dock. He also built piers, canals, the town's first water supply system, a theatre, and St George's Church.

Steers' notable successor was William Hutchinson (1725-1801) who became dock master and water bailiff in 1759. Hutchinson was born on Tyneside and went to sea as a boy; he served on an East Indiaman, was master of his own vessel in Honduras, then served with famous privateer Fortunatus Wright. Hutchinson got his own letter of marque in the 20-gun frigate *Lowestoft*, but after escaping by the skin of his teeth when *Lowestoft* was wrecked, he gave up the sea and turned to science and management.

Hutchinson founded the Marine Society, built boats, published one of the earliest books on naval architecture, established the world's first lifeboat station in Formby, invented parabolic mirrors for lighthouses (they push the beam of light further out to sea) and installed the first one in Bidston in 1763. One of the original mirrors is now in Trinity House, London.

Hutchinson and his friend Dr Thomas Houlston discovered that apparently drowned people could be resuscitated if pulled out of the water in time – they saved 26 people during their investigations.

In 1777 Hutchinson wrote a book with the following title: 'Treatise on Seamanship with hints and remarks relating thereto: designed to contribute something towards fixing rules upon philosophical and rational principles; to make ships and the management of them, and also navigation, in general, more perfect, and consequently less dangerous and destructive to health, lives and property'.

Jesse Hartley is the name most associated with Liverpool's docks: the architect of Albert Dock, the largest group of Grade I listed buildings in the country. Hartley was Liverpool's dock engineer from 1824 till 1860 and although Albert Dock might be thought his architectural masterpiece, his engineering genius led to the creation of the world's first enclosed dock system.

Up to that point, ships with split cargoes to be loaded or unloaded in different places would have to move from dock to dock by locking back out into the river and locking in to the next dock – all of which cost time and money. Hartley's solution was to build a dock system with connecting passages so that ships could move from dock to dock without worrying about the tide. He saved shipowners vast amounts of money over the years and boosted Liverpool's reputation as a port.

During Hartley's time here the docks built included Clarence (1830), Brunswick (1832), Waterloo (1834), Victoria and Trafalgar (1836), Canning (1842) and Albert (1845). In 1857 an Act of Parliament created the Mersey Docks & Harbour Board to remove control of the port from the town council and give it to its shipping and commercial interests.

Fifty years later the MDHB built the Dock Office (the Port of Liverpool Building) on the Pier Head (the site of the old George's Dock), and got permission to extend the dock system north. The largest graving dock in Europe was Gladstone Dock, opened in 1913 by George V; after the Great War work was resumed and the King came back in 1927 to open the Gladstone wet dock system. As the King cut the ribbon from the deck of the *Galatea* he said: 'The increase of commerce is of far more than local interest. The expansion of your trade implies the advancement of world commerce.'

In 1967 work started on a new kind of dock, as the world's shipping industry started to convert to containerisation. The next four years would see MDHB become insolvent; Parliament bailed the Board out and converted it to a private concern, the Mersey Docks & Harbour Company, in 1971. That year Princess Anne opened Royal Seaforth Container Dock, and in 1972 MDHC closed the south docks to shipping.

The 1970s and 1980s were hard and angry times for the docks, but after huge job losses and bitter conflicts, the docks began to be profitable once more.

More cargo goes through the Port of Liverpool now than at any time in its past – more than 30 million tonnes a year.

PLUTO was a war-time solution to the problem of getting safe fuel supplies to the Normandy Beaches. Fuel was unloaded in Liverpool (at a platform in the Mersey opposite what is now the Britannia pub – a yellow buoy marks the spot) and pumped down through pipes to the south coast and through the Pipe Line Under The Ocean to France.

Mammoth, the world's largest floating crane capable of lifting 150 tons, was given to Liverpool by Germany after WW1 and sold to Holland in 1986. The new Mersey Mammoth can lift 250 tons on its main block.

The Mersey Docks & Harbour Company showed a profit of £29.2 million (up 6.1%) on a turnover of £125.1 million (a rise of 23.7%) for the half-year ending 30th June 2001.

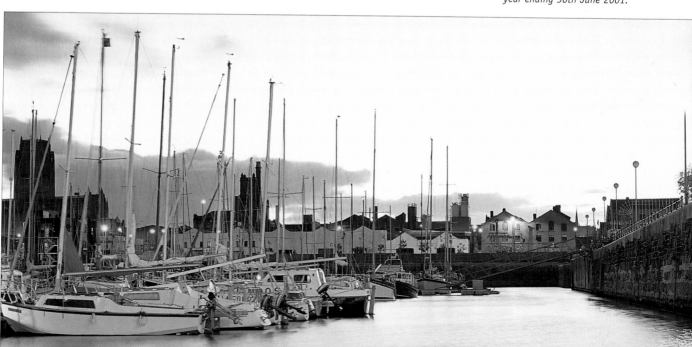

Tobacco Warehouse

Privateers were Liverpool's first great entrepreneurs. Pirates, in fact, but pirates with permission from the monarch to loot, kill and steal on the high seas. The letter of marque was a licence to print money – albeit at some considerable risk. Elizabeth I began the trend of licensing her enterprising pirates, and privateers flourished for two centuries, plundering enemy vessels for profit. An 'enemy vessel' was not necessarily built for battle, but was counted fair game by belonging to a country with which England was at odds.

Liverpool had some stunningly successful privateers, from Elizabethan swashbuckler Humphrey Brooke to the intrepid Fortunatus Wright, who died in 1757. As late as 1779 Liverpool refitted 120 merchant ships as privateers under letter of marque, after two prizes were sailed into Liverpool in 1776 netting their captors £20,000.

Two years later the Liverpool owned *Mentor* captured the massive prize of the *Carnatic* – a French East Indiaman – netting £400,000 for the privateer's owner, Peter Baker. But the *Mentor* was no swift pirate ship. Baker, a Liverpool shipwright, had built the *Mentor* for a private buyer, but she was a poor effort, with a heavy list and difficult to steer. She was refused by Baker's client, so Baker found a crew of 102 and persuaded his friend John Dawson to captain her. Dawson was no great sea captain, but he knew a bit about navigating. So the *Mentor* limped out to sea and chanced upon the *Carnatic*; the French ship had few guns – most of the ports were dummies, and she surrendered to Dawson after the Liverpool ship fired a few rounds. *Carnatic*'s captain didn't realise that most of *Mentor*'s gun ports were dummies, too. So back came *Mentor*, her rich prize in tow, and Peter Baker's fortune was made. He built the splendid new Mossley Hall, but it was the locals' nickname for the house which stuck – Carnatic Hall (the site of the University's halls of residence). As for the *Mentor*, she was lost off the coast of Newfoundland in 1881.

England wasn't the only country sending privateers out to plunder – it was common practice, making the high seas a hazardous place. During and after the American revolution, the French and the Americans were hard at it, both going for English ships. In 1779, the great American privateer John Paul Jones was much feared in Liverpool, and the riverside fort near St Nicholas (where Princes Dock is now) was fitted out with cannon and troops in case Jones attacked Liverpool.

For half a century Liverpool ships were heavily involved in the whaling industry, and many whalers went north to hunt their prey amongst the ice floes. Liverpool trader Charles Gore fitted out the *Golden Lion* in 1750 to go whaling in Greenland, and after a profitable hunt, set sail for home. But the *Golden Lion* was ambushed by a Naval frigate thinking that a whaler's crew would be useful pressed men. The whaler's crew didn't agree, and there was a bloody skirmish on shore between the press gang and the crew of the *Golden Lion* which caused such a scandal that from then on whalers' men were exempt from conscription.

There are many stories of privateers and slavers having a change of heart in later life: Bryan Blundell, who founded the Bluecoat School, William Hutchinson, who became a dock master, inventor and writer. And there was Dr William Scoresby, the scientist who made many voyages to the Arctic on whaling ships in an attempt to find the North West Passage. In later life he came to Liverpool to become Chaplain to the Mersey Mission to Seamen.

Not all seafarers were men: 19 year old 'Arthur' Douglas served on the privateer *Resolution* for three months before being discovered to be a girl; 'Jack' Roberts was really Jane Roberts, a grog-swilling, tobacco-chewing crew member of the slaver *Anne*.

Liverpool's seafarers were prepared to venture into dangerous waters: up on Greenland's desolate west coast is one of the country's most beautiful areas, and three names are a bit of a giveaway to a maritime connection with Liverpool: Scoresbysund, Rathbone Island, and Liverpool Land.

In 1588 Humphrey Brooke discovered plans for the Armada and reported them to Francis Drake – although the discovery was also claimed by two other Liverpool privateers, Nicholas Abraham and John Lambert.

During three months of 1586, when there were fewer than 190 Freemen in Liverpool, 16 vessels came from Ireland loaded with linen yarn for Manchester and hides for Garston's tanning mills. During the same period 27 ships sailed to Ireland with textiles from Manchester, knives and scythes from Sheffield, pewter goods, saddles, soap, 1,400 tennis balls and 14 racquets.

Squire Moore of Old Hall and Squire Norris of Speke Hall were importing sugar and tobacco from the southern States in the 16th and early 17th centuries.

One wool clipper covered 465 miles in 24 hours on a trip from Liverpool to Melbourne – a sailing feat never since equalled.

More emigrants sailed to Australia from Liverpool than from any other port in the world.

Maps from 1819 to 1839 show a number of shipyards on Liverpool's shore, including Humble & Mylchreest, Thomas Wilson, Clarke, Clover & Son, Forrester & Co, R & J Evans, Royden, WH Potter and Jackson.

This was a very small town in the 16th century – two devastating plagues in 1540 and 1548 had taken the population back to 13th century levels, and in 1565 the inhabitants petitioned the Queen to let them off taxes because of 'the decayed state of the town'. In 1540 only 12 ships belonged to Liverpool totalling 177 tons, with 75 seamen overall. It wasn't for another 100 years that the town would see an upturn in its fortunes. In 1647 Liverpool was made a port in its own right, independent of Chester. Then over the next decade life in the south east of England became decidedly less comfortable: Dutch wars were making the channel unsafe; and what with the plague and the Great Fire of London, many merchants thought it time to decamp north to Liverpool, well away from the European coast and the chaos of the big city. More merchants were driven up to Liverpool when the wars with the French made the channel and the southern waters a battle zone.

Still, there weren't many ships being built in Liverpool. There are records of a shipwright called John Okill in 1630 – he built small ships on land, then launched them into the river off the old dock wall. Few shipwrights are mentioned in the 18th century – a notable exception being Roger Fisher, who died in 1777. It was Fisher who, alarmed at the shortage of timber available for shipbuilding, wrote the treatise 'Heart of Oak, the British Bulwark'.

For some reason Liverpool's town council didn't encourage its nascent shipbuilding industry in the 18th century. There was great demand from privateers, slavers, whalers, merchants and the Navy; the town was perfectly placed geographically, and had the largest timber imports in the country. But apart from a few small yards where Albert Dock stands now, Liverpool created no real shipbuilding industry. So it was William Laird who exploited the opportunity, but on the Wirral bank of the Mersey. A Scot who in 1810 came to get orders for his father's ropeworks and stayed, Laird created one of the world's great shipyards (later Cammell Laird), and Birkenhead launched a long series of record-breaking ships, has a sheaf of inventions and patents to its name, and played a key role in several wars.

Liverpool had its docks, but these were for trade rather than building. It was to Liverpool that the shipowners came to set up their lines and trade with the world. Names like Cunard, White Star, Blue Funnel, Ocean Fleets, Elder Dempster, and Bibby.

The fresh-faced John Bibby was a farmer's son from Ormskirk who came to Liverpool in 1801 and founded his shipping line in 1807 (he died in 1840, murdered by footpads for his gold watch). The first ships sailed from Parkgate – then an important port on the Dee (now silted up, it is a wetland haven for waterfowl). Throughout its life the Bibby Line has continually developed and innovated, pioneering ship design elements such as the straight stem, steering from the bridge, and the tandem cabin. These days the shipping line is part of a larger family-owned group, run by Michael Bibby, the sixth generation to head the firm.

The oldest shipping line in the world is Brocklebanks, dating back to Daniel Brocklebank's arrival from New England in 1775 to join his brother, a whaler based in Liverpool. Daniel got his letter of marque and grew rich as a privateer. His sons built ships in Whitehaven, then began trading from Liverpool with links to India, China and America. Other great Liverpool shipping names include T & J Harrison, Lamport & Holt, Booth, Papayanni, Larrinaga, Booker, Canadian Pacific, Clan, Inman and Guion.

Liverpool and Birkenhead were perfectly placed to lead the race for innovation in steam, in ship design and in navigation; the speed of growth in transatlantic trade in the 18th and 19th centuries demanded faster, stronger, more unsinkable ships, and there was no shortage of money to finance these developments. Amongst the markers in shipping evolution to be claimed for Liverpool is the first ship back from Calcutta after the end of the East India Company in 1815, and *Georgiana*, the first vessel to arrive direct from China after the China Company's monopoly was broken.

Royal William was a steamship built by Lairds and powered by Fawcett & Preston. She was 617 tons, 276 horsepower, and the first ship in the world to be divided into watertight compartments with iron bulkheads. In 1838 she reached New York in 19 days and returned to Liverpool in 15 days – the fastest by far to cross the Atlantic. In 1840 the Cunard ship *Britannia* began the world's first regular steamship mail service, from Liverpool to New York, and five years later the *SS Great Britain* – the first screw steamer (as opposed to paddles) with an iron hull sailed from Liverpool on her first journey to New York.

The Elder Dempster ship *Lake Champlain* was the first fitted with Marconi wireless; the Cunard ship *Lucania* was the first to establish radio contact with both sides of the Atlantic simultaneously, in 1903. The first SOS was sent by *Slavonia* in 1909.

The last Liverpool-owned transatlantic liner sailed from here in 1967. Liverpool has wonderful reminders of its maritime glory days with visits from the *QEII*, and the stunning sight of great sailing ships at anchor in the Mersey during the Tall Ships races.

Liverpool is first and foremost associated with the river, but the city is linked to three other waterways. Liverpool's first dock master Thomas Steers made the River Weaver navigable to get salt from Cheshire's mines to the Mersey and Liverpool's refineries and docks; later the Mersey was widened above Runcorn in the mid-1700s to allow boats to take cotton up to Manchester.

The town council then commissioned engineer Henry Berry to use the Sankey Brook to reach the coal pits of St Helens. Berry began cutting the Sankey Canal in 1755 and opened three years later – the first major artificial waterway to be constructed in England since Roman times, and the first true canal (its channel is completely independent of the brook it parallels).

There was ferocious opposition to the canal, and the turnpike road trustees and packhorse owners managed to ban the use of horses to tow barges and narrowboats: teams of nine men had to be used instead.

Berry inspired a 50-year boom in canal building across the country; the longest and highest canal in Britain was the Leeds & Liverpool Canal, 127 miles long, begun in 1770 and reaching Leeds in 1816. It met the Mersey at Stanley Dock.

Benedictine monks from Birkenhead Priory ran the first Mersey ferries in 1125, taking passengers between Eastham and Liverpool in large rowing boats. The conditions could be uncomfortable and the journey take up to three hours even in calm weather – but at least passage was free for those who had to cross.

The monks' charitable ferrying ended in 1320 when Edward III granted the Priory a charter allowing them to charge passengers. Part of the monks' service was to carry passengers ashore from the boat so they didn't get wet and muddy. No landing stages in those days.

The importance of the ferry as a link between Lancashire and Cheshire meant that the Crown declared it to be a royal highway. It still is, incidentally – look for the crown at the top of the posts holding the gangway at Woodside.

The monk's charter lasted for 200 years until the dissolution of the monasteries. Following his falling out with Rome, Henry VIII confiscated the ferries along with all other Priory assets, and he sold the ferries and other properties to Ralph Worsley.

After many different owners, the ferries were taken over by the local authorities and finally became Mersey Ferries.

The ferry was, until the rail tunnel was built, the only means of getting from Lancashire to the Wirral and Chester without trekking upriver many miles to the bridge at Warrington. So although travellers could be forced to wait several hours for the weather or the tide to change, it was still cheaper and quicker than going round by Warrington (Runcorn Bridge wasn't built until the 19th century).

The first steam boat on the Mersey ran from Liverpool to Runcorn in 1815; two years later the steam ferry *Etna* began operating between Liverpool and Tranmere.

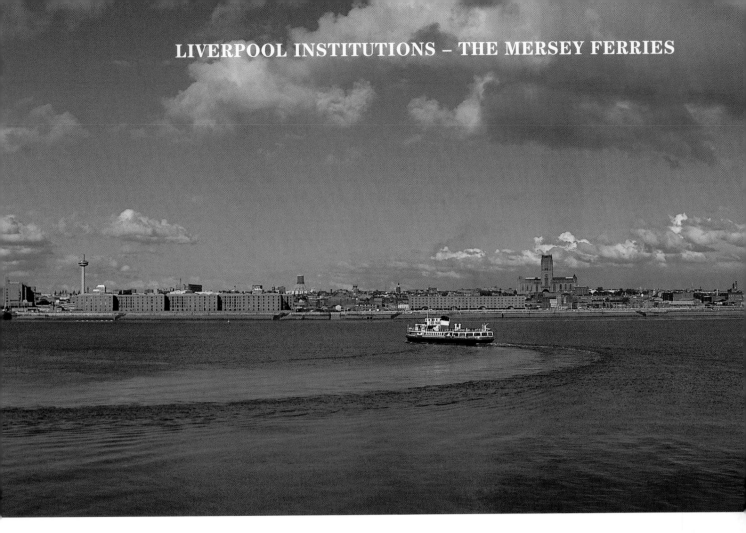

The much-improved speed and reliability of the steam ferries meant that people could work in Liverpool and live on the Wirral; this and the start of William Laird's shipyard in 1824 saw the rapid growth of Birkenhead.

The commercial viability of the ferries took a knock when first the rail tunnel then the road tunnel opened, but the ferries survived and still carry crowds of commuters at peak hours. Off-peak, the ferries *Woodchurch*, *Mountwood* and *Overchurch* take visitors on hour-long round trips up and down the river for the best possible view of the magical Liverpool waterfront, and a bit of Mersey history. And the song that welcomes them on board? Guess.

The ferries haven't always had a quiet life. Two of the Mersey's famous ferries – *Royal Iris* and *Royal Daffodil* – were given their 'royal' prefix by George V after the first World War; the ferries had led a successful operation to close the port of Zeebrugge to the Germans.

The Mersey ferries were the first to have a radar system for safe navigation in fog (1948). Even in calm weather, the tidal river's six-knot current is a challenge; piloting the 464-ton, 152 ft long ferry is like driving a bus on ice, even for a master. The ferry captains are so skilled that they bring the ferries in with the lightest of touches against the landing stage, so passengers probably don't realise how hard it is.

Quite apart from being a cultural icon for Merseyside, the ferries are a crucial part of the local authorities' efforts to get more people to use public transport and leave their cars at home. Chairman of Merseytravel Mark Dowd was awarded the OBE in 2001 for services to transport, but instead of going to Buckingham Palace, he opted to receive his gong from the Lord Lieutenant Alan Waterworth, the Queen's representative on Merseyside, on board *Royal Daffodil*.

working city

Until industry put paid to it, fishing was a good living on the banks of the Mersey, with whiting, sole and shrimp in abundance. The cockle beds of the Dee once again yield enough shellfish to keep 60 fishermen busy, with an estimated cockle harvest worth about £1.25 million a year.

Tanning has been going on in Garston for centuries, since the monks of Stanlaw Abbey built a tanning mill near the river.

Printing and bookbinding were among Liverpool specialities – John Jones and John Fazakerley had an excellent reputation.

Old Swan was at one time a centre of glassmaking. A large glassworks at the top of Edge Lane employed 40 French experts. The works closed after a scandal over fraudulent trading.

ndustry, as such, has never been a mainstay of Liverpool's economy, which has from early days been more about moving people and goods about the world. Sea-born commerce started pre-history, with the visits of Phoenician traders to the North West. There wasn't much in the way of natural resources in this area – peat moss and marsh, mostly. No minerals to mine, although there was red sandstone to quarry. Fishing was the subsistence activity for centuries, until sea trade became viable. One of the earliest Liverpool products was salt – crude brine-salt manufacture had started around 1610, but it wasn't till 1796 that the Garston salt works were built to refine rock salt extracted from the enormous salt mines in north Cheshire (still in use).

The first factory was probably built by Italian silk manufacturers on the site of Silkhouse Court in Tithebarn Street; other early industrial activities were watchmaking, pottery and printing – almost all gone now, but influential in their day. Puritan farmers in Toxteth Park began making watches and clocks as a second string; by 1800 Liverpool and nearby Prescot had become leading areas. The most famous Liverpool clockmakers were Lassell, Aspinwall and Thomas Tompian (1639-1713), who was probably the finest maker of weight- and spring-driven grandfather clocks. Peter Litherland in 1794 invented the rack lever escapement (the mechanism that makes watches tick), and Wycherley was the first to mechanise watch-making in 1817. Tobias invented a binnacle timepiece which indicated time by ringing bells, and Hartnub invented a compensation balance which was adopted by the Admiralty in 1849. The only remaining clockmaker in Liverpool now is Sewills, founded in 1800 by Sephardic Jews who fled here from Seville (from where the firm's name is probably derived).

Tobacco became a key commodity for Liverpool after the first cargo landed in 1648; tobacco goods were produced in great quantities, and in 1860 the firm of Ogdens was founded. Now part of Imperial Tobacco, the West Derby Road factory produces 120 tobacco brands, including its famous pipe-smoker's brand, St Bruno.

The Leeds-Liverpool Canal is the longest in Britain

few companies still prosper in Liverpool after more than 200 years of trading; one is RS Clare. Richard Shaw Clare's firm was producing horrible smells in 1798, prompting complaints from residents of Lord Street and forcing Clare to move to Stanhope Street, where the company is still based, as the UK's leading grease manufacturer, and an exporter of safety markings and anti-slip surfaces.

Lime Street – until 1790 called Lime Kiln Lane – saw Liverpool's earliest chemical processing; ships dumped cargoes of chalk overboard at Pier Head, to be recovered at low tide and taken up the hill to the kilns.

One of the world's great industrial giants – ICI – has its roots in Liverpool. Dubliner James Muspratt came to Liverpool and opened an alkali works in Vauxhall Road in about 1822. The stench of sulphuric acid and hydrochloric acid gases got the area the nickname of the Spice Islands and eventually forced Muspratt out to Widnes. (Until fairly recently a heavy smoker was said to smoke 'like a Vauxhall chimney'.) Sir John Brunner, born in Everton in 1842, established an alkali works with Dr Mond in 1873; Brunner Mond and Muspratts – forming the United Alkali Company in 1890 – merged with Castner Kellner in Runcorn to form Imperial Chemical Industries in 1926. ICI has now almost vanished, demerged into its component parts such as Zeneca Astra and – once more – Brunner Mond.

Speke's pharmaceutical companies now include Eli Lilley and Glaxo Wellcome (in 2001 under threat of closure), but the first of them was Evans Medical Supplies which moved to Liverpool from Worcester at first as distributors, and later manufacturing as Evans Medical, then Medeva, then Celltech – renamed with each change of ownership.

Liverpool is not associated with heavy engineering, but has in its day produced some formidable bits of iron and steel. John Cragg's Mersey Steel & Iron Company forged cast-iron sections for building churches and houses in 1812 onwards, exporting prefabricated cast-iron buildings in huge quantity all over the world. The huge Mersey Forge, founded in 1810 on Sefton Street, had a 15-ton steam hammer which could be heard on the Wirral. In 1856 the Forge built the 21-ton Horsfall Gun, then the biggest gun in the world, which could shoot a 300lb cannonball five miles.

Another maker of cannon was the firm of Fawcett & Preston (known locally as Fossetts) which was founded in 1758 by George Perry to make pans for sugar-refining; the firm achieved a world monopoly on sugar-refining machinery, supplying nine whole refineries to India. Fawcett took over in 1794 and built cannon for the Peninsular War for great profit. It was a Fawcett gun which fired the first shot in the American Civil War, and the firm made weapons for the Mexican War in 1842, the Boer War and the 1914-18 Great War.

An altogether more peaceful activity was Liverpool's pottery industry. Trading salt for Cornish china clay, Liverpool first made pottery in the 17th century; in the 19th century Liverpool potters were producing work to compete with Wedgwood's best. In fact Josiah Wedgwood sent his pots to Liverpool ceramics innovator John Sadler who, in 1856, invented the process of transfer printing. The best known Liverpool ceramics factory was the Herculaneum Pottery, opened in 1796 and closed again in 1841. Herculaneum pots are highly collectable, as are pieces by Liverpool potters Seth Pennington and Sam Gilbody.

Another famous name that has bitten the dust is match-makers Bryant & May who introduced the first continuous match-making machine in 1896. The splendid Mersey Works on Speke Boulevard was the largest match factory in Britain, and the second largest in Europe; it finally closed in 1994, no longer able to compete with Eastern Europe and China.

The Boulevard Industry Park in Speke, on the site of the old Lockheed factory

Half of all Britain's rubber came through the port of Liverpool. Dunlop's tyre factory in Speke was one of the largest.

The first recorded cargo of sugar to Liverpool was in 1677, and Liverpool swiftly became one of the world's leading sugar refinery centres, eventually with 40% of the world's output. Arguably the most famous sugar name is that of Tate & Lyle. Henry Tate (1819-99) was a young entrepreneur, buying his first shop in Manesty Lane at 20. By 1855 he had six shops, and in 1859 bought into the sugar industry, with the patent for making cube sugar and the innovation of granulated sugar, which could be poured into bags at exact weights. His refinery in Love Lane opened in 1872; the Lyle name came into the business in 1921. The refinery's closure in the 1970s caused massive unemployment in Vauxhall – which influenced the decision to site the Tate Gallery's northern venue in Liverpool.

Joseph Heap & Sons opened in 1796 to become sugar refiners and rice millers. It is now the only rice mill in Liverpool, but still the largest in the country.

Confectioners Barker & Dobson were the first to wrap individual boiled sweets in twists of protective paper.

Foodstuffs coming in through the port of Liverpool were an irresistible opportunity for entrepreneurs, so Liverpool has a solid history in food-processing and manufacture, from sugar to flour. Tate & Lyle has come and gone, but more than 70% of Britain's unrefined brown sugar is still imported and packed by Billingtons, the family firm now in its fifth generation. The business was founded in 1858 by Edward Billington, the youngest of 10 children who left the family farm in Cheshire to join a firm of importers in Liverpool. He set up on his own to import sugar, tea and coffee, but it was the sugar that made his fortune. Billingtons bought Criddle & Co, makers of animal feed, and began making cattle cake in Great Homer Street in 1900; today Billingtons produces over 180,000 tonnes of feed. The company also dealt in spices, acquiring in 1936 the old Liverpool firm of Wright Crossley, makers of Lion pepper and spices.

Also derived from sugar imports was the Nelson Preserving Company, founded by Tom Porter in 1921, making jams using fruit and sugar imported through the docks. Almost next door to Nelson's in Aintree is the home of the Cream Cracker, Twiglets and Club biscuits – Jacob's – founded in Dublin, but moved to Liverpool in 1910. The famous Cream Cracker, incidentally, was first made in 1885; its secret recipe involves a 14-hour baking process. No simple biscuit, this.

Five years before the Jacob's cracker burst on to the world stage, William Simpson and Frank Roberts went into partnership and began importing canned lobster and became the world No1 at it; they went on to import red and pink salmon from British Columbia, Alaska, Japan and Siberia in vast quantities. By 1914 it was canned crab, then Californian pilchards, then fruit – pineapples from Singapore, mandarins from Japan, and on they went. The brand was Princes, and in the 1960s the company changed its name to Princes Foods – the UK's top importer of canned foods.

Sweets, of course, are natural products of a sugar town like Liverpool – the original Everton Toffee Shop was in business in 1790. William Taverner starting making Minto toffees and chews in 1890, and by 1931 his son Henry had invented the chocolate eclair. Taverners' favourite Olde English fruit drops were so popular they were put into army rations in the Second World War. The factory off Edge Lane now makes 6,500 tonnes of sweets a year for 38 different countries – keeping dentists in work all over the world ....

As for drink – Higson's Brewery was the first built in Liverpool, in 1780; the brewery is now Robert Cain's, producing award-winning real ales. Threlfall's was another local brewery, and the biggest was Walker's – its founder (and Liverpool mayor) Andrew Walker built three of Liverpool's most splendid art nouveau pubs, and donated a large chunk of the profits for the building of the Walker Art Gallery.

Engineering and design has always been strong in Liverpool, from the precision of watchmaking and the delicate scientific instruments made by Casartelli in Hanover Street, to the giant ocean liners of the White Star Line; craftsmanship from stonemasonry to glass-engraving and ceramics. Designers, from mechanical inventors to today's style gurus, abound in Liverpool. The Reverend Thomas Wilkinson, minister at St Chad's Church in Kirkby around 1756, invented the gold balance as well as several other ingenious machines.

One of the most prolific inventors to come out of Liverpool was the exotically-named Sebastian Ziani de Ferranti, born in Bold Street in 1864. An electrical engineer, Ferranti took out 176 patents during his lifetime, and founded a business that would become one of the world's great companies before its demise in the 1990s.

Not so well-known a name is Thomas Brassey, born in 1805, a local surveyor who progressed to building roads (including the New Chester Road) and then to railroading. He won an unparalleled reputation as a railway contractor, building all of France's major railways and many others across Europe, and then in Canada, Australia and India. The greatest railway contractor the world has ever known.

Ironically, three of Britain's most famous engineers never got a foothold beside the Mersey, but not for want of trying. Marc and Isambard Brunel submitted plans for a tunnel under the Mersey, and a ship canal to Manchester – both ideas were ridiculed. Thomas Telford, in 1816, designed a bridge to cross the Mersey at Runcorn – again rejected, so he built it across the Menai Straits instead.

Liverpool builders known for entirely opposing reasons are Costain, the main contractors and civil engineers (founded here 1865) and Jerry Brothers, the dreadful housebuilders of the 19th century, who gave the term 'Jerry-built' to the language.

As well as producing its own home-grown engineers, Liverpool must have sparked thousands of engineering and mechanical careers with its most famous toy: Meccano. Invented by Frank Hornby in 1901, the Meccano constructor systems were superb early training. It had more commercial uses, too. Nobel prize-winning physicist Sir Harry Kroto remembers that Meccano was used to hold paintbrushes on the production line at his father's balloon factory.

Fantastic innovation of process and product can be credited to Liverpool-born or based engineers and designers in road, rail, sea and canal transport. Not everything came quickly, though. It took another 100 years after the Brunels proposed a Mersey tunnel for the thing to be built.

Banking in Liverpool can be traced back at least to 1593, and the sign of the Grasshopper (*see picture, right*), a tavern where an astute moneylender was the embryonic version of what was to become Barclays Bank. The Grasshopper merged with the Bank of Liverpool's Liver Bird to create the town's first joint stock bank in 1831; it was swallowed by Martin's Bank, which was in turn acquired by Barclays. The Royal Bank of Scotland has Liverpool connections through Heywoods, and NatWest has several local links, including the National Bank of Liverpool and the Manchester & Liverpool District Banking Company.

Like the Grasshopper, some of today's biggest commercial concerns started life as something rather different. Liverpool Victoria Friendly Society and Royal Liver Assurance began life as burial clubs. Liverpool Victoria, in 1843, had mostly Irish members to begin with; its first president was William Fenton, a customs officer. Growing at enormous speed, the society moved to London in 1884 and is now the world's largest friendly society.

Royal Liver was founded by nine working-class men in 1850, at the Liver Inn in St Anne's Street. Within five years the society had agents in 25 towns, and by the time King Edward VII died, the society was wealthy enough to commission a new headquarters on the site of the old George's Dock. The new office block was to become the unmistakable emblem of the city – the Royal Liver Building, topped by its two 18ft-high Liver Birds. Not commonly known is that Britain's welfare state was born in this building. David Lloyd George's scheme for National Health Insurance was devised according to the advice of Royal Liver staff, who then put the scheme into place.

The story of Liverpool's insurance companies needs a book to itself. For a start, Liverpool Underwriters' Association was formed in 1803 – the oldest in existence. Marine insurance was a specialism, of course; motor insurance was pioneered here, as was electrical and mechanical insurance. All these can be claimed by what is now Royal & Sun Alliance, which began as Royal Insurance in 1845, formed to fight back against domination of the insurance industry by London firms. After 150 years it gave in, moving its corporate HQ to London, although keeping a serious presence in Liverpool.

A curious link to the past is provided by property company Beetham Developments. An old Liverpool name, dating back to the Norman Conquest, it was the polymath Edward Beetham who made his mark here. Beetham was an actor who in 1782 invented Beetham's Royal Patent Washing Mill, which could clean 60 shirts in an hour. Two years before he died, Beetham backed his friend Sir William Rawlins in the formation of a new insurance company – the Eagle – and became a director of what was to become Eagle Star.

Another in the long list of firsts is the Liverpool Society of Accountants, formed in 1870, 10 years before the National Institute of Chartered Accountants. The accountancy profession has changed almost beyond recognition since then, as indeed has commercial law, corporate finance and debt provision. Liverpool can, however, hold its own against Manchester; although a smaller professional community, there is strength in depth and some impressive professional muscle.

Completing the professional group are Liverpool's surveyors, architects, consultants and creatives from the brilliant Dutchman Thomas Steers and the extraordinary Captain William Hutchinson, through names such as Hartley, Waterhouse, Reilly, Cockerell, Foster, Brodie, to the creators of today's city such as Professor Ken Martin and Peter Carmichael, and of tomorrow's Liverpool, names such as Jon and Miles Falkingham.

Heywoods Bank, founded in 1773 in Brunswick Street, specialised in African trade. Some of its customers were illiterate and records have descriptions such as 'thick-lipped old woman of 45' and 'rings on her fingers and about twelve hands high'.

Martin's Bank (now Barclays) in Water Street stored 1,700 boxes of gold in its vaults after the fall of France in 1940. The bullion was part of Britain's gold reserves, sent here to be ready for shipment to Canada in the event of a German invasion.

The book Whisky Galore *by Compton Mackenzie was based on the real life wreck of the* Politician *on the shores of a Hebridean island. The ship was insured by the Liverpool firm C Danson & Co.*

The NatWest bank built a branch in Prince's Road that had one distinction: it is Britain's first drive-in bank.

Brokers and traders met in the open air behind the Town Hall; on her visit to the town in 1851, Queen Victoria looked down to the Flags from the balcony of the Town Hall and remarked that she had never before seen so large a number of well-dressed gentlemen collected together in one place.

The Corn Laws (1360-1846) regulated the trade of wheat to protect farmers' incomes. The laws were bitterly resented by the working-classes because they kept bread prices high; manufacturers hated them because it left the populace little money to buy their goods.

In 1755, when the new Town Hall opened, the Mayor and Bailiffs of Liverpool gave up their claim to the local corn tolls in exchange for enormous annual fair dinners.

Men meeting on street corners to talk about cotton, slaves, tobacco, sugar, timber, and to do deals – this was the beginnings of the 'exchange'. They soon began to gather on Exchange Flags, and gradually the systems became more sophisticated and Liverpool's exchanges formally established. The earliest of them was the Corn Exchange – the only one in England – built in 1805, although Liverpool is the oldest grain port in the country, trading with Ireland for centuries.

As demand in Britain for wheat outgrew domestic production, Liverpool merchants grabbed the opportunity to exploit the market. In Brunswick Street the Futures market was founded, making Liverpool the wheat barometer of the world once the Corn Laws were abolished in 1846.

Liverpool's corn trade flourished; corn traders built huge new grain warehouses and formed themselves into the Liverpool Corn Trade Association in 1853; by the end of the century Liverpool's stocks of wheat were the biggest in any European port. On Strand Road was the world's biggest silo built for bulk grain and, once Liverpool had built the first mill in the country to process wheat without using traditional millstones, Liverpool became the world's second largest flour-milling centre (after Minneapolis). The city's mills processed 700,000 tons of wheat in 1927 alone.

The first Corn Exchange in Fenwick Street was destroyed by bombs in the May Blitz of 1941; the second, designed by Hinchcliffe Davis in 1953, is on the same site.

While the cotton merchants wheeled and dealed on Exchange Flags in wind, rain and sun, Liverpool's Stock Exchange had its origins in the Merchants' coffee house on the Strand near St Nicholas's Church. In 1837 this was the place to deal and gossip; there were commodity auctions held, and speculation indulged in. A group of accountants and insurance agents banded together as a Sharebrokers' Association.

The Stock Exchange moved into the Royal Bank building in Queen's Avenue, but it was thrown out after a series of drunken evenings which included fireworks and a dancing bear. For 10 years, till 1879, the Stock Exchange was housed in the east wing of Exchange Buildings (not the Stalinist-style buildings there now). The brokers eventually built their own premises in Exchange Street East, early in the 19th century.

To counteract the pressure being put on regional exchanges by London, the exchanges of Liverpool, Manchester, Huddersfield, Leeds, Sheffield, Newcastle and Oldham formed the Northern Stock Exchange in 1965, but in the mid 1980s Liverpool lost its Stock Exchange (although its administrative centre carried on till 1990) as trading changed radically with the introduction of telecoms, computers and new regulations.

The city's band of stockbrokers and investment managers has diminished, too, with mergers, acquisitions and relocations having thinned out the number of firms operating in Liverpool at the start of the 20th century to the half dozen still here: Rathbones, BWD Rensburg, Charterhouse, Quilters, Tilneys and Blankstone Singleton. Even Rathbones has moved its corporate HQ to London, despite its deep roots in Liverpool stretching back past its century of stockbroking to its banking and shipping traditions.

Tilney is another long-established Liverpool firm, founded in 1836 by Thomas Tilney and his son George. Tilney senior was a Geordie who tried the Tyneside shipping business before coming to try his luck in Liverpool – changing the company name to Tilney with the arrival of third son Robert. In 2000, after a roller coaster ride through the 20th century, Tilney was acquired by American firm Refco.

J Bibby & Sons, founded in 1878, introduced family allowances to staff 27 years before the national scheme. In 1924 Bibby's pioneered the five-day working week and inaugurated a non-contributory pension scheme for employees.

Owen Owen pioneered the weekly half-day holiday for his staff.

A woman going to work in the Crawford's factory in 1911 remembers: 'When I first walked into the machine room, I was terrified by all the noise and bustle. Great machines crashing away, driving belts screeching in protest, dough mixers grinding away ... the staff shouting and whistling to each other.'

Working conditions in Liverpool haven't always been marvellous; employment legislation and health and safety regulations have improved things beyond all recognition in the last 30 years, but there are still plenty of unpalatable, filthy and downright dangerous jobs to be done. Even the man who replaces the light bulbs in the city's 59,000 street lights gets bricks hurled at him in some areas.

Dockers haven't had an easy time of it. The casual labour system could be desperate, with men coming to hiring pens each morning, hoping to be picked for work. By 1929 there were 239 stands along the seven-mile dockland waterfront. Every docker had his hook – the tool used to shift heavy sacks. A good hook could save a docker's hands – after a day handling up to 100 tons of cargo, hands could be bleeding, red raw and blistered.

Skilled craft workers established trade associations in the 18th century, but it was only in the 19th century that trade unions began to form to fight for better terms and conditions for unskilled workers; dockers didn't get a union till 1889, but they made their voices heard in the following 100 years or so. Union power has been much reduced in the last 20 years, but passions continue to run high, as the Mersey Docks & Harbour Company discovered to their cost in a vicious dispute that ran for three years from 1995 to 1998. The MDHC says it lost no profits because of the strike, but the dispute didn't exactly help the company's plans.

Although Liverpool gained a reputation for militant industrial disputes in the 1970s, strikes were happening all over Britain then. Liverpool's private sector has seen very little strike action, or even unrest, in the last 20 years; the 1990s dock strike was a rarity. Management attitudes (as well as the law) have changed radically since the 1970s – not before time.

Some of Liverpool's shops have made a dent in retail history: the jewellers Boodle & Dunthorne, for instance, have been around since 1798 and were so well-known that the word 'Boodle' became slang for jewellery, as any reader of the Raffles stories will know.

Littlewoods is known primarily for its football pools business, and only later as a mail order catalogue and chain of stores. But it was the mail order that came first, if only in embryo. John Moores (born in Eccles in 1896) was working as a telegraph operator in Ireland, when he began sending for supplies from England and selling them on for a commission. In 1924 John Moores and two friends (one called Littlewood) started the pools business; the mail order business was revived in 1932 and the first store was opened in Blackpool in 1937. Littlewoods became one of the largest privately-owned companies in Europe, and is owned by 32 members of the Moores family.

Liverpool had early branches of Woolworths and Marks & Spencer: Frank Woolworth opened his first European store in Liverpool in 1909; the 3d-and-6d store (the equivalent of the American five-and-dime) was at 25 Church Street, and the shop sign can still be seen on the side of the building, along with the American coat of arms.

David Lewis was one of the city's most innovative retailers, founding his store in 1856 at the top of Ranelagh Place, opposite the Adelphi Hotel. His was the first group of department stores to introduce central buying, through its purchasing office in London. Heavily bombed in the war, Lewis's was rebuilt, and over its main entrance is Epstein's famous male nude statue *Liverpool Resurgent.* Heaven only knows what 1950s patrons thought of it.

Owen Owen came to Liverpool in 1868, from a village in deepest Wales, with £300 in his pocket and opened a store in London Road. He started with two staff and ended up with 6,000. Owen Owen gave credit – in fact he was so well-known for it that 'Owen Owen' became the synonym for 'on the never-never'. The store merged with TJ Hughes in the 1930s, demerging in 1992. (TJ Hughes, the discount store in London Road, has grown enormously, floated on the Stock Exchange, and opened 34 branches around the country.)

Comedians may dress Scousers in shell suits and give them perms but fashion store Wade Smith, started by brothers Robert and David Wade Smith in 1982, says that Liverpudlians have a very sharp fashion sense and spend a good deal of money on designer clothes, knowing quality when they see it.

Liverpool has plenty of big high-street names, but its bedrock is small family businesses who survive despite supermarkets and out-of-town retail parks: the bakery run by Mrs Kinsey (born in 1915) and her two sons Charles and Peter, for instance. The shop in Aigburth Road opened in 1956 and both the shop fittings and the quality of service has remained the same. Traditional, top quality food for local people (try the blackcurrant pie).

Islington Market, on Shaw's Brow (now William Brown Street), was established in 1818 but was affected by the opening of St John's Market Hall in 1822 and was eventually demolished in 1856. St John's, with its 25ft high thin iron columns, was replaced in the 1960s by the current two-storey building with its famous 450ft high Beacon.

George and Henry Lee started their business selling straw bonnets in the 1850s; they were soon selling everything from lace to saucepans. By 1897 they had 1,000 employees and a splendid building in Church Street. Now part of the John Lewis chain, Lee's is, like Lewis's, a Liverpool retail landmark.

In the 1960s there was only one place for snappy dressers to buy their suits: Abrams Brothers, tailors in Lord Street, made suits for the Beatles, the Dave Clark Five, the Animals, and Liverpool's followers of fashion.

Fifteen years before the Rochdale Pioneers formed their society, John Finch formed the Liverpool Co-operative Society in 1829. Members pooled their resources to buy necessities at the best possible prices.

Clayton Square

Roger Phillips (above), award-winning voice of BBC Radio Merseyside, is one of the city's key media figures.

Communications used to mean talking to one another; these days it tends to mean the ways in which messages, goods, people and money are shifted from A to B, through fibre optic cables, on paper, down motorways, bounced off satellites, along rails, or through the ether. Speaking of ether (what a lovely old-fashioned word) none of the broadcast media would have been possible without the work of a physics professor at Liverpool University. If you thought that Marconi invented radio, think again: it was Oliver Lodge who sent the first radio message. More of Lodge later.

Along the way, a Liverpool factory made the first automatic telephone exchange in 1912, and the heart of Britain's subscriber trunk dialling (STD) system in 1958 (the factory was then the Strowger Works, later Plessey, then GEC, then – ironically – Marconi.

Before radio was born the Liverpool optician William Chadburn invented a ship's telegraph in 1870 – they were soon installed by all the major steamship companies. Thirty years later, the Elder Dempster line in Liverpool was the first to install a Marconi ship's wireless, on board their ship *Lake Champlain*. Two years later the first ship to establish simultaneous radio contact with both sides of the Atlantic was the Cunard Liner *Lucania*.

Moving forward, Liverpool was in the early 1990s the city with the biggest cable network (per capita) in the country. Liverpool's two main local radio stations – BBC Radio Merseyside and Radio City – have the biggest audiences in the the UK. (Radio City, by the way, has the most perfect perch at the top of St John's Beacon.) Radio Merseyside became a focus in April 1997 when thousands of visitors were stranded in Liverpool overnight because of the Grand National bomb scare; the station pumped out news and ran a phone-in to match stranded visitors with kind locals offering sofas, beds and floors for the night.

Liverpool's newspapers today are the morning *Post* and evening *Echo*. The *Daily Post*, when it was first published in 1855, was probably the country's first penny newspaper. The first editor was Michael J Whitty; the Irishman had started out as a journalist, then in an intriguing career jump became Liverpool's Head Constable when the police force was established here in 1836. The *Liverpool Echo*'s first editor, in 1879, was AG Jeans; today the paper has one of the largest circulations of any provincial daily.

There were earlier publications: the *Leverpole Courante* was published in 1715, but didn't last long. The first edition of Williamson's *Advertiser* (1756) contained 30 advertisements, and was successful enough to run for 100 years. In 1844 the *Telegraph & Shipping Gazette* was the country's first provincial newspaper.

With the advent of the world wide web, email and digital telecoms came the new economy. Liverpool is well-equipped for the digital age and fairly aggressive in its determination to make sure everyone has some kind of access to a computer and a modem. In the early days of IT, Martin's Bank in Liverpool was the first in the country to use a computer (1960) which could cope with 30,000 accounts in five hours. Two years later, the Mersey Docks & Harbour Board was the first port authority to install a computer.

The city has its fair share of web consultancies such as Amaze, Merseysite, Enzyme, Web Shed, New Mind, and is in the forefront of computer game development and publishing with names like Sony Psygnosis and Rage leading the way.

Liverpool University is the first British university to offer a degree in e-business, and was the first in Europe to launch a fully interactive Internet-based degree – an MSc in IT. In its first year (2000) it took 300 students from more than 3,000 applications worldwide.

This isn't Liverpool: it is Moscow, Chicago, St Petersburg, Dublin, London, Berlin, New York, Prague, Venice, even Manchester. Thirty years after taking a starring role in *Gumshoe* (with Albert Finney as the Scouse detective), the city of Liverpool might as easily appear on the silver screen as almost any city in the world. Since setting up the UK's first film office, Liverpool has become a leading stand-in for the movie industry, offering skilled technicians, actors, musicians, writers, experienced contractors from unit caterers to scaffolders, throngs of willing extras, and co-operative police and local authorities prepared to make life easy for the producers.

Since 1989 production companies coming here to make films, TV, music videos and commercials have injected many millions of pounds into the local economy – this is good business, declares film office director Lynn Saunders. The success of Liverpool's film office sparked similar offices in London and elsewhere in the UK, all vying to lure the movie dollar.

Alex Cox, director of cult classics *Repo Man* and *Sid and Nancy*, came back to Liverpool for the city's 'epic qualities' and its relatively low cost of living; he has since teamed up with producer Colin McKeown to set up the Liverpool Film Consortium and build the city's first fully-equipped film studio.

During 2000 there were six feature films shot in Liverpool; early 2001 saw three features being shot at the same time. Among them was *51st State*, a thriller starring Samuel L Jackson and Robert Carlyle. *My Kingdom* is a modern King Lear, starring Richard Harris and Lynn Redgrave; and Alex Cox's *Revenger's Tragedy* is another 17th-century play transposed to modern Liverpool with a cast including Derek Jacobi, Eddie Izzard and Sophie Dahl.

Underpinning the visiting productions is Liverpool's resident TV company, Mersey Television – maker of *Brookside* and *Hollyoaks (pictured below)* – headed by Phil Redmond. All told, the moving images industry now brings over £20 million into Liverpool each year.

Liverpool was the setting for the world's first feature film Liverpool Scenes, *flickering images of the city captured by Monsieur Lumiere in 1896.*

The Parole Officer, *the comedy starring Steve Coogan and released in August 2001, was set in Manchester but mostly filmed in Liverpool.*

For the Oscar-nominated film Hilary and Jackie, *about cellist Jacqueline du Pré, locations around Liverpool such as Abercromby Square and the Walker Art Gallery were turned into five different European cities.*

To capture the flavour of 1940s Liverpool in the film An Awfully Big Adventure, *they had to film in Dublin as Liverpool was no longer shabby enough.*

Exchange Flags

King Cotton gave Liverpool the boost she needed in the early 19th century, once the appalling trade in human lives had been abolished. Cotton was first imported into Liverpool in 1757, when 6,720 pounds of raw cotton were auctioned – the first such sale anywhere. At first, raw cotton was brought back on the third leg of the triangular trade, bought with profits from the slaves. Cotton garments and goods produced in Lancashire mills (as well as wool or linen) were then exported to Africa on the outgoing journey.

Merchants such as Rathbone, Holt, Ewart and Blundell were soon deep in cotton. The plant fibre from the Confederate States of America (the South) became increasingly important, so the disruption to trade caused by the American Civil War caused bankruptcy – and for the jobless cotton workers, starvation. With the transatlantic trade halted, Liverpool's traders had to look elsewhere in the world. It was John Gladstone (father of Prime Minister William Gladstone) who first explored the potential for cotton in the East Indies. His ship, *Kingsmill*, was the first Liverpool ship to sail to India after the East India Company's monopoly was broken.

The risks of transatlantic sailing meant that early news of a ship could make the difference between profit and loss; it was cotton money that had the lighthouse built at Hoylake, and set up Bidston as a flag station to warn of a ship as soon as it was sighted off the Bar. Cotton, again, was one of the driving forces behind the Liverpool-Manchester railway in 1830.

Distance was risk; given the length of time it took to sail back from the United States with a cotton cargo, the merchant could lose a small fortune. Between buying the cotton by letter, and the ship docking in Liverpool, the price could drop and force the merchant to take a loss.

Two factors made the trade more sophisticated: the first transatlantic telegraph cable in 1866, and John Rew. Liverpudlian cotton trader John Rew came up with an ingenious solution – hedging. News of any purchase made in America could now be wired straight back to Liverpool. On receipt of the news, Rew immediately sold the same amount at the same price in Liverpool. Then, if the price did drop before his ship docked, he was covered. The technique of hedging was adopted by traders in all Futures markets, and the current complex trade in derivatives has taken Rew's invention a quantum leap further on.

The Cotton Brokers' Association was established in 1841, and 41 years later was succeeded by the Liverpool Cotton Association. The cotton traders took offices in the Albany when it was built in 1856, as well as basement rooms around the courtyard where they could display samples. (One of the young men working at the Albany was Thomas Armstrong, author of the novel *King Cotton*.)

When Liverpool's Cotton Exchange was built in 1906 and traders abandoned the Flags for the weatherproof building, it was not only the first in Britain, but the most advanced exchange in the world of its type, with a transatlantic cable direct to the New York Cotton Futures Market. The Old Hall Street building was a demonstration of Liverpool's wealth, and boasted lavish hospitality. For one banquet 200 waiters travelled up from London on a specially chartered train, bringing with them six turtles and 200 pheasants to tickle the taste buds of the cotton traders.

At its peak in 1911, Liverpool's Cotton Exchange imported five million bales and held one million in stock: the city was the world's greatest market for trade in spot cotton. The trade declined over the coming decades, and control was ceded to London. Even the old Cotton Exchange was demolished, making way for an altogether inferior building.

But although Liverpool's Cotton Exchange is no longer the focus of the world's trade, the Association – with members in over 60 countries – is still the forum for traders throughout the world. Almost 70% of the world's raw cotton for export is still sold under Liverpool arbitration.

St. George's Hall

chapter 7
2D-3D

Art is alive and well in Liverpool; not only does the city have more world-class collections than you can shake a stick at, but its home-grown talent has made and continues to make an impact on the art world. As for architecture: there are some 2,500 listed buildings in Liverpool – more than in any other city outside London. Liverpool's pre-eminence as a world city meant that there was the money and the civic pride to invest in the best architects, with some stunning buildings as a result. So much has been lost, either through over-enthusiastic town planners or the thousands of bombs dropped by the Luftwaffe during the May Blitz of 1941.

The Customs House, for instance, was badly damaged in the war and demolished – some say it could and should have been restored. And its neighbour overlooking the Pool was the extravagant-looking Sailors' Home, of which chunks have been rescued, and other chunks are still languishing in a hole in Canning Place. St John's Market was another casualty, this time of the town planners, who replaced it with the charmless building there now. (St John's Beacon, incidentally, is wrapped around the market's ventilation shaft.)

Luckily the planners were cheated of their demolition plans for the Albert Dock complex, the North Western Hotel and gems like Bluecoat Chambers; rescued and converted to new uses, all are now part of the city's rich built environment. Some of the worst excesses of the post-war civic design, such as the Roe Street Gyratory, and the tower blocks of flats on the city fringes, are being expunged. (Perhaps in another century pundits will be cursing the lack of vision that destroyed these 1950s and 1960s works of genius – oh, the joys of hindsight.)

Liverpool is not a high-rise city. There are few tall blocks (100 Old Hall Street, Concourse House in Lime Street and St George's Hotel opposite are the only examples in the centre of the city), which might reflect the lack of demand for commercial space in the post-war period, but which has allowed the city to be dominated by the huge Liver Building at sea level, and the even huger Anglican Cathedral (which appears as the city's key landmark looking over the Wirral from the A55 in North Wales) up the hill on St James's Mount.

Liverpool's marvellous collection of visual art – buildings, public sculptures, paintings, photographs and glass – should not overshadow the contemporary scene of local artists, enterprising private galleries and international festivals such as Visionfest (until its demise in the 1990s, the biggest visual arts festival in the UK), the prestigious John Moores Painting Competition, and the Liverpool Biennial.

Working today, either locally or further afield, are Liverpool-born sculptors such as Tony Cragg, Stephen Broadbent, Mark Warwick, John Haymes-Hogg, Tom Murphy; painters Nicholas Horsfall, Richard Meaghan, Clem McAteer and Amanda Relph.

In 2001 Liverpool lost the polymath Adrian Henri – who died aged 70. Famous as one of the Liverpool 8 Poets, Henri was first and foremost a painter who exhibited widely, won prizes and carved a niche in British art. George Melly said of Henri's 1960s works: 'Like his poems they reflect not an abstract reaction to the universal, but the packet of washing powder by the sink, the cornflakes on the breakfast table or the recently emptied bed.'

Henri described himself as one of life's magpies – a great hoarder of ideas; he was open to an enormous range of artistic influence, from Sickert and Whistler to jazz and poetry and politics, and chance meetings. Adrian Henri was a creative force in Liverpool for almost half a century, was loved and is much missed.

Liverpool has produced its fair share of artists, and continues to do so; of all of them, the best known name around the world is probably George Stubbs, the supreme animal painter of his time. Stubbs, born in 1724 in Ormond Street (behind what is now Mercury Court in Tithebarn Street), was the son of a currier and developed enormous strength heaving about animal skins for his father's business (dressing and colouring leather) – even carrying dead horses upstairs on his back. Stubbs was a self-taught painter, and learned anatomy by dissecting animals and humans (he published *The Anatomy of the Horse* in 1766). The result was superbly accurate paintings – Stubbs was the pioneer in realistic animal portraits, as well as leading the way in painting English landscape without continental influence. He had a lot of commissions from the wealthy to paint their horses; one of the most remarkable was *Whistlejacket* – a lifesize portrait of a half-rearing chestnut horse, painted on a plain, pale background so that nothing distracts from the vision of this spectacular animal. (There is, by the way, a spooky similarity between Stubb's *Horse Frightened by a Lion* and the image of a fat pony frightened by a small girl disguised as a ghost, by another Liverpool genius, Norman Thelwell ....)

Liverpool had two other world-class animal painters: William Huggins, born here in 1820, was declared 'second only to Landseer', but was known as an eccentric, experimenting with colour (eg purple donkeys). Considered Liverpool's greatest 19th-century animal artist, Richard Ansdell's picture *The Hunted Slaves* was sold (for £700) to raise money for Lancashire cotton workers threatened with starvation during the American Civil War.

Another remarkable Liverpool artist was Sarah Biffen (whose grave is in St James's cemetery, by the Cathedral). Born in 1784, she was only 39 inches tall, and was born without arms or legs. She spent 15 years as a freakshow with a travelling circus, but was taught to paint by the circus manager by fixing her paintbrush to a loop on her right shoulder, and moving the brush with her mouth. Biffen became a miniature portraitist with four monarchs as patrons (from George III to Victoria) and had work hung in the Royal Academy; befriended by the Rathbone family, she lived at 8 Duke Street and died aged 66.

Other local painters of note include the master of chiaroscuro, the 'Liverpool Rembrandt' William Daniels (died 1880); marine artist Richard Wright (who died in 1775); and Richard Caddick, an 18th-century portrait painter who invented the technique of engraving glass through a chemical process. William G Herdman (1805-82) would not have made it into the pantheon of painters – he was neither particularly good nor original – but for his 2,000-plus watercolours of old Liverpool townscapes; these were mostly contemporary scenes, but he would use earlier paintings and drawings, often 'improving' on these artists' work. Masterpieces they were not, but Herdman's watercolours were hugely popular in his day, and still sell like hotcakes. They certainly gave the city a rare pictorial record of its past.

Sculptors of the town include John Gibson and Warrington Wood, both of whom found fame in Rome; the 18th-century eccentric John Deare (who habitually prayed in the nude) was an eminent sculptor. In the 20th century, Herbert Tyson Smith had his studio at the Bluecoat Chambers, heated by a stove given to him by Augustus John; up the road in Seel Street worked the great Arthur Dooley, an ex-docker who died in 1994, of whom many affectionate stories are still told in Liverpool pubs.

At 59 Rodney Street lived the brilliant photographer E Chambré Hardman; not only does Liverpool have his stunning collection of photographs, but the National Trust is now restoring his house and studio, a 1940s time capsule.

The British Journal of Photography evolved from the photography magazine founded in 1853 by the Liverpool Amateur Photographic Association. Two of the LAPA's members invented the dry-plate process in 1864.

The Merseyside Film Institute, based in Bluecoat Chambers, was founded in 1933 and was the oldest and the largest outside London. It lasted until the early 1990s, but has now finally faded to black.

Sandon Studios (which in 1907 evolved into the Bluecoat Society of the Arts) was a group of leading figures in the arts including Augustus John, and Wilson Steer, under the aegis of Miss Fanny Dove Hamel-Lister.

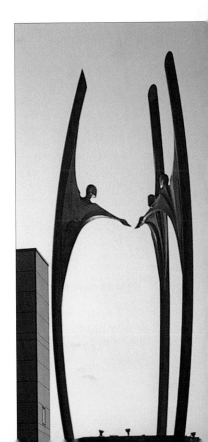

The extraordinary colour thrown by the stained glass in the Catholic Metropolitan Cathedral

In Harrington Street is the sculptural equivalent of two fingers to a London architect, who once said that 'Art is to architecture like lipstick is to a gorilla.' The piece, which can be seen on the terracotta keystone over the arched opening of the Cavern Walks car park) depicts a gorilla applying lipstick, and was done by terracotta manufacturers Hathernware. Ya boo sucks.

One of Liverpool's most infamous statues is 'the man exceedingly bare' who stands on a ledge above the entrance to Lewis's department store. By Jacob Epstein, the 1957 nude is Liverpool Resurgent *– the spirit of the post-war city.*

Around Liverpool there are over 90 listed monuments and statues – the most important collection outside London – from classical figures to modern abstracts and contemporary irony. The Victorian monuments to the great and the good, the memorials to the dead and the living in several wars; iconic figures, mythic figures, symbolic figures. Abstracts and concepts, the sad and the sarcastic; fountains and fairies, columns and obelisks; of wood, fibreglass, steel, bronze, stone, marble and concrete.

In the whole of Britain there are 26 royal equestrian statues: four of them are in Liverpool. Queen Victoria and Prince Albert (by Thorneycroft) are on St George's Plateau; Edward VII (by Goscombe John) is on the Pier Head in front of the Cunard Building, and in Monument Place is George III (by Richard Westmacott) who is dressed as a Roman general.

There are several statues of Queen Victoria, including a bust in Gateacre, and the huge memorial in Derby Square. On the site of the old castle now stand four groups of columns supporting a dome, under which stands a rather poe-faced Victoria. The architects of this 1906 creation were Professor FM Simpson and Willink & Thicknesse, whose best idea was the brickwork on the square, designed to represent the ramparts of the castle. The sculpture was by Charles J Allen – eight rather fine groups – the lower four representing agriculture, commerce, education and industry, the upper four representing the virtues of the Queen: wisdom, justice, charity and peace. Over the whole lot stands the figure of Fame. Until recently, there was a rather splendid gents' loo beneath the monument – now removed.

War memorials feature large in Liverpool's collection, unsurprisingly. The very first public sculpture (1813) in the city was the spectacular Nelson memorial on Exchange Flags, behind the Town Hall. Rather macabre, the sculpture was designed by Matthew Cotes Wyatt and fabricated by Richard Westmacott. A naked Nelson stands on the body of the enemy, touched by the skeletal hand of Death just as he reaches for a fourth great naval victory. Britannia kneels weeping, and around the base are four chained figures – not slaves, as often thought, but representing the four victories of St Vincent, the Nile, Copenhagen and Trafalgar. (In St John's Gardens there lie buried 230 French prisoners of war who died in the Tower of Liverpool during the Napoleonic Wars; a plaque to their memory was erected on Armistice Day 1924.)

Also in St John's Gardens is a memorial, by W Goscombe John, to the King's Liverpool Regiment, put up to remember the dead of the Boer War. The Museum of Liverpool Life now has a gallery devoted to the King's Regiment, opened by Prince Charles in 2000.

On St George's Plateau is the Cenotaph, designed by Lionel Budden, professor at Liverpool University, with sculpture by Herbert Tyson Smith (he, his wife and son are amongst the carved figures: Tyson Smith stands to the right, his hand tucked into his jacket).

At the Pier Head are a number of memorials to the seamen and women of World War II: to the Royal Navy and Merchant Navy, Norwegian, Belgian, Canadian and US sailors, airmen and army troops. Most were put up after the war; but the most recent is the 1998 Merchant Navy Memorial by John Schimmin.

Outside Lamb Brothers ship's chandlers on Wapping is a very yellow sculpture by Taro Chiezo. Seven tons of steel and concrete, Super Lamb Banana was fabricated by local artists Andy Snall, Julian Taylor, Ray Stokes and Tommy Reason from the artist's 1:50 scale maquette. The Yellow Peril, as the locals named it, outraged the public on its unveiling in 1988, but it has acquired almost cult status.

In the churchyard of St Andrew's in Rodney Street is a pyramid, the tomb of W Mackenzie who died in 1868. The legend is that Mackenzie – a keen gambler – is buried sitting upright at his card table holding a winning hand.

In Stanley Street is a stone bench, on which sits a bronze figure – Eleanor Rigby. Sculpted by singer Tommy Steele and sold to the city for half a sixpence, the sad little figure often has a bunch of fresh flowers at her side, but who puts them there has never been known. Inside the statue is a four-leaf clover, a page of the Bible, a football sock, copies of the Dandy and Beano, and four sonnets.

Beatles-inspired sculptures include the life-size figure by David Webster of the young John Lennon, leaning against the wall in Mathew Street near the site of the old Cavern. Inside Cavern Walks shopping mall is a group sculpture of the Beatles by John Doubleday, and outside is a terracotta piece by Cynthia Lennon, John's first wife. On the ledge over the door of the Beatles shop is another group – From Me to You – by David Hughes. Possibly the most famous Beatles piece is the bronze by Arthur Dooley, up on the wall opposite the Cavern. It depicts Four Lads Who Shook the World; Mother Liverpool is cradling three of her sons, but the fourth has grown 'Wings' and flown away.

Around the Dooley bronze is the Mathew Street Wall of Fame (pictured right), which lists every band and solo singer who has performed at the Cavern since it opened in 1957, including Stevie Wonder, the Rolling Stones, the Who and Bono.

Possibly the most unusual war memorial is in the English Garden at Calderstones Park. Dedicated to Jet of Iada, the first rescue dog of World War II. Having saved over 50 lives of people trapped in bombed buildings in London, Jet was given the canine VC – the Dickin medal; and in 1947, having saved the lives of rescuers after a mining disaster in Whitehaven, Jet was given the RSPCA's Medallion for Valour.

Over in Princes Park is the grave of another well-loved animal – this time the donkey Judy, 'who during 21 years' service in this park was the children's friend'. Judy was 26 when she died in August 1926, and fresh flowers on her grave show she is still remembered.

There are a number of obelisks in Liverpool. The largest – a memorial to the Scot, Samuel Smith, cotton broker and philanthropist – is on the north side of Sefton Park; 60 feet high, of red granite, it was designed by Willink & Thicknesse and unveiled in 1909. It was Smith who led the search for a new source of cotton when the American Civil War stopped cotton imports from the southern states; he was also involved in founding a society to prevent cruelty to children (now the NSPCC), and supported Dr Barnardo in his work for orphans.

There is an obelisk in Princes Park dedicated to the park's creator, Richard Vaughan Yates; Yates died in 1856 and the obelisk went up two years later.

The obelisk near the Oratory on St James's Mount is a much smaller affair, dedicated to Maurice Gandy by the firm he founded, the Gandy Belt Manufacturing Company. Down Rodney Street, next to the pyramid in St Andrew's Churchyard, are two more obelisks.

A rather sad-looking obelisk is that to Lord Nelson put up by a Mr Downward. A sugar refiner, he offered the obelisk to the city, but was declined; the comment being that such a thing was unworthy of a place in Liverpool's streets. So Downward took back his obelisk and erected it in the grounds of his house, Springfield, in Knotty Ash. The last stone needle, south of the city centre, on Allerton golf course, is a sandstone obelisk from Allerton Hall; it marks a spot exactly five miles from Liverpool Town Hall.

Every city needs at least one chap on a column. Liverpool has Wellington, standing 14-foot high on top of his 132-foot Darleydale stone column, near St George's Plateau. The statue of Wellington, by Glaswegian sculptor George Lawson, is cast from melted-down cannon salvaged from the battlefield after Waterloo.

A much smaller column is in front of the Cunard Building on the Pier Head; this one is the Cunard War Memorial and carries the bronze figure of a nude male on top of its Roman Doric column.

Liverpool has two splendid fountains, both of which stood dry for many years, and are now both restored and flowing again. At the top of William Brown Street is the lush cast-iron circle of the Steble Fountain, designed by W Cunliffe and built in 1879, as a gift from Richard Fell Steble, former mayor of Liverpool. The *Porcupine* – a satirical weekly paper – was scathing about the engineering, suggesting that 'a barman washing the windows of a grogshop by the use of a hose' would produce a better effect than the 'lop-sided squirt of dirty water'.

On Beetham Plaza to the east of the Strand is the splendid 1966 *Piazza Waterfall*, engineered by Richard Huws. 'It is a waterfall of a strange new kind which hurtles down unexpectedly in detached lumps in all directions,' said Huws. Twenty steel cups of varying sizes are hung on axles between bronze posts; the cups fill with water and tip over, pouring into the pool below. A wonderful game for bored office workers with windows on to the plaza, gambling on which cup will spill next.

Liverpool, being a waterside city, should have many more fountains and cascades – it would be an ideal marker for the city's 800th anniversary in 2007, for instance.

Another fabulous sculpture – this time to underline Liverpool's bid for status as European Capital of Culture in 2008 – is that proposed by award-winning local artist Tom Murphy. A spectacular and monumental piece, 150-ft long and 60-ft high, Murphy's *Neptune* would sit on a sandbank of the Mersey, so that the head and chest would be visible at high tide, and all of him would be seen at low tide. Murphy reckons it would cost £3 million, but says the city needs something to wow the world, like the Eiffel Tower or the Statue of Liberty.

Religious sculpture in the city ranges from the staid monument marking the site of the old West Derby Chapel, to four striking modern pieces depicting Christ. The 1970s *Crucifixion* by Arthur Dooley is a gaunt Christ figure, on the Methodist Centre at the corner of Princes Avenue and Beaconsfield Street; by the Chapel Street entrance to St Nicholas is the 1971 *Christ on an Ass*, by Brian Burgess; and over the great West Door of the Anglican Cathedral is the huge *Welcoming Christ* – originally known as the *Risen Christ* – the last commission completed by Dame Elizabeth Frink. Around the entrance to the Catholic Metropolitan Cathedral is a rather startling sculpture of a fierce-looking Christ, by William Mitchell.

Just in case London thought it was the only city with an Eros, think again. Liverpool's *Eros*, a casting of Alfred Gilbert's statue in Piccadilly Circus, stood on its fountain from 1932 to 1993 when Eros was taken for restoration, leaving the fountain looking rather bereft. Eros now dominates the cafe of the Conservation Centre. Nor does London have the only Peter Pan – presented by George Audley (as was Eros) to the city, *Peter Pan* (designed by George Frampton) stands in Sefton Park (or will do again, after its restoration in 2001).

There isn't room here for every sculpture in the city: statues to a string of worthies from Father Nugent to assorted Rathbones, from Gladstone to Florence Nightingale. There are some terrific abstracts: Barbara Hepworth's 1963 *Squares With Two Circles*, Charlotte Mayer's *Sea Circle*, S English's *Seven Seas*, Nicholas Pope's *Unknown Landscape*, and Stephen Cox's *Palanzana*. Tom Murphy has a dozen figures and groups around the city, from the Blitz Memorial to statues of Sir John Moores and Bill Shankly; look for Stephen Broadbent's *Community Wall*, and his stylised groups *Coming Together* and *Reconciliation*; the 12-ft high *Mother and Child* by Terence McDonald outside the Women's Hospital, and the intriguing *Case History* by John King, which includes references to Arthur Askey, Josephine Butler, Charles Dickens, Kwok Fong, Margaret Simey, Lennon and McCartney.

There is no title on the memorial (below) topped with gold flame to the north of the Liver Building; it was designed by Goscombe John as a memorial to those who lost their lives on the Titanic, but due to local sensitivities, the name Titanic *is not mentioned anywhere, and the piece is now dedicated to all engine-room men lost at sea.*

Leaning out of a niche in the wall of Flanagan's Apple in Mathew Street is the top half of archetypal psychologist Carl Gustav Jung, who in 1927 said: 'Liverpool is the pool of life'.

The 12-ft high group in Church Street is by Edward Cronshaw. The Great Escape is of a man and a rearing stallion, representing 'the power of life and death, the horse and figure trapped in a never-ending cycle of birth and rebirth, life and death, a continuous battle of wills between the body and matter, the mind and spirit'.

The Tate's opening exhibition included the Liverpool equivalent of Carl Andre's pile of bricks – a piece titled Bed *by Antony Gormley, which consisted of 6,000 slices of white bread which, although waxed, went mouldy over the exhibition's run, causing much fevered arts analysis, and many barbed Scouse jokes.*

n giving local people access to art, as in so much else, Liverpool took the lead. Andrew Walker, the brewer and mayor of Liverpool, put up the money to build the first public art gallery in the country. The Walker opened in 1877, was extended five years later, again in the 1930s and once more in 2001. The gallery now has one of Europe's finest collections of paintings, drawings, sculpture, furniture and decorative art from the 14th to 20th centuries, and every two years runs the internationally renowned Liverpool John Moores Painting Competition. The winner in 2000 was Michael Raedecker's *Mirage*; previous winners have included Hockney, Peter Doig, John Hoyland and Bruce McLean.

The former Midland Railway Goods Depot was in 1996 transformed into the Conservation Centre, European Museum of the Year 1998, the first in the country, and the only one open to the public. World-class conservators preserve and restore everything from ancient archaeological treasures to fine art and space suits – and the public can watch them at work and get advice on their own heirlooms. In the cafe named after him, the original Eros perches on his toes, bow and arrow poised. On one hand it is wonderful to see such an icon at close quarters, face to face; on the other, it is a wicked shame that the world-famous statue cannot be replaced on his fountain in Sefton Park for fear of damage by pollution, ignorant vandals or clued-up art thieves. A replica will be placed in the park instead.

Another conversion is the jewel in School Lane: Bluecoat Chambers. A charity school from 1716 to the early 1900s (when the school moved to within a stone's throw of the Beatles' Penny Lane), it was the University's School of Architecture for a few years, and is now an arts centre with the Bluecoat Gallery at its heart.

In the leafy suburbs to the south of the city is Sudley House, set in parkland with stunning views across the Mersey to Snowdonia. The former home of shipowner George Holt, Sudley is unique in that it houses a private collection (including work by Landseer, Turner, Corot, Gainsborough and Reynolds) in its original setting, so visitors see not only the paintings, but a beautiful example of a wealthy Victorian merchant's home. The exterior of the house is no great architectural jewel, admittedly, and the gardens – including what must have been a great walled garden – have been all but lost. A grand restoration project for a 21st-century philanthropist, indeed.

The Tate Gallery – the London gallery's first 'branch' to be opened (now joined by the Tate in St Ives and Tate Modern in London) – was created from warehouse space in the Albert Dock by Liverpool-born architect James Stirling. As a boy, Stirling explored the maze of riverside warehouses and colonnades, and remembers 'the perfect plaza of water' in the Albert Dock quadrangle. Part of the master plan to revive Liverpool's fortunes, the Tate was opened in 1988 by the Prince and Princess of Wales. As well as housing a stunning collection of 20th-century British art, Tate Liverpool's special exhibitions are world-class, from solo shows and retrospectives to numbers such as *Emotional Ties* in 2001 (including work by Picasso, Hockney, de Chirico, Chagall, Bonnard, Munch).

Alongside Liverpool's great public galleries are its museums, from the Museum of Liverpool Life (opened in 1993) to the Customs & Excise Museum (1994). The Maritime Museum (1980) gives visitors a hint of how it felt to be aboard an emigrant ship in the 1800s, or on board the pilot boat *Edmund Gardner* on World Cup Final Day 1996.

Liverpool Museum itself has collections that each rank in the UK's top 10 – together they are difficult to match anywhere in Europe: more than a million specimens and artefacts from Egyptian mummies to 350,000 botanical specimens and 2,500 scientific instruments.

Galleries aren't all big and public. Liverpool has a growing collection of private art galleries showing and selling work by local and visiting national and international artists, plus a whole slew of restaurants and bars that mount exhibitions for local artists. The Hub Cafe, for instance, has its own artist in residence, and the cafe at No7 Falkner Street houses the Ainscough Gallery.

Visual art galleries include the Acorn in Newington, the Hanover Galleries, the John Lennon Gallery, Ktisis in Allerton Road, and Static in Roscoe Street.

Architect Ken Martin established The View on the sixth floor of Gostins Building in Hanover Street in the mid-1990s, and built such a good reputation for the space that he opened the stunning View 2 in Mathew Street, and then moved the original View to a much larger space in Gostins. His faith in Liverpool's arts community and the buying public has, thank god, been justified; Martin now charges commission on work sold (he didn't for the first five years), but doesn't charge artists to exhibit, nor the public to come in and look.

The Open Eye Gallery in Bold Street began in the 1970s to support local photographers, and has established a great reputation. Film, both still and moving, plays a big part in Liverpool's art sector: Video Positive is a month-long showcase for avant garde video and film-makers (the next is in 2003); and in 2000 work started on the FACT Centre, a major international centre for film, video and new media with three galleries, cinemas, public spaces and online archive.

A joint venture by John Moores University and Phil Redmond's Mersey TV is the International Centre for Digital Content – Liverpool's latest addition to its tertiary level arts teaching, a 21st-century neighbour to Liverpool Art School.

Liverpool's first academy for painting, the Society of Artists of Liverpool, was founded in 1769, but it was William Ewart, a local man and Liverpool MP, who drove forward the art school system in Britain, and sponsored the Museums Act 1845.

At the end of the 20th century, the man who created the National Museums & Galleries on Merseyside (NMGM) was Richard Foster. Given the task by Michael Heseltine of enlivening a disparate group of existing institutions, creating new ones and investing the whole group with energy (and cash), Sir Richard Foster became one of Liverpool's champions. It was said of him: 'He gave Liverpool back its dignity.' Foster died suddenly in 2001, aged 59.

Ken Martin's gallery The View

The archetypal look of the elegant colonial houses in America's southern states came from the Liverpool home of the Rathbone family. Greenbank House (built in the late 18th century), is a delightful mixture of Georgian and Gothic styles, with the addition in about 1815 of filigree screen of cast iron on the side facing the garden. This style of decorative cast iron was extensively used in Liverpool, and spread to the colonies in America, Australia and New Zealand. Greenbank House was converted in 1964 into a university club.

For a city that is not known for its manufacturing, let alone its iron and steel industries, those metals have had quite an impact on Liverpool and, as a result, on the wider world. Key figure in the cast iron story of the city is John Cragg, owner of the Mersey Iron Foundry in Tithebarn Street; born in 1767, Cragg made a fortune from iron and was its greatest promoter. It was Cragg who helped Thomas Rickman design the first cast-iron churches in Everton and St Michael's, and Cragg who then built the prefabricated pieces in his foundry. Cragg also built the hamlet of St Michael's, in Aigburth – which is a hymn to Cragg's great passion, with cast-iron columns, gate-posts, window-frames, fireplaces and stairs.

Two hundred years on, one architect is going back to timber and turf as the building materials of the future. Tayo Aluko, of Aluko Brooks, has designed the city's first truly green house, to be built from woodchip, old newspapers, timber beams and turf. The four-bedroom house has a very modern price – Aluko estimated around £350,000 in 2001 – and is designed for a plot in Woodlands Road, Mossley Hill. The three-storey house would be built of woodwool blocks on a timber frame, then plastered. Newspaper pulp will be sprayed inside wall cavities for insulation, with solar panels on the roof; rainwater will work the water-saving loos, exterior paints and finishes will be eco-friendly, and one section of the roof will be turfed, both for insulation and for the benefit of Mossley Hill's smaller wildlife.

Today, new housing is, by and large, either traditional semis and detached on landscaped estates by the likes of Morris Homes and McLean Homes, or by the new breed of inner city developers such as Urban Splash, Space and Beetham (all Liverpool-based). It was Urban Splash that kicked off the trend for stylish, affordable apartments in converted buildings written off by more conventional developers as too difficult. Now every redundant building is a target, from an old Post Office depot to an eyesore of a 1960s office block; such is the demand for inner city living space that prices have rocketed, and the resident population of the commercial and retail heart of the city trebled in the last eight years of the 20th century.

The new developers are reversing the redundancy of old buildings; it would be a little eccentric to do the opposite. But Joseph Williamson wasn't just a little eccentric – he was out on his own. For more than 30 years he built structures that were of no use whatsoever. Known either as the Mole of Edge Hill or the King of Edge Hill, depending on who you asked, Williamson made a fortune out of tobacco. Born in 1769, he left his family and came to Liverpool, aged 11, to find a job. Later, he worked for Richard Tate in his tobacco and snuff business, married the boss's daughter and bought the business when the old man died.

In the first years of the 19th century Williamson built several houses in Mason Street in the rural area of Edge Hill; already employing a large gang of men, Williamson began to be besieged by unemployed men looking for work, so rather than turn them away Williamson got them to dig into the sandstone and build tunnels. He employed thousands over the next 30-odd years, many of whom became skilled masons and craftsmen and went on to build the railway infrastructure that would run from Lime Street, through Edge Hill and on inland.

Williamson's tunnels vary in size, design, direction and shape from the so-called Banqueting Hall (70ft long, 25ft wide and 30ft high) to mere channels in the rock the width of a skinny tunneller; beautiful vaulted passages and elegant arches over yawning underground pits. Several miles of tunnels were burrowed out; few remain intact now, but the Friends of Williamson's Tunnels are campaigning to get the remaining tunnels restored and opened to the public and, with funding promised, work has begun again.

The roof of the southern hangar at the old airport terminal in Speke was a revolutionary design by German engineers Fokker (later famous for building fighter planes in WW2). Sadly for the designers, the hangar was completed shortly before hostilities broke out, and when the German architects sent in their bill they were politely told to Fokker off.

JA Brodie, Liverpool's brilliant city engineer (1858-1934) gave this city its wide tree-lined boulevards and its ring road.
It is less well-known that he laid out the road system for New Delhi, working alongside architect Edwin Lutyens.

The extravagant Mersey Tunnel ventilation shaft

Coming to Liverpool for the first time, visitors are often dumbfounded at what they see around them. Expecting – what? – grey urban grunge and dereliction (if they believe what they read in the papers), they come face to face with some of the country's most stunning buildings. There are more listed buildings in Liverpool than in any other city outside London: 2,500 of them, ranging from the delightful 18th-century Town Hall and the 19th-century Palladian splendour of St George's Hall to an art deco ventilation shaft and two rare telephone kiosks. A tour of the city's architectural gems would not fit into an afternoon unless whizzed around on the back of the guide's motorbike.

The great civic buildings, the evidence of the city's pride in its own success, its temples to education and the arts, its palaces of travel, and – proof of affluence – the purely functional turned to decorative splendour ... Liverpool's great wealth and influence brought great architects here, and promoted local architects to greatness. How rich must a city be to house the ventilation shaft from an underground road tunnel in a tower of Egyptian-influenced art deco elegance? Herbert Rowse's 1934 Georgian Dock Building is part of a matching set with the tunnel mouths, the monumental lamp standards and the other ventilation shafts.

All of Liverpool's key points of departure have been housed in splendour, from the original airport at Speke, the great curved skin of Lime Street, to the Pier Head. Speke (the airport opened in 1933) was the first municipal airport building in Europe, and one of the first purpose-built air terminals in the world. Completed in 1937, the Grade II listed terminal was designed by Arthur Landstein in the shape of an aircraft – at the suggestion of barnstorming aviator Alan Cobham. Liverpool Airport moved in the 1980s to a new site, and after more than a decade of neglect, the art deco terminal has been revived as a four-star Marriott Hotel, sensitively refurbished and extended by Liverpool architects Falconer Chester.

A century earlier, the world was turned on its head by the arrival of the railway. In Edge Hill a small, unremarkable sandstone building is a world No1: this is the first passenger railway station in the world. Built in 1836, it is the terminus of the Liverpool-Manchester Railway which only later was extended through the deep cutting to Lime Street.

Lime Street itself saw three stations built in 40 years, the first in 1836 and the fourth – which we have today – was completed in 1879, designed by William Baker and CR Stevenson for the London & North Western Railway.

Built in 1871 to serve the railway company's passengers, Alfred Waterhouse's North Western Hotel was fit for kings – then the city's largest and most luxurious hotel with 300 rooms on seven storeys. It prospered for 60 years, but the hotel was closed in 1933 and, after 30 years as offices, it was threatened with demolition in 1969 and stood empty till 1995 when it was converted by John Moores University into student accommodation.

The hotel that did for the North Western was the world-famous Adelphi; in 1912 Frank Atkinson, architect of Selfridge's store in London, designed a luxurious hotel to house wealthy travellers heading off across the Atlantic. It has an impressive marble foyer and an elegant palm court, and the ballroom is of a similar design to that of the White Star line's great ocean liners.

Sitting quietly on the Mersey itself is one of Liverpool's superlatives: the floating landing stage, built by engineer G Fosbery Lyster in 1876 (the first in 1874 was destroyed by fire) it was 2,000-ft long. Over the years it was extended to become the largest floating structure in the world, nearly half a mile long (these days it is back to its shorter self).

Oriel Chambers' reflected glory

The Old School House in Walton has a datestone marked 1548.

Waterhouse's magnificent Victoria Building was the original 'red brick university', the term coined from the building's distinctive pressed red brick exterior.

The Lyceum, built in 1800 as a gentleman's club, housed Europe's first proprietary circulating library in its public news and coffee room. Minus books, the great circular room is now a stylish café and bar.

School architecture doesn't impress children, on the whole, but in Queen Anne's reign the Bluecoat charity school was housed in a gem of a building set around three sides of a fringed courtyard. Probably designed by Thomas Ripley, the Bluecoat in School Lane is one of Liverpool's two surviving 18th-century jewels (along with the Town Hall). The school has long since moved out, and Bluecoat Chambers is now an arts centre with a delightful oasis of a garden courtyard – a well-loved green haven in the heart of the city.

Dating back to its 1785 origins, Blackburne House on Hope Street became the Liverpool Institute High School for Girls in 1844, opposite the Art School and the Liverpool Institute for Boys (1835). One hundred and fifty years later the girl's school was reborn as the Women's Technology Centre; the brilliant conversion by Liverpool architects Maggie Pickles and Gladys Martinez won the RIBA's award for Building of the Year in 1995.

Tucked away in Colquitt Street, the Royal Institution in 1814 took over the house of Thomas Parr the merchant, for the promotion of literature, science and the arts; William Roscoe gave the opening lecture in 1817. Some of the house's features – its stone portico and Palladian wings – were much copied by wealthy merchants for their own houses.

The Medical Institution – on a triangular site between Hope Street and Mount Pleasant – was built in 1836 to a design by Clark Rampling; the elegant curving facade with its Ionic columns is rather overshadowed by the neon-lit bulk of the Everyman Theatre next door.

The rival to the Liverpool Institute was the Liverpool Collegiate in Shaw Street, founded in 1839; it was the first of the great Victorian public schools (followed by Marlborough, Lancing and Wellington, amongst others). In what was then fashionable and affluent Everton, the Collegiate was designed in glorious Gothic style by the 26-year-old Harvey Lonsdale Elmes; fire-damaged in the 1980s, the Collegiate has been transformed by Urban Splash into flats.

Alfred 'Slaughterhouse' Waterhouse excelled himself with the design of the Victoria Building in 1887, although it wasn't to everyone's taste then, or since. Professor of architecture Charles Reilly wrote: 'In colours of mud and blood it struggles to reach the sky, out-Nuremburging Nuremburg itself in its efforts to be picturesque. It has towers and turrets, long oriel windows, and all the trappings of romance … and yet remains the hard prosaic thing we know it to be.' The Victoria Tower is possibly best seen at dusk, when the clock face is lit.

Liverpool University has grown from its beginnings at the top of Brownlow Hill to a substantial campus stretching north to Pembroke Place and south to Myrtle Street, with a sweep of architectural styles from the Georgian elegance of Abercromby Square to the modern 1950s and 1960s buildings of Sir Basil Spence (Physics Building, 1958), Gerald Beech (Wyncote Sports Pavilion, 1961), Brian Westwood (Arts Library, 1962) and Yorke Rosenberg & Mardall (Department of Electrical Engineering, 1963) whose white-banded building won the RIBA prize. The Wyncote Sports Pavilion has perhaps the most contemporary look; designed by Geoff Holland, the pavilion, looking like a Japanese temple, is set against the greenery of the Geoffrey Hughes Memorial Ground in Mossley Hill. The pavilion won a Civic Trust Award, and is one of the best post-war buildings in the city.

Arguably the best piece of 1990s architecture in Liverpool is the award-winning Aldham Robarts Learning Resource Centre in Maryland Street. A 1994 addition to John Moores University, this geometric structure of steel and glass is a light, airy building which is at its best when lit at night.

Turning from education to civic centrepieces, Liverpool is blessed with some gems. One, built as a gift to the city from banker Henry Yates Thompson, is the Palm House in Sefton Park designed by McKenzie & Moncur. A glorious meringue of white iron framework glazed with 3,720 panes of glass, the Palm House was opened in 1896 and was one of the city's best-loved buildings until the glass was shattered in the May Blitz of 1941. It was reglazed, but in the 1970s and 1980s the Palm House was left to rot, at the mercy of stone-throwing vandals and dismissed as a symbol of Liverpool's bourgeois colonialist past by those then in charge of the city's fortunes. Nevertheless – after a long and relentless campaign by the Friends of the Palm House, the glorious building has finally been restored at a cost of more than £2.5 million, its statues (including the UK's only statue of Columbus) replaced, new palm trees imported from Italy, and – sadly – a 10-ft high steel fence to keep the building secure. The reinvigorated and sparkling Palm House was reopened on 6th September 2001 to much deserved cheering and popping of champagne corks.

The Technical School (now an extension to the Liverpool Museum) at the bottom of William Brown Street is adorned by two beautiful bronze lamp-posts by FW Pomeroy, who also sculpted the Minerva on the pediment. Pomeroy is best known for the figure of Blind Justice on top of the Old Bailey in London.

In Exchange Street West, beside the Town Hall, are two red telephone kiosks designed by Sir Giles Gilbert Scott. The K6, designed in 1936, is unusual; the K2 (1924) is very rare. Both of these landmark phone boxes are listed buildings.

In Nelson Street, Liverpool now boasts (thanks to the great generosity of the city of Shanghai) the biggest Chinese arch outside mainland China. Unveiled in September 2000, the arch is of typical Northern Chinese design by architect Mr Zhang. It was built by the South Linyi Garden Building Company in Shanghai before being dismantled, brought to Liverpool and reconstructed by eight Shanghai craftsmen who worked furiously for three months on the site chosen by feng shui masters.
On the arch are 200 dragons, 12 of which are pregnant (very good fortune); each colour in the arch relates to the five elements – fire (red), earth (yellow), wood (green), water (black) and metal (white). As a powerful symbol of the relationship between the two cities – officially twinned in 2000 – the arch augurs well for our linked futures.

A Case History

The Town Hall and Martin's Building

Declared the greatest classical monument of the 19th century, and one of the great edifices of the world, is St George's Hall. Queen Victoria said the hall was 'worthy of ancient Athens'. The design by the brilliant Harvey Lonsdale Elmes – then aged 23 – won the open competition in 1838 for a new concert hall. Elmes (1814-1847) also won the competition to build the new Assize Courts; the Corporation decided to combine the two schemes, and appointed Elmes to do it. But Elmes died of tuberculosis aged 33, before the building was finished, and much of the interior was designed by Elmes' mentor and friend Sir Charles Cockerell. Like Pushkin, Mozart, Mendelssohn, Byron – all of whom died in their 30s – one wonders what Elmes might have achieved had he lived longer.

Elmes combined the spatial engineering of classical Rome with beautiful Greek detailing; inside is the Great Hall (measuring 169ft by 74ft with a vaulted ceiling 84ft high), the exquisite Concert Hall (used by Charles Dickens for his readings) and the two courtrooms. The sheer weight of masonry was a major construction problem, solved by using hollow bricks to save 400 tons in the ceiling. Unusually, Elmes collaborated closely with heating engineer Dr Boswell Reid, designing a remarkable central heating and ventilation system into the fabric of the building.

In the Great Hall is the stunning Minton floor of 30,000 ceramic tiles in a complex geometric pattern; 10 enormous chandeliers each weigh 15 cwt and have 120 lightbulbs; the six pairs of great bronze doors each weigh 43 cwt and carry the letters *SPQL* – a cheeky distortion of the motto of Rome, *Senatus Populusque Romanus* to 'the Senate and People of Liverpool'. The organ was the largest in the world when installed; with its green and gold pipes 'like a great pile of golden syrup tins' (according to *Echo* arts editor and organist Joe Riley) the St George's organ is still one of the world's great instruments.

At the heart of Liverpool's civic life is the stunning Town Hall, facing Castle Street and with Exchange Flags behind it. Another classical gem, but of a very different order to St George's Hall, this is Liverpool's third town hall, built in 1749 by John Wood the Younger of Bath (his father was Liverpool's first choice, but was too busy). The Corporation was not entirely happy with Wood's building and, when it was gutted by fire in 1795, James Wyatt was called in to reconstruct it. He added the Corinthian portico on the front, and built a more impressive dome on a high drum, with Felix Rossi's graceful gilded statue of Minerva on the top, watching over her city.

The interior of the Town Hall is beautiful – the staircase beneath the high dome (*right*) tends to cause a sharp intake of breath, and the reception rooms were said by Edward VII to be second only to the Winter Palace in St Petersburg. On the ground floor is the council chamber, remodelled by Thomas Shelmerdine; the council offices, however, are in the Municipal Buildings at the top of Dale Street.

Again – no space for the rest of Liverpool's great public buildings, from the lost Sailor's Home, to the Picton Reading Room and Central Library; the Victoria clock tower matched only by one in Moscow; the art deco Forum Cinema and the earlier Futurist and earliest of all, the Paramount Studios. The Wellington Rooms and the Playhouse, Walton Gaol and the sadly neglected International Garden Festival Hall; Everton waterworks ....

The briefest of mentions for the Grade I-listed 1934 Philharmonic Hall, by Herbert Rowse. The elegant brick building in the Dutch style with its stunning Deco interiors has perfect concert hall acoustics and the world's only remaining rising cinema screen. Marvellous.

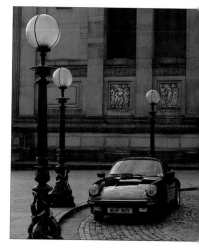

The pillared front and steps of St George's was used as a location for Indiana Jones & the Last Crusade *(where Indy sees Hitler watching the ritual burning of books in Berlin).*

WS Gilbert, rather more famous for writing lyrics for Arthur Sullivan, was a barrister who acted in trials in St George's courts; he was rather better as a lyricist than a lawyer, apparently.

Port of Liverpool Building (above)
and Royal & SunAlliance:

Half-hidden amongst the majestic commercial buildings in the city centre is another of Liverpool's world-class masterpieces. Peter Ellis (1804-1884) was a Liverpool architect of whom relatively little is known. Way ahead of his time, Ellis's two buildings in Liverpool – Oriel Chambers in Water Street, and 16 Cook Street – foreshadow by many years the Modern movement in architecture. Oriel Chambers, built in 1863, were Ellis's solution to bringing light into a building overshadowed by its enormous neighbours. Cast-iron construction (very early cantilevered cladding design) and a honeycomb of plate-glass oriel windows broke every rule for commercial buildings of the time; Ellis was slated by the critics for this and his Cook Street building, begun the following year. It is the back elevation which is important here, foreshadowing the work of Charles Rennie Mackintosh – the most striking feature is the astonishingly modern glazed spiral staircase. Ellis's work made a deep impression on John Wellborn Root, an American youth sent to Liverpool by his father to avoid the worst of the American Civil War. Once back in Chicago, the architect Root and his partner Daniel Burnham built some of the earliest skyscrapers such as the Monadnock Buiding. The Rookery has a spiral staircase clearly modelled on Cook Street. Peter Ellis, however, was destroyed by the criticism, and apparently built nothing else.

Liverpool's oldest commercial buildings are, unsurprisingly, dock-related. The Ropewalks (Bold, Wood, Fleet, Seel and Duke Streets) were originally enormously long yards for spinning the great ship's cables; they grew into fascinating mixtures of Georgian merchants' houses, warehouses and factories; in 2001 the Ropewalks are gradually and (with a bit of luck) sensitively being brought back to mixed-use life, with offices, artists' studios, shops, cafes, bars and apartments exploiting the riches of three centuries' architectural evolution.

In the commercial area of the city, a wander round will yield some stunning 19th-century buildings, the earliest of which are Heywood's Bank (now the offices of Silverbeck Rymer) in Brunswick Street, and the Union Newsroom (now the HQ of the Bibby Group), both built in 1800. One of the most architecturally important buildings is Halifax House (1835) in Brunswick Street – one of the world's first purpose-built office blocks.

In Dale Street, look for the pretty facade of the Queen Insurance Building (1837) and round the corner, the complete contrast of 3-5 Castle Street (1839) with its delightful mosaic frieze of sailing ships. Further along Castle Street is Charles Cockerell's 1845 masterpiece, the Branch Bank of England (now Lloyds TSB). Quentin Hughes says of it: 'Its main facade consists of a free adaptation of pure Greek detail used in a way that no 5th-century Greek architect would have adopted, probably because he would never have thought of it.' Opposite this, on the corner of Brunswick Street, is the old Adelphi Bank (now the Co-operative Bank) the bronze doors of which are covered with panels depicting friends and brothers ('adelphi' is Greek for 'brothers') including Castor and Pollux, Rowland and Oliver, Achilles and Patroclus, David and Jonathan.

In Old Hall Street the graceful Albany contrasts with the graceless sandcastle of Royal & Sun Alliance, the blob of the Post & Echo building and the dull Cotton Exchange.

On the north side of Water Street is the 1927 Martin's Bank building by Rowse (where Britain's gold reserves were stored in WW2); on the south side is Rowse's stunning India Buildings, which houses the Liverpool passport office amongst many other activities.

On the Dale Street side of the Town Hall is the Royal Bank of Scotland, built in 1856 by Cockerell ('there is no more original and satisfactory public door in England').

O f the great warehouses that used to line Liverpool's dock road, one of the remaining few is the gargantuan Tobacco Warehouse at Stanley Dock. Covering 36 acres, rising to 12 storeys above ground, and sinking as far below ground, this is the biggest brick warehouse in the world. Built in 1900 of 27 million bricks, the Tobacco Warehouse is so vast it could swallow St George's Hall whole.

Stanley Dock, the link between the Mersey and the Leeds-Liverpool Canal, was built by the great Jesse Hartley, almost 10 years after his masterpiece, Albert Dock.

South of the Pier Head, the Albert Dock complex is the largest group of Grade I-listed buildings in Europe, designed in 1839, opened six years later. Everything at and around Albert Dock is on an enormous scale; the steps, gateposts, walls, keystones, columns – but their solidity and bulk are offset by light and movement from the huge sky and living water.

There are those who regret the loss of the empty docks, abandoned in the 1960s when container ships were too big to get into the enclosed Albert Dock. The dark brooding bulk of the brick warehouses looming over silted-up docks had a romantic charm, but after threats to pull them down and fill in the docks, their survival depended on clever redevelopment; now Albert Dock draws about five million visitors a year to see the Tate Gallery and the Maritime Museum – and Fred's floating weather map (still used by Granada TV). The only disappointment is the concept of 'festival shopping' that was all the rage in the late 1980s. Crystals, African handicrafts and scented candles do not draw local people across the Strand to shop, and the average tourist can only buy so many sticks of rock and toy Titanics.

The rest, however, is terrific – worth spending a day drifting about looking at Jesse Hartley's beautiful detailing and what the Architects' Journal called 'Cyclopean Classicism'.

For half a century, Albert Dock ruled the south docks, but in the first 15 years of the 20th century, the Pier Head and George's Dock were transformed by an architectural trio that were dubbed the 'Three Graces'. First came the Port of Liverpool Building to the south; architect Sir Arnold Thornley married an Italian merchant's palace with a classical church dome (it is said that this was based on one of the losing designs submitted for the Anglican Cathedral competition).

Then, in 1908, came the design for the Royal Liver Building – topped by its two Liver Birds, this has come to be the distinctive symbol of Liverpool. Designed by Walter Thomas (compare the graceful Gothic curlicues of his State Assurance Building in Dale Street, and his avant garde Tower Buildings, glazed in white faience tiles). Charles Reilly, professor of architecture at Liverpool University, wrote of the Liver Building: 'A mass of grey granite to the cornice, it rose into the sky two quite unnecessary towers, which can symbolise nothing but the power of advertisement. It seems to say "I am a great awkward sentimental creature, unused to civilisation, but I have strength, and whether you laugh at me or not I shall get what I want."' Reilly declares the Liver Building as plebeian as the Cunard is patrician, and the Port of Liverpool building 'because it appears to use clothes which belong to another walk of life, one might perhaps, without offence, call nouveau riche'.

Its architectural importance, though, lies in its construction: the Liver Building is one of the world's first large-scale steel-framed reinforced concrete buildings, a technique that made the building of huge skyscrapers possible later in the century.

The most recent of the Three Graces is the middle one, the elegant Cunard Building, designed by architects Willink & Thicknesse. Could the next decade produce something of bold 21st-century distinction to match this splendid trio?

The Liver Building clock, with its four faces, is called Great George, *and was started on 22nd June 1911, at precisely the moment that King George V was crowned in Westminster Abbey; this was achieved by an engineer in Liverpool and an observer in the Abbey talking over a telephone link. The faces of the 'Dockers' clock' are the biggest in the country, and 2'6" bigger than Big Ben; the minute hand is 27-ft long. The chimes of Great George are not bells, but made by piano wires struck by beaters, and the sound is amplified by domes under the female Liver Bird on the clock tower.*

The Liver Birds, at 18-ft high, are taller than a double-decker bus. They were designed by a German, Carl Bartels. When the First World War broke out, Bartels – who had lived in London since 1900 – was arrested, interned on the Isle of Man and forcibly repatriated.

Thomas Rickman – designer of Cragg's iron churches – came to Liverpool when he was made bankrupt in London and worked for an insurance firm before he met up with Cragg. Rickman coined the architectural term Perpendicular. *Rickman designed New Court and St John's College Cambridge, and also invented a system of book-keeping.*

The 1960s Metropolitan Cathedral was swiftly given two nicknames: Paddy's Wigwam, and the Mersey Funnel.

The Oratory, a Greek temple built in 1829 by Hellenophile John Foster Jnr, was the only building on St James' Mount for 75 years – until the foundation stone was laid for the Cathedral.

Just up the road from the delightful Swedish Church is the Catholic church of St Vincent de Paul, notable for its curious little belfry perched on one gable end.

n a leafy corner of Toxteth Park, where the Dingle flowed down the hill towards the Mersey, a tiny school was founded in 1611 for the children of nonconformist Puritans; on land given to them by Richard Molyneux (a Roman Catholic) the Puritans then built a chapel in 1618. These days traffic thunders past the Ancient Chapel of Toxteth, hemmed in on the corner of Park Road and Dingle Lane, but the little chapel still holds Sunday services for its tiny congregation.

Of all the churches in Liverpool, possibly the one of greatest architectural and engineering importance is also one of the dullest. St James, on the corner of Upper Parliament Street and St James' Place, was built in 1774 by Cuthbert Bisbrowne has little aesthetically to recommend it. This church, though, contains the earliest recorded structure in cast iron to survive in Britain – several decades ahead of the cast-iron revolution in which Liverpool led the world. But although it is meant to have been cared for by the Redundant Churches Fund, St James is quietly falling to pieces.

Forty years later, in 1812, Thomas Rickman and foundryman John Cragg built St George's in Everton into the history books. This was the earliest experiment in using large-scale prefabricated dry construction – the cast-iron sections were made in Cragg's foundry, then taken to Everton, bolted together and given a stone casing. Their second project, the church of St Michael-in-the-Hamlet, was two years later – on this building there is much more cast iron visible outside, around the brick cladding. The success of these churches led to a great volume of prefab iron buildings being exported from Liverpool around the world.

Evidence of the passion for classical Greek architecture is not hard to find in Liverpool; St Bride's Church in Percy Street is a Greek temple complete with Ionic portico. The interior, though, was remodelled by the Victorians.

This obsession with all things classical was exhibited by two Liverpool architects above all others: John Foster Jnr and Charles Cockerell. Having met on the Grand Tour in 1810, they discovered the Aegina marbles, and were inspired to recreate a modern Athens in Liverpool. It was Elmes who crowned Liverpool with the ultimate – St George's Hall – but the Neoclassical tradition continued with Sir Charles Reilly well into the 20th century.

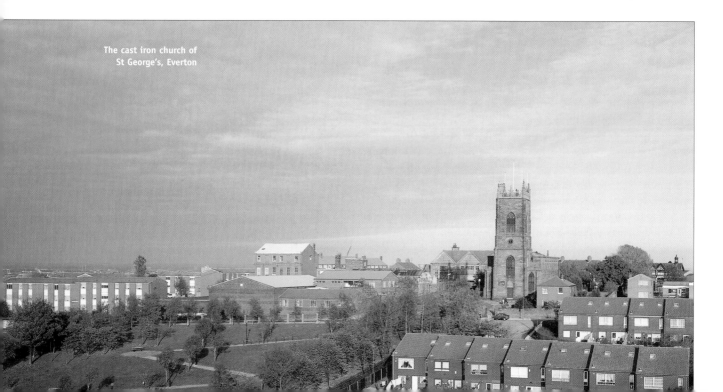

The cast iron church of
St George's, Everton

At the north end of Prince's Avenue is a collection of religious buildings well worth investigating. The Greek Orthodox Church of St Nicholas, right next to the drive-in NatWest Bank, is a handsome mid-19th century Byzantine church serving the 3,000-strong Greek community since 1865.

Across the road is the magnificent Synagogue – one of the most beautiful in Europe – built in 1874 by W & G Audsley; the brick and stone exterior hides a sumptuous interior, with its spectacular vaulted roof and great rose window.

To serve the community of Swedes, Norwegians and Danes in Liverpool, the Swedish Seamen's Church (Sjomanskyrkan) was built in 1882. Architect William Caroe – son of a Danish consul in Liverpool – translated a traditional Norwegian Stavkirche from timber to red glazed brick; the result is a highly distinctive building on Park Road.

Liverpool's long tradition of nonconformism has left its mark on the city's architecture. In 1773, for instance, there were Liverpool churches catering for Quakers, Baptists, Methodists, Presbyterians and Unitarians as well as Anglicans. For a long time after the Reformation Catholics met in secret – the second church to be built in England after Henry VIII's split with Rome was the Jesuit chapel in Lumber Street, destroyed 23 years later in a religious riot. The oldest remaining Roman Catholic church is just about surviving, although only its skin remains after being gutted for conversion in 2001. Known after the war as the Polish Church, St Peter's in Seel Street was built in 1788, but has been redundant for several years and is now destined for other uses.

But if anyone thought all Nonconformists held on to the Puritan ethic of plainness, they should go immediately to Ullet Road to see the Unitarian Church there, completed in 1902. Part of one of the country's finest group of Nonconformist buildings, this was designed by Unitarian architects Thomas Worthington & Son with backing from some of Liverpool's most influential families such as the Holts and the Rathbones. The exterior of brick and red sandstone is ornate, but the interior is astonishing. Rich decoration – painted ceilings, carved wood, beaten copper, stained glass, ornate door handles and light fittings.

For all its Nonconformism, Liverpool is strongly Catholic, too. The tide of Irish refugees from the famine in the mid-19th century put strong Catholic roots back down in Liverpool soil. They needed a cathedral, and in 1930 the Archdiocese under Archbishop Richard Downey bought the massive Workhouse site at the top of Brownlow Hill and commissioned Sir Edwin Lutyens to design the cathedral. Lutyens came up with a building that would have dominated the entire city, even the massive Anglican Cathedral then under construction. Lutyens's cathedral was to be the biggest in the world, and work began in 1933. At the outbreak of World War II the crypt was complete, but by 1952, when work could start again, Lutyens was dead, and there was not the money to complete his design. There was no option but to start again, and the competition was won by Frederick Gibberd (designer of Heathrow Airport). This was a radical modern design – circular, tapering to a lantern topped by a crown of thorns. Gibberd said that his scheme was: 'a precise geometric structure on a precise geometric base, growing out of irregular rocky surroundings'. From the air, the little cone of the building looks rather farcical perched on one end of Lutyens' gigantic base, but at ground level it is an impressive structure. The exterior of the building is not universally loved, but inside the Metropolitan Cathedral of Christ the King never fails to astonish visitors with its breathtaking, exquisite colour. The saturated reds and blues cast by the stained glass in the lantern and down the drum fill the great circular space.

For a city of Liverpool's size and importance, to have no cathedral was extraordinary. Now there is 'one to spare', as the song says. The two cathedrals are, appropriately enough, at either end of Hope Street.

Giles Gilbert Scott, architect of the Anglican Cathedral, was a Roman Catholic. Frederick Gibberd, designer of the Catholic Cathedral, was an Anglican.

The Crown of Thorns topping the Cathedral lantern

One of the best modern Catholic churches is the Church of Christ the King, on Queens Drive in Wavertree. The architects Pritchard Son & Partners have designed a copper sheeted pyramid on a plain brick base, the lines clean and unfussy. The church was completed in 1967 – the same year as the Metropolitan Cathedral.

The Anglican Cathedral - designed by the 21-year-old Giles Gilbert Scott – dominates the Liverpool skyline, sitting on St James's Mount, one of the city's highest points. A completely 20th-century building – built between 1904 and 1978, the cathedral is one of the last great buildings in the Gothic tradition.

Designed and begun when Liverpool was at the height of its prosperity and importance as a world trading centre, it was finished when Liverpool was almost at its lowest point, with unemployment at destructively high levels, confidence at rock bottom and image sinking into the silt that filled the south docks. The cathedral, then, was one of the few symbols of faith in the city and its future, and is now so much a part of its fabric – and its skyline – that it's hard to imagine how Liverpool looked without it.

Scott died in 1960, before the cathedral was completed; his grave is near the steps to the West Door, and his memorial stone is at the centre of the cathedral, directly below the tower. This central space is an area of over 15,000 square feet, unobstructed by columns and with an uninterrupted view of the altar and pulpit. As Scott said: 'Don't look at my arches, look at my spaces.' It's hard not to look at the arches, towering 107 feet high. And the under-tower space is high enough (175 ft) for Nelson and his column, if Nelson removed his hat.

Built of red sandstone from Woolton Quarry, this is the largest Anglican church in the world and the biggest cathedral in Britain. Its list of superlatives is lengthy: the highest Gothic arches ever built; the highest and heaviest peal of bells in the world; the longest nave, and so on.

Sir John Betjeman wrote of Liverpool Cathedral: 'This is one of the great buildings of the world ... the impression of vastness, strength and height no words can describe ... suddenly one sees that the greatest art of architecture, that lifts one up and turns one into a king, yet compels reverence, is the art of enclosing space.'

The great West Window is by Carl Edwards; 16,000 square feet of glass, each of three lights 52 feet high, and the fanlight 31 feet wide. Full of colour during the day, as the light fades the window turns almost completely blue (blue is the last colour to fade).

Above the visitors' centre is the sculpture *Spirit of Liverpool*, designed by cathedral architect Keith Scott and made by Alan Boyson in 1984; the stone carvings on the doors along the central space are by local sculptor E Carter Preston, with arts and sciences on one side, and virtues on the other.

The organ is astonishing. The biggest cathedral organ (and one of the biggest of all) in the world, there are 10,000 pipes, from the half-inch Top C to the 64-footers which can be felt more than heard. The main console has five manual keyboards and the pedals; in 1989 Victor Hutson donated a splendid ground-level concert console to the cathedral, linked to the organ by fibre optics. The organist, Ian Tracey, is regarded as one of the best of his generation; his predecessors have included Noel Rawsthorne and Henry Goss-Custard.

Two tiny details in this vast building delight visitors: the church mouse (*left*) on the Derby Memorial – whose little bronze head gleams gold from being rubbed for luck – and the monk in one of the bottom right diamonds in the window above the memorial (the stained glass windows were made by the Whitefriar Studio: it's their signature).

The Lady Chapel shows how the cathedral might have looked; Giles Gilbert Scott's design won the competition, but because of his youth, he was supervised by the president of RIBA, GF Bodley, who is reputed to have told Scott that they would build his design 'over my dead body'. Having completed the Lady Chapel in Baroque style, Bodley died, leaving Scott to rethink his design with the backing of the building committee and the Dean and Chapter.

In the Lady Chapel – which served as the cathedral from 1910 till 1924 – is a 15th-century Madonna by Giovanni della Robbia, and on the stairs, the Women's Window, commemorating Liverpool 'saints' such as Agnes Jones and Kitty Wilkinson. Two more recent additions to the cathedral's works of art are Frink's figure of Christ above the West Door entrance, and *Crucifixion*, a painting by Craigie Aitchison, hanging behind the altar in the Chapter House.

A curio, both functional and ironic, is the red phone box by the lift to the tower. Designed by Gilbert Scott, it is his smallest creation inside his largest. There are two lifts to the tower, then 108 steps to the top, from which the views to Liverpool Bay, across to Wales and inland, are spectacular.

It may be a 20th-century building, but there is more magic about Liverpool's cathedral than one in a nearby city with more than 1,000 years of history. A remarkable building and unmissable by any visitor, regardless of creed.

dark days

When disaster strikes – whether it hits an individual, a family, a community, a nation – life is changed for ever for those who survive it. No-one is immune from violence, catastrophe, ruin, disease or random chance – it is part of the human condition. A city containing hundreds of thousands of people is going to see its share of dark days; Liverpool is no exception. For some of these disasters, big and small, Liverpool's people and its governors must take responsibility or, if not of their doing, accept the burden of recovery and change. In every case, learning the lessons and moving ahead is the only way to cope with such devastating events.

This is being written on 12th September 2001, the day after the shattering destruction which fell on New York out of a clear blue sky. No Bruce Willis or Will Smith to save the world this time; no stuntmen to get up and walk away; no aliens or monsters to blame.

Amongst the thousands dead (as yet uncounted) in the rubble of the World Trade Centre are hundreds of Britons, and quite possibly some Scousers. It is beyond imagining how it felt to be in that place at that time; so hard for families, friends and survivors to cope over the coming months and years.

The world has been deeply shocked, most of all, because we watched it happen, live, on television. Like Heysel, Hillsborough, this was a media event happening in our kitchens and living rooms. It is harder for us to feel for people we never knew, in hells beyond our experience, with no sounds or pictures to help us understand. Men and women in slavery, families fleeing from famine, children abandoned and starving, slow death from grinding poverty, neighbours killing one another over religion and politics. All these things affected Liverpool in the past ... all these things affect people living elsewhere in the world today.

The mark of a city, or rather its people, is how the community copes with disaster, whether anything positive can be made of a negative, and whether the future is better because of the changes that come about.

Victoria Memorial

Ships, submarines and aircraft of the Allied Forces fighting the Battle of the Atlantic during World War II were plotted in the basement of an unremarkable office building in Liverpool's Rumford Street: this was the Combined Headquarters of the Western Approaches. Round the corner, in the deep vaults of Martin's Bank, was stored gold bullion from the Bank of England. Through Liverpool's docks came millions of tons of supplies and vast numbers of troops, and the Mersey's shipyards and related industries were churning out weapons and munitions.

These four factors made Liverpool the prime target outside London for Hitler's bombing campaign – Liverpool paid a heavy price for its war effort. Between July 1940 and January 1942, German bombers made 68 raids on Liverpool, in which 3,966 people died and the city was flattened. By far the greatest damage was done over eight nights, from 1st to 8th May 1941; the May Blitz was the most savage and sustained attack of the war so far, and Liverpool's anti-aircraft guns were poor defence against the Luftwaffe's bombers.

In those eight nights alone nearly 2,000 died, over 1,000 were badly injured, and more than 75,000 were made homeless. On 14th May a mass funeral was held at Anfield cemetery, at which 1,000 people were buried in a common grave.

In Bootle, 80% of houses were hit or set on fire. Bodies lay in the streets or were buried under rubble; hospitals and mortuaries were crammed; factories, warehouses, shops and offices were reduced to rubble. Ships lay wrecked and burning in the river and the docks. The ammunition ship *Malakind* was in Huskisson Dock, ready for sea, when it caught fire and exploded; bits of wreckage were found more than two miles away.

But life continued; the city may have been flattened, but the people weren't. Although the trams couldn't run and the telephones were out of action, Liverpudlians kept on with 'normal' life as best they could. Union Jacks fluttered from windows that survived the bombs. When the Corn Exchange was hit, traders did business in the street, as their forebears did centuries before. The ferries kept sailing back and forth across the river, theatres and cinemas stayed open for packed houses.

There were desperate stories of whole families killed and children orphaned. People who survived the loss of their homes were left with nothing but the clothes they stood up in. Liverpool's Lord Mayor Sir Sydney Jones set up the Air Raid Distress Fund to help victims of the bombing. But their courage and resilience was remarkable, as was that of the firemen, special constables, auxiliaries and volunteers who kept going with little or no sleep, to rescue the trapped, find the dead, put out fires and keep the city functioning.

There was enormous damage to property, from historic buildings like the Customs House to priceless treasures in Liverpool Museum. The Museum and the William Brown Library were gutted by fire; Bluecoat Chambers took direct hits, as did the Three Graces on the Pier Head. St Luke's Church was gutted (as it remains today, the 'Bombed-out Church'), the Anglican Cathedral – then only half-built – was hit, although it escaped serious damage.

It's easy to see where the worst damage was inflicted: from the top of the Cathedral tower, look for the green spaces and the modern buildings; from James Street to Hanover Street there is precious little left of pre-war Liverpool. The Victoria Memorial in Derby Square was untouched, but surrounded on three sides by heaps of rubble: Lord Street, Paradise Street, South John Street and the Strand looked like brickfields; South Castle Street was completely destroyed. It is a miracle that so much of the city's 19th-century heart survived, and a gift to post-war generations that so many badly-damaged buildings were restored.

Nonconformism was well established in Liverpool by the 1640s, and the Puritans provided lively opposition to the Tory ruling class such as Sir Edward Norris and the Stanleys.

On Everton Brow was a small building known as Prince Rupert's Cottage. In fact it was a penfold for stray sheep.

Once the monarchy was restored in 1660, the castle of Liverpool was destroyed by order of Charles II. The King did not like the spirit which the inhabitants of Liverpool had shown during the Civil War, and in 1667 he issued a charter which diminished the privileges of the burgesses.

The Civil War broke over Liverpool in May 1643, when Parliamentarian Colonel Assheton took the town and penned the Royalists up in the Castle before driving them out of town with the loss of 300 prisoners and 80 dead. There were 1,000 Parliamentarian horse and foot soldiery in Liverpool under the authority of Colonel John Moore; Parliament meanwhile sequestered the tithes of the parish of Walton (which then included Liverpool).

With Liverpool in Roundhead hands, the King lost his supply route from his Lords Lieutenant, the Stanleys, in Ireland. Plans to attack by sea from Chester were made and abandoned; in February 1644 Lord Byron (an ancestor of the poet) was despatched by the Crown to attack Liverpool, but was defeated at Nantwich. In June the same year, having captured Bolton, Prince Rupert descended on Liverpool with a force of 10,000 men and declared that it would be an easy matter to take the town. Liverpool was stronger than he realised, protected by water, fortifications and Colonel Moore's defenders. It took Rupert a week and cost him 1,500 men; his forces fought from trenches dug in Lime Street, and finally stormed the castle at night, attacking through the Old Hall and Lancelot's Hey.

Later that year the Roundheads besieged Liverpool with Major-General Meldrum's forces on land, and Colonel Moore's blockade of the river. After a dreadful three months, the castle was given up when soldiers betrayed their officers.

A sum of £20 was given to widows and orphans of those killed in the siege, and in 1645 £10,000 and 500 tons of timber were taken from the estates of Derby, Sefton and other royalists to compensate the citizens of Liverpool for losses during the siege.

Liverpool came late to the slave trade – Captain Hawkins, who made a profitable slaving trip in the royal ship *Jesus* was given a great reception in Elizabeth I's court, and slaving became 'respectable'. Slavery had, of course, been going on for centuries in Europe, the Middle East, Africa and Asia – often prisoners captured in battle.

Slave ships from England first carried white slaves – convicts, beggars and the unlucky caught, transported and sold in America for tobacco. Bristol and London had been dominant in the European trade of 'black gold' before the *Liverpool Merchant* reached Barbados in 1700 with its cargo of 220 African slaves for sale. For the next 40 years Liverpool ships did not join the trade in any number, but for 60 years to the turn of the 19th century, Liverpool was the leading port for slave ships, sending between 40 and 100 ships on the infamous triangular journey each year and accounting for up to half the world's trade in slaves from West Africa to America.

In 1771 Liverpool's 105 slave ships carried more slaves than the entire population of Liverpool. By the turn of the century, a quarter of Liverpool's ships were engaged in the slave trade – a tenth of Liverpool outbound shipping tonnage went to Africa carrying textiles, guns, iron, alcohol and beads. These goods would be exchanged for men, women and children who might have been debtors or convicts, or prisoners of war, or sold by relatives or elders. Of the two million slaves taken from West Africa, fewer than 750,000 survived until 1825, either dying on the long journey, or from brutality and disease on the other side of the Atlantic. Slaves were packed like rows of books on shelves or herrings in a barrel, with a space no more than 18 inches wide – less room than in a coffin; they were chained to each other hand and foot for up to 14 weeks, the period it took to cross the ocean. Brutality and violence from and between crewmen was the order of the day. Ships' captains had an incentive to keep slaves alive and saleable, but they were mostly barbarous men. One captain, irritated by an African woman's anxiety for her sick child, snatched the baby from her, smashed its head against the side of the ship and threw it overboard.

In Liverpool an industry grew up making slavers' instruments: branding irons, handcuffs and shackles and the speculum oris, used to prise open a slave's mouth for force-feeding.

Men like William Rathbone, Dr Binns and William Roscoe campaigned, against ferocious opposition, for the abolition of slavery, founding the Society for Abolition in 1787 – the Act was passed in 1807, no thanks to 64 petitions from Liverpool slavers to Parliament.

In August 2001 Liverpool saw a ceremony of cleansing and forgiveness performed by African chiefs, after the city of Liverpool made formal apologies for its part in the slave trade. The ceremony was part of the International Day for Remembrance of Slavery and its Abolition, organised by Liverpool both to acknowledge the shameful past and to celebrate the city's multicultural inheritance.

*There is no evidence of a ship docking in Liverpool with a cargo of slaves, but some slaves were sold here. In 1758 Williamson's Advertiser announced:
'A beautiful negro boy for sale, well-proportioned, mild, sober and of honest disposition.'
And another: 'A healthy negro girl aged about 15 years, speaks good English, works at her needle, washes well, does housework, and has had the small pox.'*

*Although there were some fabulously profitable voyages made by slavers, the average profit on a slave cargo was less than 10%, and some slavers made a loss. The key to making money, then, was volume.
In 1702 alone, some 40,000 slaves were packed like sardines into the holds of Liverpool ships for sale in the Americas.*

There is a myth that the Goree Warehouses (demolished after the Second World War) had iron rings to which slaves were chained. Not true – the Goree Warehouses (named after the slaving island of Gorée off West Africa) were not built until 1793; 21 years earlier, in 1772, a slave became free as soon as he set foot on English soil.

Granby, the triangle of streets bounded by Upper Parliament Street, Lodge Lane and Princes Avenue, combusted during the summer of 1981, along with St Paul's in Bristol, Brixton in London and Handsworth in Birmingham. In Granby, tension between the police and the local community – mainly black – simmered, boiled and finally blew up, leaving hundreds injured, millions of pounds worth of property destroyed and a community in tatters.

What was dubbed 'the Toxteth Riots' by the press began after the heavy-handed arrest of a young black man; the fracas turned into 'disturbances', and then into a full-blown riot, with pitched battles between police and Granby youths.

The Merseyside police force of the time had a bad reputation for heavy-handed policing and racist attitudes, with officers using the infamous 'sus' laws (which allowed police to stop and search anyone who looked suspicious) to the point of harassment. Police were accused of planting drugs on youths – a practice known locally as 'going farming'. There were too many accusations of random beatings of black men by police to be dismissed.

Feed into the mix chronic unemployment, bad housing, poor education, racism and little hope of a decent future, and it is easy, with hindsight, to understand the ferocity of the riots. At the time Chief Constable Kenneth Oxford said the riots were down to 'thieves and vagabonds' who needed no excuse for violence and destruction. The Chief Constable and the Chair of the Police Authority, Margaret Simey, had fierce and very public rows; she accusing him of failing to acknowledge the possibility that social issues had sparked the violence. The powerful church duo of the Anglican Bishop David Sheppard and the Catholic Archbishop Derek Worlock also weighed in to the fray, to the anger of the establishment and the enduring respect of the community.

The police and the city authorities were taken by surprise – the rage that boiled into the streets turned vehicles to ash, firebombed a bank and burned out the Rialto ballroom. White youths from other areas of the city joined in, and it looked as though the whole city would be engulfed in the mayhem. Then came the controversial decision by the police to fire CS gas cannisters at the mob – the first time they were used in Britain.

The worst of it lasted for three days; the whole affair took nine days to cool down. Liverpool, already with a reputation for industrial unrest (there had been strikes all over the UK in the 1970s, but Liverpool's articulate strikers got more media coverage) now became known as Riot City. Do people think of riots when they hear the names Birmingham or Bristol? Will the same label be stuck on Burnley and Bradford after the summer of 2001?

The 20 years since the riots have produced a disappointing lack of social change. There has been a marked improvement in policing, thanks to a change in attitude right at the top. Even the fierce champion of Granby, its former councillor Margaret Simey, approves of the new style of leadership on Merseyside, but waits and watches to see how the style is translated into action at street level.

However ... while public and private sector investment pours into the city, there is still a gaping hole in Granby. Princes Avenue looks fine now; the Rialto has been replaced, and there are organisations with the right sounding names – this development trust and that housing scheme; new homes are being built, and a big project or two is in place. But black people still don't have a place in Liverpool's public or private sector hierarchy; there are still too many black kids with no hope of prosperity or even higher education. Crime is still high and fear of crime even higher; the split between wealth and poverty is growing wider again.

In the mid-1800s a commentator reported: 'I have seen more beggars in one week in Liverpool than I have ever seen in all my life. The streets are full of them; at every step you are arrested and often followed by the pitiful cries of distress and want. Poor, ragged and haggard wretches, with four and five barefooted and poorly clad children. The most of these distressed beings are Irish, and have been driven over the channel by the approach of starvation. Some of these poor creatures may be undeserving of charity, but most of them, I doubt not, are proper objects of Christian benevolence and kindness.'

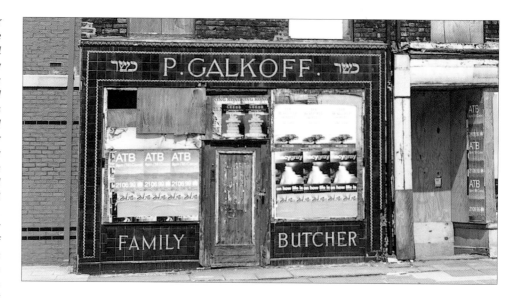

Despite Liverpool's Confederate bias, in 1863 the city of Philadelphia sent a gift of clothing and 5,000 barrels of flour on the barque Achilles, *'for the relief of Lancashire Distress'.*

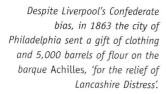

Famine is probably not a word readily associated with a seaport of the size and wealth of Liverpool in the 18th and 19th centuries. But beneath the glittering, glossy surface was a morass of poverty which, in bad economic times, turned swiftly to starvation and destitution. The two sieges of Liverpool in the Civil War caused great distress and hardship in the town; many families buried those caught between Roundheads and Cavaliers.

Two centuries later the American Civil War had a devastating effect on Liverpool and Lancashire, throwing half a million cotton workers out of their jobs when the blockade of the southern States halted cotton imports for Lancashire's 2,000 mills. Merchants and banks were ruined; only 72,000 bales of cotton came into Liverpool during 1862 compared to 2.5 million two years earlier, before the war. During the American Revolution trade had also been badly disrupted; Gore's Advertiser in 1775 declared that 'all commerce with America is at an end!' and since so much of Liverpool's trade was with America, its interruption was economically disastrous for the town. Even slave ships were affected – one slave ship owner cut the wages of his crew, resulting in a riot that lasted several days and saw many lives lost. Thousands of unemployed sailors rioted; cannon were dragged up from the quayside into Castle Street and fired on the Town Hall, taking chunks out of the walls.

Eighty years later, in 1855, the lower classes protested once more, plundering bread and flour shops and rampaging through the town in such numbers that trade was brought to a standstill. The desperation of the poor was recognised this time, and money was raised to help those in distress.

Poverty and destitution isn't an historical phenomenon; in the 20th century there was trouble in 1911, the General Strike in 1926, and the Depression in the 1930s. After the war, when containerisation changed the docks for ever and big employers started to leave the city, unemployment became endemic, with people facing a lifetime of living off the dole.

In the 1990s Liverpool's gradual resurgence began to produce new investment, new jobs, and hope for the future. But it is a slow, slow process.

The White Star Line's headquarters were in Albion House, the 'streaky bacon' building on the corner of the Strand and James Street. The company was founded by TH Ismay in 1869 and, in competition with Cunard, ran sumptuous ocean liners such as the *Oceanic*, the *Olympic*, and the *Majestic*. Then Ismay commissioned Harland & Wolff, the Belfast shipyard, to build the world's largest and most luxurious liner.

The *Titanic* was registered in Liverpool, but sailed from Southampton on her maiden voyage to New York. But she was not to arrive. Shortly before midnight on Sunday, 14th April 1912 *Titanic* was holed by an iceberg off Newfoundland, and less than three hours later the 'unsinkable' ship sank in mirror-calm but ice-cold seas. According to one survivor, the Liverpool purser said, as the ship was sinking: 'Boys, it will be sand for breakfast in the morning.' There were 711 people rescued from the North Atlantic that night, but 1,490 men, women and children died.

Among them were the eight men of the ship's band, who are remembered for their extraordinary courage, continuing to play as the ship sank, in a gallant attempt to keep passengers calm. The musicians: Theodore Brailey, Roger Bricoux, Fred Clarke, Jock Hume, George Krins, Percy Taylor, JW Woodward and the leader, violinist Wallace Hartley. They weren't White Star employees, but worked for Blacks of Liverpool and had second-class tickets on *Titanic*. Legend has it that the band were playing *Nearer My God to Thee* as the ship slipped beneath the waves, but given *Titanic*'s angle of descent, this seems impossible. Wireless operator Harold Bride said the last piece played was a hymn called *Autumn*. Other accounts suggest it was the *Londonderry Air*. But whatever they played, it is not the song, but their courage that is remembered.

Titanic sailed from Southampton, but many of the crew were Scousers, and as news began to filter through, Albion House was surrounded by an angry, frightened crowd; White Star Line officials had to shout down the latest news from the balconies of the building.

J Bruce Ismay, son of the White Star's founder, was on board the Titanic, *but got a place in a lifeboat and was rescued. His reputation was ruined and he lived the remaining 25 years of his life in seclusion. His American wife lived to the age of 96, and almost until she died in 1963 she was still haunted by* Titanic *and her husband's failure.*

Many Liverpool ships have been lost at sea over the centuries; Titanic *to an iceberg, others to storm or fire. But the Cunard liner* Lusitania, *on her way back home from New York on 1st May 1915, was torpedoed by a German submarine off the Irish coast. She sank in less than 20 minutes with the loss of 1,198 lives. There was anti-German rioting in Liverpool, and it helped push America into the war. What wasn't known until much later was that the* Lusitania *was carrying large quantities of explosives and ammunition.*

The Titanic Memorial near the Liver Building

> ❛ Football's not that important. No game of football is worth that. ❜
>
> **Kenny Dalglish**

Bill Shankly once famously said: 'Football is not about life and death – it's more important than that.' But that was before the two disasters involving Liverpool Football Club in the 1980s which proved, after all, that Shankly was wrong. The names of two stadiums – Heysel and Hillsborough – have been carved painfully into Liverpool culture, and have had far-reaching effects not only on the game of football but, sadly, on the lives of the 135 families most closely affected, and thousands of others.

On 29th May 1985, Liverpool FC were due to play Italian club Juventus in the final of the European Championship at the Heysel stadium in Belgium. Juventus won 1-0, but few remember the match, let alone the score. What most people remember from the news reports is that Liverpool hooligans rioted, and were responsible for the deaths of 39 Italian fans crushed by a collapsing wall in the stadium.

Kenny Dalglish, Liverpool's manager at the time, remembers it differently, and points out that Liverpool FC were very concerned about the poor condition of the stadium, the lack of police presence and the failure to keep the two sets of fans segregated. They warned Uefa, but nothing was done. Dalglish also points out that Liverpool fans had been abused and attacked at the European Cup Final in Rome: 'Our supporters were attacked in alleys; coaches were ambushed by Roma fans tossing bricks at them. A year later, the seeds of chaos bore fruit.' When Juventus fans starting hurling stones and missiles at Heysel, and waving a banner saying 'REDS ANIMALS', some Liverpool fans retaliated.

n the scramble a wall collapsed, crushing 39 fans to death. Provocation is no excuse, and it is true enough that the English game had a serious problem with hooliganism throughout the 1970s and 1980s. Liverpool FC and its fans bear a heavy responsibility, but, said well-informed commentators, Uefa, the Belgian organisers and the Juventus fans should face up to their part in Heysel.

Hillsborough, by contrast, was nothing to do with club rivalries, hooliganism or even bad behaviour. It was a desperate tale of incompetence, naivety and bad communication.

At the 1989 FA Cup semi final at Sheffield Wednesday's Hillsborough ground, Liverpool were playing Nottingham Forest. At 2.45pm that afternoon, when most of the Forest supporters were in their seats, there were still about 5,000 Liverpool fans waiting to be let in to the Leppings Lane end. When the gate was opened by a police officer eight minutes before kick-off, thousands of fans rushed through the tunnel and into the back of the pens, pushing those at the front up against the steel mesh fence keeping them off the pitch. At 2.54pm when the teams came on to the pitch, the fans at the back surged forward to get a better view, unaware that people were being crushed at the front.

At 3.06pm the referee stopped the game, as people were being dragged out of the crush and on to the pitch or lifted up on to the balcony above. Ninety-five people died that afternoon, of whom seven were female. Most were under 30; the youngest was a boy of 10. One young man was badly injured and after being in a persistent vegetative state for months, finally died, bringing the sad total to 96. There were also 766 people injured, and thousands traumatised; several suicides have been attributed to the events at Hillsborough.

The city was appalled by the loss of life, and messages of sympathy came from football fans all over the world. In the week following, over a million people visited Anfield, and on the Sunday people queued for hours to get into the ground. The sight of scarves of every club colour draped over the Kop railings, and the pitch covered in flowers reduced many to tears. Just before 3pm, the gates were closed, and those in the ground ushered to seats for a brief memorial service. Dalglish and the players were on the pitch dressed in dark suits, as was Prince Charles. At 3.06pm there was a minute's silence, during which there was no sound at all – all the traffic outside had stopped. The Salvation Army Band played Liverpool's anthem, *You'll Never Walk Alone*, but where voices usually raise the roof, this time few people could sing.

Years of court cases and inquiries have followed; some blame has been apportioned, and major changes have been made both in football and in policing. But the families of the 96 still feel that justice has not been done, and fight on.

Liverpool may have football in its blood, and passions run high. But as Kenny Dalglish said after Heysel: 'Football's not that important. No game of football is worth that.'

Hillsborough had nothing to do with club allegiances – Juventus, Everton and Manchester United scarves were among those tied to the Shankly Gates.

On Sunday, 16th April, thousands of people of all faiths gathered at the Metropolitan Cathedral for a memorial mass. On 29th April at the Anglican Cathedral it seemed the whole of Liverpool was present at the ecumenical Service of Remembrance. The Hillsborough Memorial stone is in front of the South Door of the cathedral.

'This town's a corporation full of crooked streets; Death's in the marketplace, where all men meet. If life was merchandise that men could buy, the rich would always live, the poor would die.'
(Carved on a plague gravestone.)

The scandal in 1999 over the organs of dead children taken without parents' permission and held by pathologists in hospitals and medical schools all over the UK involved Liverpool's Alder Hey Children's Hospital, which had the largest collection. The backlash from the row, whipped to a frenzy by the media, has resulted in doctors getting hate mail and pathologists quitting their jobs for fear of attack.

In 1827 William Gill, a 'respectable teacher of anatomy' and a middle man between body snatchers and doctors, was arrested and later tried for arranging for bodies to be stolen from Walton churchyard. Gill was convicted, but only fined.

Cholera was never the most deadly disease to hit Liverpool – typhus and tuberculosis killed many more – but it was a terrifying disease, striking in epidemics and killing swiftly. Disease was a fact of life for the poor in the stinking cellars and filthy overcrowded back streets of 18th- and 19th-century Liverpool; records show an endless litany of plagues from the 13th century onwards. But in 1832 the cholera epidemics in Liverpool sparked riots in the streets. They were directed against the city's doctors. There were eight separate riots in the city during two weeks in the summer of 1832; cholera was everywhere in Britain, with more than 20,000 deaths in about 18 months. In Liverpool there were 5,000 cholera cases, of whom 1,500 died. Doctors could do little for sufferers other than offer brandy and opium which could at least dull the excruciating pain. Doctors would often worsen matters by bleeding and purging.

The first riot happened on 29th May, when a doctor took dock worker Mr Clarke and his wife from their cellar in Perry Street to the hurriedly-organised cholera hospital in Toxteth Park. A mob of more than 1,000 'women and boys of the lowest order' gathered outside. The *Liverpool Chronicle* reported the attack: 'Stones and brickbats were thrown ... several windows were broken, even in the room where the woman, now dying, was lying, and the medical gentleman who was attending her was obliged to seek safety in flight. The park constables were apparently panic-struck and incapable of acting.'

Doctors and medics had abuse hurled at them along with missiles; the crowd shouted that doctors wanted to get the poor in their clutches 'so they can Burke them'. The mob accused medics of 'giving patients stuff which killed them and made them turn blue'. (Cholera victims turn blue with cyanosis before they die.)

Burking referred to the murderers Burke and Hare who were tried (only Burke was hanged) in Edinburgh in 1829 – they had sold bodies for anatomical dissection, and the rioters in Liverpool and other cities believed that doctors were killing people for experiment and blaming it on the cholera. Frightened and angry people, not told the truth, believed rumours; arrogant medics saw no reason to enlighten them about dissection and medical research. How history repeats itself.

The inscription on Kitty Wilkinson's gravestone reads: 'Indefatigable and self-denying, she was the widow's friend, the support of the orphan, the fearless, and unwearied nurse of the sick, the instigator of baths and wash-houses for the poor.'

Many people call this extraordinary and selfless woman a saint; it isn't hard to see why. Her entire life was devoted to others, and despite being poor herself, managed with the support of her husband, to feed, nurse, house, help and teach those worse off than herself.

Kitty Wilkinson's heroic work for others is almost beyond believing: her story reads almost like Dickens at his most mawkish. But it was all too grindingly real for Kitty.

Catherine Seaward was born in Ireland in 1786; wanting to find a better life, her parents took the family on the ferry to Liverpool, but her mother and sister were drowned when the boat struck the Hoyle Bank. Kitty went to work in a cotton mill in Lancashire when she was 12, studying at night school to improve her education.

She married a sailor, but was soon a widow with two babies and – her father now dead – a blind and senile stepmother. When the old woman died, Kitty came back to Liverpool and earned a living by taking in washing, and adopted three orphaned children. She met and married Tom Wilkinson, a porter working for Rathbones, and they set up house in Denison Street.

When cholera broke out in 1832, Kitty Wilkinson had the only boiler in the street, so she turned her cellar into a wash house for fever-tainted clothes and bedlinen. In one week she washed over 2,000 articles infected with cholera.

The epidemic made many children orphans: Kitty set up a class for 20 of them each morning, which grew into the first public infants' school. She also sent food and clothing to those in distress, lent what little money she had without interest, helping everyone whatever their religion. To pay for all this she collected waste paper and sold it, sold her sewing work, did any work to earn enough to keep her family and help her neighbours. Her tenement home was open to anyone who needed help; she nursed the sick, fed the hungry, looked after the very young and the old.

Kitty's example, and the success of her wash-house, prompted the Corporation to open the first public wash house in 1842. Four years later Kitty and her husband Tom were appointed superintendents of the first ever public

baths in Frederick Street. (The Jewish community had their own wash houses in Frederick Street before this, but the Wilkinsons' were the first open to the general public.)

Tom Wilkinson died in 1848; Kitty in 1860, at the age of 73. She is buried in St James's cemetery, and her portrait is amongst those of Liverpool's 'noble women' in the stained glass window of the Anglican Cathedral's Lady Chapel.

chapter 9
the law

Statistics may not tell the whole story, but they can give some important clues. In 2000, Liverpool was down at No22 in the crime league of Britain's 45 principal towns and cities. Far from being the crime capital of the world – as you might believe from the press – there is a lower rate of violence per capita in Liverpool than in Bedfordshire, Gwent, Humberside and Staffordshire; there is less vehicle crime per capita than in Cambridgeshire, Avon, Somerset, Gloucestershire and all other metropolitan areas. Residents of Lincolnshire, Kent, Gloucestershire and all other metropolitan areas are more likely to be burgled than if they lived on Merseyside.

That's not to say there isn't a pile of crime in the city. But when you stuff half a million people in to a relatively small patch of land, there will be trouble. But there is less in Liverpool than in any other British city today. Norman Bettison, Chief Constable of Merseyside, appointed in 1999, has a fight on his hands to change the image of Merseyside as crime-ridden: 'There were 23 homicides in the county in 1998, most of which were domestic incidents. In a county of 1.42 million people, that is a minuscule proportion. This is a very safe city to live in.'

Liverpool's police force was established in 1835, with 390 officers, along the lines recommended by Sir Robert Peel, since when the force has racked up a number of firsts, from wearing helmets to being armed with cutlasses. In 1884 the City Police replaced their wheeled stretchers with a horse ambulance, and in 1889 they were the first force to be equipped with rubber-soled boots for night duty. Before a separate fire service was established, Liverpool was the first force to introduce a motorised fire engine (1901). This was the first force to have two-way radio communication, first by Morse code, then voice. (The transmitter at Old Swan could reach France, and once a trawler at sea off Norway.)

This was the first force to set up a juvenile liaison scheme, was the first force in the North to have a Flying Squad. More recently, Liverpool's force was the first to use CCTV (1964) and, during July 1981, the first to fire CS gas at rioters.

Deep flaws exposed and painful lessons learned in the Granby riots have slowly led to more sensitive policing, a greater emphasis on community liaison, and a commitment from the chief constable to rid his force of any vestiges of racism. He has the sceptical local community to convince first. Ingrained attitudes are hard to change.

There's some way to go, but PC Paul Hurst has shown it can be done. Community policeman of the year in 1998, Hurst patrols the Granby area on foot, without a long baton: 'I feel safe on Granby Street ... it's a nice community and I feel very passionately about it.'

> ❛ *The [Liverpool] force is directed by an unusual intelligence ... in all respects it tempers its remarkable vigilance with a still more remarkable discretion.* ❜
>
> **Charles Dickens 1860**

Riots crop up quite regularly in Liverpool's history – over poverty, local rivalry, bad conditions, political and sectarian fervour. These days, Liverpool's economic regeneration, its ecumenical culture and lessons learned 20 years ago about policing a multicultural community, mean a relatively peaceful city.

The earliest record of civil unrest in Liverpool was on St Valentine's Day in 1345, when rioters 'interfered with the King's Justices'; many rioters were pardoned and sent on military service. The long-standing rivalry between the Molyneux family and the Stanleys (later the Earls of Sefton and Derby) meant flare-ups from time to time: in July 1424 Henry IV had to put a stop to a pitched battle between Sir Richard Molyneux and Sir Thomas Stanley, who had mustered about 2,000 men each.

In the mid-18th century there was a serious riot during which the Catholic church in Lumber Street was destroyed, and in 1775 sailors, angry about poor wages, rioted for several days. Cannon were brought into Castle Street to control the mob, and many lives were lost. Seamen's wages were the cause of another uprising in 1801.

Irish troubles began brewing in Liverpool in 1819, when there was an affray between the dock police and a party of Irishmen. Later the same year, there was a riot when an Orange march was attacked by Catholics on 12th July. Not quite 30 years later, there was a panic over the 'turbulent spirit' in Liverpool connected with insurrectionary movements in Ireland. To curb the potential riots, another 500 policemen were recruited, and more than 20,000 special constables. The authorities even brought in 2,000 soldiers, billeting them in Everton.

In 1881 there was a determined Fenian attempt to blow up the Town Hall with dynamite, a few days after trying to blow up the police station in Hatton Garden.

In 1911, with the population of Liverpool at 747,000 – up 6% in 10 years, there was a railway strike. The Lord Mayor threatened to read the Riot Act, and brought in extra police from Leeds and Birmingham, as well as 200 Royal Irish Constabulary. Later that year, on 11th August, the Riot Act was read to a mass meeting of strikers on St George's Plateau; when the police tried to disperse the crowd, 12 policemen and over 100 strikers were injured. A mob erected barricades in Christian Street that night, and again the Riot Act was read.

Lady Eleanor, Duchess of Gloucester, was charged with witchcraft and confined in Liverpool Castle in 1440.

The Earl of Derby had the Parliamentarian Colonel Birch trailed under a haycart at Manchester; in revenge, Birch, when governor of Liverpool during the Commonwealth in 1648, had the Earl's children locked up in the Tower of Liverpool for 18 months, refusing even to give them bread so they were forced to beg for subsistence.

Ma Smyrden, a landlady of a seamen's lodging in Pitt Street, was notorious for conning crimps ('agents' or press men) into shanghaiing a corpse.

The Robin Hood of the Liverpool slums was the mysterious gentleman Mr Boon, who in 1875 carried out some audacious burglaries, leaving polite notes explaining what he had done and why. He stole jewellery and £4,000 from the Aigburth home of millionaire William Graves, and took £1,000 from the wallet of rich miser, the cotton merchant Angus Critchley, while he was sleeping in the Adelphi Hotel. To one victim, Boon left a note saying: 'Pray, do not fret. I am merely distributing your wealth to the needy.' He had disguised himself as a widow with a black veil, tying up the elderly butler before escaping. Mr Boon told Chicago philanthropist DL Moody that his 'kind and humane nature' were his inspiration.

f legislation today seems restrictive, with speed cameras, CCTV and European directives governing every sneeze, life in 16th-century Liverpool wasn't exactly free and easy, either. For one thing, in 1571, Liverpudlians were told that: 'none of the Queen's lieges are to be frightened by monstrous beasts or vision voyde or vayne without licence from the Mayor'. Then take a look at this set of local laws, which demanded: 'that apprentices should not play at cards or dice; that tanners should not leave horns or hides in the streets; that no ballast should be thrown into the sea, lake or pool; that the curfew bell should toll at eight o'clock; that suspicious persons should not walk in the streets after nine o'clock at night; that sheep should not be turned out without a shepherd nor swine without a swineherd; that persons afflicted with pestilence should be kept separate from the rest of the inhabitants; that waites should be appointed to play musical instruments morning and evening every day except Sunday; that carts should pay fourpence a year each towards mending the roads ...'.

Funnily enough, no mention of prostitution. Liverpool, being a port, did a thriving trade in sex, around Lime Street and Paradise Street till the 20th century, then among the Georgian terraces of Liverpool 8. Tich Maguire, Mary Ellen, the Battleship, Harriet Lane, Jumping Jenny, Cast-iron Kitty and The Dreadnought were all famous 19th-century prostitutes; Maggie May was immortalised in song.

There is nothing more uncomfortable to the rich than having poverty thrust in their face; in 1640 a load of beggars were scooped off the streets and shipped off to Barbados – the colonies were useful places to dump the poor, the indigent and the convicted.

At least (until 1696) debtors were given a break – for 10 days before and after each Liverpool Fair (on 25th July and 11th November) debtors could walk between the two sanctuary stones (one survives, near 20 Castle Street) without fear of arrest, as long as they were on legitimate business.

Two criminal trials that excited local interest in the last ten years were those of comedian Ken Dodd for alleged tax offences, and local politician Derek Hatton for allegations regarding a horsebox. Both men were acquitted, to markedly differing reactions from the public; Ken Dodd's trial and acquittal were greeted with laughter and cheering, at the poor old taxman's expense. Doddy has been cracking jokes about the Revenue ever since.

Liverpool's Registrar continues to hold the ancient privileges of the Court of Passage – being moss reever and burliman, administrator of leather sealers and scavengers, alefounder and taster, and fryer of seized shoes. Liverpool's original Court of Passage was a franchise granted by the royal charter of 1229 (Henry III) and dealt with merchants visiting the Liverpool Fair, and sea-custom; by definition, itinerant merchants and seamen needed justice dispensed swiftly, and with an eye to commercial common sense. These pie-powders (from pieds-poudres – 'the man with dusty feet') or Mayor's Courts were more appropriate for traders than other options; not many merchants would appreciate being offered trial by battle or wager of law as a means of settling disputes.

Until Liverpool got its own registry in 1853, the town relied on the Court of Chancery in Preston – the King's Court of the County Palatine of Lancashire (Liverpool was a Lancastrian city until the boundary changes in 1974 created Merseyside). There was a Registry established in Liverpool in 1853, and a year later, when St George's Hall was opened in 1854 Liverpool got its own Assizes, sited in the two magnificent courtrooms at either end of the Great Hall.

As for lawyers, Liverpool has produced its fair share of characters. As well as the country's first woman judge, Rose Heilbron, Liverpool also provided the country with two Lord Chancellors – FE Smith (later Lord Birkenhead), and David Maxwell-Fyfe. Liverpool's Law Society was founded in 1827 as the Law Library, with its first president Joshua Lace and members including Samuel Brabner and John Holden; President in 1893 was JW Alsop. The Law Library was the biggest outside London, until the May Blitz in 1941, when the building was bombed, and 30,000 legal books, many dating back to the 16th and 17th centuries, were lost. The names of those early Law Society members all survive in present-day law firms; Brabner Holden, Berrymans Lace Mawer, and DLA (Dibb Lupton Alsop, as was). Through Joshua Lace, Berrymans can claim the title of oldest firm in Liverpool; Lace was originally part of the firm of Aspinwall & Roscoe, dating back at least to 1740.

Liverpool's commercial law firms, such as Mace & Jones, Hill Dickinson (marine insurance specialists), Weightman Rutherford and Cuff Roberts, can trace histories back a century or more, but newer names have been added to the roll: Davies Wallis Foyster was founded by Jim Davies and Guy Wallis in 1977, and in 1998 JST Mackintosh was set up by four partners leaving another firm to carve out their own niche.

Rex Makin, who qualified in 1950, is now a living legend regarded with affection, fear, admiration and loathing in equal proportions, depending on who one asks. A razor-sharp litigator with a wicked sense of humour and an elephantine memory, he has acted for the famous, the good and the downtrodden, as well as 'a better class of murderer', as he put it.

He doesn't care much for his fellow solicitors and is well-known for his style of letter-writing which is brusque, to say the least, but there are probably many clients who would like their own solicitors to be as brief and clear. No greeting or farewell in letters to other solicitors: 'They are not dear to me, and I have no intention of being faithful to them,' he says. Often the body of the letter is a single word response – 'No.' In the generous tradition of Liverpool philanthropists, the Makin name is attached to various bits of Liverpool's arts and education establishments, and although he calls himself an iconoclast, he makes his presence felt in the goings-on of the city. The grit in the city's legal oyster, Makin is a Scouse original and has been a part of Liverpool life for several decades; he will be missed if he ever decides to retire, even if there is a collective sigh of relief from the legal profession.

The burliman administered the Byrlaw (today's by-laws) – the local ordinances governing boundary disputes and the like, which could be settled by the burliman without going through the court process.

Europe's first purpose-built prison was built in Great Howard Street in 1786.

In Calderstones Park there is an oak tree, known as the Laghok or Law oak. Under its spreading branches sat the Hundred Court ... a thousand years ago. The tree still flowers each spring.

The last duel in Liverpool was between Colonel Bolton and Major Brooks; the duel took place in a field at the corner of Pembroke Place and Boundary Place, on 20th December 1805. Colonel Bolton was found guilty of murder at the inquest, but was never charged, as he had public opinion behind him.

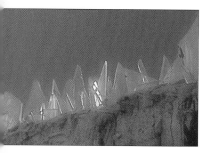

The only man to assassinate a British Prime Minister lived in Liverpool. John Bellingham – a timber contractor – was from St Neots, and lived in Duke Street for several years. When he went to Russia on business, he was arrested for debt and thrown into jail, having been refused help by the British Ambassador. When he was released, he went back to Liverpool, and demanded that the government do something about his unjust treatment, but got nowhere. So in May 1812 Bellingham went to London, bought two pistols, went to the House of Commons and, in the lobby, shot Prime Minister Spencer Perceval dead. Bellingham was tried, convicted and hanged the same week. Coincidentally, not only was Perceval's family Liverpudlian and owners of the mansion house in what is now Calderstones Park; but Perceval's successor as Prime Minister was Lord Liverpool.

Cities these days may be thought of as dangerous places to live; Liverpool is, in 2001, one of the safest in Britain. It wasn't always so: apart from the riots that blew up from time to time, life in a seaport could be hazardous and fairly lawless. In 1573 Liverpool was 'much pestered and charged' with soldiers on their way to Ireland, and the same year Irish insurgents murdered the crew and passengers of a Liverpool ship stranded near Carrickfergus. Two centuries earlier, in 1337, William Blount – sheriff of Lancashire – was murdered in Liverpool; there is no record of his murderers being caught.

By contrast, an infamous murderer who killed in London, was caught in Liverpool. Dr Crippen, who killed his wife, was on his way to America with his mistress Ethel le Neve. Ma Egerton, a Liverpool landlady, had met Crippen and le Neve in a pub, and had recognised a piece of jewellery owned by Crippen's wife, who Egerton had known well. She tipped off the police; Crippen's wife's body was found, and the police sent a message by the brand new technology of wireless to the *SS Montrose* (one of the first uses of ship-to-shore wireless), and Crippen was brought back for trial and execution.

The most spectacular public execution in Liverpool was in 1863, only five years before public hangings were banned. There had been no public executions in Liverpool before 1835 as only then did Liverpool have its own Assizes, in the courts of St George's Hall. The 1863 hangings, in Kirkdale Gaol, brought people in droves from all over the North to see four men die. Convicted murderers, John Maria Alvarez, John Hughes, James O'Brien and Benjamin Thomas were executed by hangman Calkraft.

Hanging wasn't reserved for murderers: in 1788 Silvester Dowling and Patrick Burns were convicted of robbing Mrs Graham in Rose Hill, and were the first men to hang since 1715, when some of those involved in the first Jacobite rebellion were executed on the gallows in London Road.

In the late 20th century, the scourge of every city has become drug-related crime; Liverpool doesn't escape – but neither do its criminals, scot-free. A number have been murdered, usually shot, by rivals – although the numbers are well down on Manchester and other cities.

The first death ever caused by a police marksman on Merseyside happened in July 2001, when Andrew Kernan, a diagnosed schizophrenic threatening police with a sword, was shot in Wavertree. It was the second shot fired by Merseyside police in more than 20 years.

English legal history was made by two sensational murder trials at St George's Hall in Liverpool, the first in 1899 of Florence Maybrick, the second in 1931 of Herbert Wallace – the man from the Pru. Both escaped the hangman's noose – just – on appeal.

American-born Mrs Maybrick was accused of murdering her husband James by feeding him with arsenic scraped off flypapers. Conflicting evidence and the judge allegedly misdirecting the jury made for a sensational trial, at the end of which the jury returned a guilty verdict.

Maybrick was sentenced to death, but a petition was sent to the House of Lords, and Florence Maybrick's sentence was commuted to 15 years' imprisonment – the first time in England that a death sentence had been commuted.

Mrs Maybrick served her time and was released – she came back to Liverpool for the Grand National in 1927, but returned to America, where she died in poverty.

The second case, of Herbert William Wallace, intrigued many; even Raymond Chandler was hooked by the mystery, saying: 'The Wallace case is unbeatable; it will always be unbeatable.'

Insurance collector Herbert Wallace, aged 52, and his wife Julia – a devoted couple, by all accounts – lived at Wolverton Street, Anfield; on 20th January 1931 the 70-year-old Julia was found with her head bashed in, and Wallace was arrested and charged with her murder.

Wallace's alibi was that he had gone to see a prospective client – a Mr Qualtrough, of 25 Menlove Gardens East – who had asked him to come and discuss business at 7.30pm that night. Qualtrough had phoned the previous evening, ringing the City Cafe in North John Street where Wallace was to play in a chess tournament (Qualtrough left a message with the chess club captain, Samuel Beattie).

Wallace insisted that his wife had been alive when he left his house the next evening at 6.45pm – only to find that Menlove Gardens East did not exist. He went home; finding the front door locked he went to the back, meeting his neighbours John and Florence Johnston in the alley. Together they went into the house, to find Julia dead in the front parlour.

The forensic expert, Professor MacFall, testified at the trial that Julia Wallace had been dead at 6pm or before, but it later transpired that MacFall had simply looked at the blood around Julia's head and decided it to 'be quite old'.

Wallace was lucky that milk delivery boy Alan Close had spoken to Julia at about 6.45pm, and their conversation was witnessed by a newspaper boy delivering the Echo next door.

Even so, the jury returned a guilty verdict, and Wallace was sentenced to hang and taken to Walton gaol. On appeal, legal history was again made when the Court of Appeal quashed the conviction, and Wallace was acquitted. He got his job back, but was shunned in the street and had doors shut in his face by his customers. He died two years later of kidney disease.

So who did kill Julia Wallace? Liverpool journalist and local mysteries expert Tom Slemen researched the case with criminologist Keith Andrews, and says that all the evidence points to the Wallaces' neighbour, John Johnston. Johnston and his wife Florence were burgling the house when they were surprised by Julia Wallace, and Johnston beat her to death.

chapter 10
society

King John's charter in 1207 gave Liverpool's guild merchant a monopoly: 'No person unless of that guild shall make merchandise without the consent of the burgesses.' This held good for several hundred years: in 1567 one James Byrnie, not a freeman of the town, was fined for opening his shop and selling his wares on week days without having the town's permission to do so.

An order made in 1617 stated: 'If any person speak ill of the Mayor he shall lose his freedom.'

Liverpool was once granted a charter by a foreign king: Philip of Spain and his wife Mary I jointly signed the 1556 charter.

In 1793 Liverpool printed its own money – £300,000 – the Corporation members had to pledge their estates as security.

Mike Storey, leader of the city council

Society: not just the polite bit, but the whole structure of the city and how it supports the lives of hundreds of thousands of individuals living hugger-mugger in a few square miles. For a sociologist, Liverpool must provide one of the most intellectually fascinating studies – the town's slow start, rocket-fuelled growth over two centuries, and its nose-dive after the war to a bleakly high profile state of desperation in the 1970s and 1980s. Extreme wealth and grotesque poverty living in parallel streets; fierce resistance to change on one hand and ferocious demand for change on the other. Power for some and powerlessness for others; a demand for respect from one group without offering respect to the other. Little wonder, then, that politics have flared white-hot from time to time both between local factions and between Liverpool and central government.

Local government from the time of King John's charter in 1207 was not exactly sophisticated, but then Liverpool was not exactly a large conurbation, consisting of 840 inhabitants and 168 burgesses. The names of the first few mayors are lost – the first record is of William Adamson in 1351; in 1398 Thomas de la More of Banke Hall is down as being mayor for the twelfth time – but that is no great political feat since the town (like most towns in those days) was ruled by a self-elected oligarchy of the wealthy and powerful.

In 1626 when Charles I grants his charter to Liverpool, he creates the town as a body corporate and politic (on 4th July – Liverpool Independence Day). The borough's first mayor is James Strange, Lord Stanley; the first bailiffs were Richard Tarleton and James Southern, and Richard Dobson was the first town clerk.

In the next 100 years the town would take bad hits from plague and two sieges in the Civil War, but got its independence as a port, its own parish, its first enclosed dock, the first turnpike roads and navigable waterways inland to Manchester and south to the Cheshire salt mines. By the mid 1700s administrative control was split between the town council and the Select Vestry – an ecclesiastical committee of considerable power. Distribution of poor relief was organised by the Overseers of the Poor; by 1771 the workhouse was built and five years later the House of Correction.

It was only in 1773 that the streets in the town were named and the houses numbered. In 1777 the manorial rights to Liverpool were bought from Lord Sefton for £2,250, finally giving control of the town to its inhabitants.

Political corruption was, of course, commonplace – to get elected mayor could cost the candidate £10,000 since a freeman's vote cost £40 or more, and there were other expenses to be met. The 1757 election of William Goodwin as mayor was so scandalous that it caused a riot; hustings were destroyed and most of the Exchange windows broken.

The 1832 Reform Act did much to sort out some of the worst excesses of the old Corporation, abolishing many rights and privileges; the new council sacked the town surveyor and the town clerk (whose salary and perks were more than £7,000 a year).

After Liverpool became a diocese in 1880, Queen Victoria granted Liverpool city status and a little later granted the new city the right to have a Lord Mayor – the first was Robert Durning Holt. Liverpool gave the country its first female local councillor, Eleanor Rathbone, in 1909 (when of a population exceeding 739,000 only 85,000 were eligible to vote: no women). The first female Lord Mayor was in 1927 in the shape of Margaret Beavan.

In 1767 the town was divided into five administrative divisions or wards, to be named St Nicholas's, St George's, St Peter's, St Thomas's and St John's.

On 18th October each year (till 1832) was the beating of the bounds, when the mayor, the bailiffs and the rest, in full regalia, tucked into pigeon and shrimps washed down with rum and brandy, before going to watch the bear-baiting on Exchange Flags.

The municipality was enlarged in 1895 to take in Walton, West Derby, Wavertree and Toxteth Park; Garston joined in 1902, and Fazakerley in 1905. In 1907 there were 112,654 municipal voters (population: 739,000+).

Jews were not officially allowed to be members of Parliament or take municipal office until 1858. But in Liverpool Elias Joseph, head of the Jewish community, was elected to the parish council from 1803 to 1819, and his brother in law Morris Mozley was then elected to the Watch Committee every year until 1932.

When Charles Mozley was elected to mayor in 1863 – the first Jewish mayor in Liverpool – the vicar of St George's (the Corporation Church in Derby Square) preached violent anti-Semitic sermons. He was surprised to see the next mayor's Sunday procession pass by and on to St Peter's in Church Street.

I n modern times the image of Liverpool has been until very recently a left-wing city, strike-bound, riot-torn, ravaged by unemployment and falling to pieces. The Militant Tendency through its motormouthpiece Derek Hatton were grabbing headlines and alienating central government and much of the rest of Britain, courtesy of the media. Hatton was never leader of the city council, only deputy leader – but few people can remember the leader's name. It was John Hamilton, for the record. Nor was the city council heavily Labour-dominated; until 1983 it was under Liberal minority control, and even during the Militant period was fairly marginal.

Hatton lost his grip on the city in 1987 having been finally and very publicly expelled from the Labour Party (along with the rest of Militant) by Neil Kinnock after a bit of steamy repartee at the party conference in 1985. Degsy Hatton went into public relations, and the political leadership went to Keva Coombes and then in 1990 to Harry Rimmer, an old-school Labour man. Coombes had started the shift away from the bloody-minded isolationist stance of Militant, recognising that if Liverpool was to drag itself out of the hole it was in, it needed help, even it was from Margaret Thatcher's Tory government. Rimmer quickened the move towards pragmatic partnerships and began to cool down the Merseyside political furnace; he appointed the energetic Peter Bounds as his chief executive to sort out the administrative chaos created by years of poor management and political idiosyncrasy.

After the 1998 elections Liverpool had its first Liberal Democrat council leader, Mike Storey. David Henshaw moved across from Knowsley to become chief executive after Bounds retired, and with a cabinet style council in place, there was talk of an elected mayor and more reform. Considerable effort will be needed to boost interest in local democracy: in recent national and local elections the turnout in Liverpool has been abysmal.

In 1559 the town was given an order to pay the expenses of its MP, Ralph Seckerston, for the amount of £2 3s 4d.

There have been seven prime ministers with Liverpool connections: Spencer Perceval (an old Liverpool family), Lord Liverpool, Lord Derby, George Canning (Liverpool MP 1812-1823), William Gladstone, Harold Wilson (MP for Huyton) and Tony Blair (his wife is from Liverpool).

Francis Bacon, lawyer, philosopher and essayist, was MP for Liverpool from 1588. Bacon, who said: 'Riches are a good handmaid, but the worst mistress', was found guilty of bribery and corruption in 1621, fined £40,000 and banished from office and Parliament.

The first record of Liverpool sending burgesses to Westminster as members of Parliament was in 1295: Adam son of Richard and Robert Pinklowe. In 1306 it was Richard More and John More, and the next record is in 1545 when Nicholas Cutlyer and Gilbert Gerard were elected. Perhaps the word 'elected' is a little misleading: those able to vote were restricted to the great and the good, the town's freemen or burgesses. It is worth noting that the 'new industrial towns' of Manchester and Birmingham only got parliamentary representation after the 1832 Reform Act.

Votes were bought in parliamentary elections just as they were in local council elections. In 1694 Jasper Mawditt was elected MP by about 400 of Liverpool's freemen, but the man returned to Parliament by the mayor, Alexander Norris, was Thomas Brereton – despite his having won only 15 votes. For such blatant misconduct Norris was made to beg pardon on his knees in the House of Commons, given a fine and seven weeks in prison.

Nothing much had changed by 1830, when William Ewart and JE Denison fought to win the votes of 4,335 freemen. The row went on from 23rd to 30th November and eventually Ewart was returned to the Whig benches, but the election was condemned because of gross bribery and corruption. Ewart's campaign expenses came to £65,000 – men were paid £80 each for their vote. This was one of the scandals that drove the fifth William Rathbone to dedicated opposition to electoral corruption.

At least when the fourth Earl of Derby was elected in 1822 it was to an acknowledged rotten borough. The Earl was prime minister three times between 1852 and 1868 (at one stage had two of his sons in the cabinet) and drove through the 1867 Reform Act which was to double the electorate by giving the vote to all householders and £10 rent payers in the towns, enfranchising many working class people for the first time.

The Earl of Derby's family, the Stanleys, had been at the heart of English politics since the 12th century – one of the most influential families in the kingdom.

Minerva, goddess of wisdom, watches over Liverpool

William Gladstone was the key political figure for Liverpool of the Victorian era, prime minister four times between 1868 and 1894. The son of Edinburgh-born shipowner John Gladstones (the family dropped the 's' in 1837), William Ewart Gladstone was born at 62 Rodney Street in 1809, the fifth of six children, and became a Tory MP in 1833 before crossing the floor to the Whigs. Queen Victoria thoroughly disliked him, preferring his opposition leader Disraeli; she said: 'He speaks to me as if I were a public meeting,' and in a letter to Lord Lansdowne in 1892, wrote: 'The danger to the country, to Europe, which is involved in having all these great interests entrusted to the shaking hand of an old, wild and incomprehensible man of 82, is very great!'

If Gladstone was the outstanding Liverpool-born politician of the Victorian era, then it was two women in the first half of the 20th century: Eleanor Rathbone and Bessie Braddock.

Eleanor Rathbone (1872-1946) was the daughter of the sixth William Rathbone; hers was one of the wealthiest merchant families in the city, but from a long tradition of nonconformist philanthropy and liberal politics. 'Her philosophy came down to the respect of other people: that was her moral foundation,' said Margaret Simey, Rathbone's student and assistant in the 1920s when Rathbone set up the School of Social Sciences at the university. She became the first woman councillor in 1909, an MP in 1929, and the first female minister; her greatest achievement was her book *The Disinherited Family* (1924) and the campaign that led to the introduction of family allowances in 1945.

Bessie Braddock (1899-1970) was in many ways the antithesis of the reserved, Oxford-educated Rathbone. Battling Bessie was the imposing and forceful embodiment of socialist Liverpool. A councillor in 1930, she was elected as MP for Liverpool Exchange in 1945 and became vice-chairman of the Labour Party in 1968; she fought like a tiger for the poor and disenfranchised people of Liverpool. A formidable character who made enemies, Braddock was much loved, a generous woman, whose many kind acts were mostly unpublicised.

Bessie Braddock was taken to her first political meeting when she was three weeks old; Bessie's mother Mary Bamber was a prominent figure in local politics. Bessie was also with her mother on St George's Plateau on Bloody Sunday in August 1911, when police charged thousands who had gathered to hear Tom Mann speak at the transport workers' strike meeting.

Jack Braddock, leader of the city council in 1964, was speaking at the dinner for the John Moores autumn art exhibition at the Walker Art Gallery. He sat down at the end of his speech, collapsed and died.

By the age of 25, Eleanor Rathbone was a manager of the Granby Street Council School and secretary of the Women's Industrial Council.

A hospital for decayed seamen was built in 1752, maintained by a monthly payment of sixpence from the wages of every sailor in Liverpool.

In 1843, of Liverpool's 57 miles of streets less than half had any sewerage provision at all: 32 miles of streets had to dispose of sewage in pits, on dung heaps or in the gutters.

Due to ferocious campaigning by Dr William Duncan and town surveyor John Newlands, Liverpool obtained the first ever Sanitary Act in 1848 (national Acts would follow). But such was the resentment of the conservative lobby that the Act was repealed ten years later.

In the 1830s Liverpool's water supply was controlled by two private companies who would force up prices by creating deliberate shortages. Some 'customers' could use a pump for 15 minutes every other day, and then often only at night.

The first X-ray machine in Britain was at the Southern Hospital, installed in 1896. The first medical diagnosis by X-ray was done by Oliver Lodge, when he found a bullet in a child's wrist.

The first provincial hospital dedicated to children's health was the Royal Liverpool Children's Hospital in Myrtle Street; the first children's ward was opened in 1857 at the Southern Hospital.

Public health was a bit of a joke for most of Liverpool's history – as it was throughout Europe. China, of course, has had a scientific system of medicine for 5,000 years, still in use today and catching on fast in the advanced West. Until the mid 19th century life was a bit of a lottery, healthwise. Surviving birth (for mother and child) was not exactly guaranteed; infant mortality was high – hence the enormous families born by exhausted women. People aged fast and died young, compared to life expectancy in England today. Liverpool followed the pattern of most towns and cities in the country in its history of health and medical science – until the population explosion of the 18th and 19th centuries. In 100 years Liverpool's population went from 80,000 to 800,000, and the town could not support it. By 1840 Liverpool was the unhealthiest port in western Europe.

There were 142,000 people per square mile in Vauxhall, compared to a European urban average of 25,000. The Georgian developers who built such stunning houses for the rich also built the slums – dark, smelly cramped courts, no running water, dank cellars... Poverty was not just grinding, but deadly. Food was scarce and poor, water was dirty, the air polluted, and contagion unstoppable. The average life expectancy in Vauxhall was 17 years.

The father of Liverpool's medical profession was Sylvester Richmond, who lived from 1616 to 1692 and was known as a professor of physick and chirugery – the town's first 'proper' doctor. The year he died, Richmond gave £100 towards the building of almshouses on Shaw's Brow (which was the site for Liverpool's first infirmary, opened in 1749 and the first in the north of England). The year the infirmary was opened, Liverpool got a local Act passed for street cleaning, years before a similar national Act was passed by Parliament.

Thirty years on, the first dispensary was opened in 1778 in Princes Street for 'such sick and lame poor as were formerly in the care of the parish apothecary'. The dispensary moved to bigger premises in Church Street three years later, built on a former fruit garden and apple orchard. By 1820 the dispensary had 20,000 patients.

At the end of the 1700s, poverty was reprehensible; mental illness was a crime. Blindness, deafness and physical disabilities – congenital or caused by injury – were just tough luck.

Edward Rushton went blind at 19, from an eye disease he caught while trying to tend slaves on board ship. He raised support to open the first school for the blind in Commutation Row. Rushton's Asylum was also the first school to teach disabled people a trade or skill (some learned to play the harpsichord and got jobs as church organists). To cope with demand it moved first to London Road, then to Hardman Street, and later to its current site in Church Road, Wavertree. Rushton later recovered his sight after an operation, and became a poet, newspaper editor and bookseller.

The year after Rushton's school opened, the remarkable Scot Dr James Currie – first physician of the infirmary – opened a Lunatic Asylum in the infirmary gardens. Currie was the first to realise that madness was not the will of God, not due to the moon, not a crime, but an illness: inmates were not to be bled, kept in dungeons and beaten till exhausted. Currie had to fight prejudice and indifference, but won his battle. He later pushed through plans for the first fever hospital, the first recognition of isolation as a means of stopping contagion (he died before it opened in 1805).

Without doubt the most influential doctor in Liverpool's history was Dr William Duncan (1805-1863). He wrote a shocking report to the town council in 1844 and despite fierce resistance, the council ordered the cleansing of infested houses, courts and cellars to kill parasites and cockroaches and remove filth. But that year and the next was when the tidal wave of Irish fleeing from the potato famine overwhelmed Liverpool, with dozens forced to share each cellar; 15,000 immigrants died of fever and famine in 1847 – the year that Dr Duncan was appointed the first ever Medical Officer of Health, after the 1846 Liverpool Sanitary Act. Duncan faced a constant political battle, as well as massive resistance to change and, hardest of all, complete indifference. Why, among Liverpool's umpteen statues to the great and good, is there no memorial to Dr Duncan, other than a pub name?

Dr Edward Bickersteth was the first surgeon to use carbolic spray and antiseptic catgut. He was also the first to wear a surgical gown instead of a topcoat.

The UK's first purpose-built ambulance was in Liverpool; William Joynson, chairman of the Northern Hospital, had seen horse-drawn ambulances in New York and brought the idea back.

Britain's first epileptic colony was in Maghull, opened in 1889.

Liverpool was the first city, in 1898, to appoint a municipal bacteriologist: Professor Rubert Boyce of the University College.

Liverpool pioneered health visitors and infant welfare clinics.

Appalled by the conditions suffered by the sick amongst the 5,000 inmates of the vast workhouse on Brownlow Hill, Rathbone offered to pay the costs for three years if he could put in a proper nursing system. He asked Agnes Jones (born 1832) to be superintendent of the workhouse hospital; she arrived in 1865 and worked herself to the bone, with her team of 40 nurses and an army of scouring women, to clean the workhouse and run the hospital. Agnes Jones caught typhus and died in February 1868.

In 1776 ether was first used publicly as an anaesthetic in Liverpool.

In 1900 Liverpool built the first public sanatorium in Britain for the open-air treatment of tuberculosis, among the pine trees of Delamere Forest.

Although there had been nurses at the infirmary since it was first built in 1749, they weren't what we know now as nurses. There was, after all, precious little medical science; pharmacology was in its infancy, and there was still little understanding of contagion and infection. These 18th century nurses were paid £4 a year 'to behave with tenderness to patients, with submission to their superiors and civility and respect to all strangers'.

When in 1858 William Rathbone's wife Lucretia fell ill, he hired Mary Robinson, a nurse trained by Florence Nightingale; Robinson's care and professionalism so impressed Rathbone that, after his wife's death, he wrote to Florence Nightingale asking her to come and train local women to nurse the poor in their own homes. Nightingale didn't come to do the training herself, but offered her advice and support. Rathbone and Mary Robinson began a district nursing scheme – the first – in 1862 and nurse training was provided for infirmary nurses. Rathbone later married Emily Lyle, the lady superintendent of district nurses.

Back in 1796, the Ladies Charity had been founded to help women in childbirth at home, providing bedlinen and food; but the charity could do little about the pain and danger of childbirth, in which a high proportion of babies and mothers died.

Fifty years later, David Waldie – a Liverpool chemist – realised the potential of liquid chloroform (it had first been used by Liverpool surgeon Dr Formby), and told Sir James Simpson (who is credited for its discovery). A friend of the great Dr Duncan, Waldie, Duncan and another doctor experimented with chloroform on each other, putting themselves 'under the table in a minute or two'.

Simpson gave chloroform to women in childbirth to ease their pain, but was denounced by a priest as going against God's word. God, apparently, wanted women to bring forth children in sorrow as punishment for Eve's problem with apples and serpents. Simpson neatly turned the tables, by quoting the world's first surgical operation: 'the Lord God caused a deep sleep to fall upon Adam, and he slept: and He took one of his ribs, and closed up the flesh instead thereof'. Not only anaesthesia, but wound closure too. (In 1933 at the Liverpool Maternity Hospital Dr Robert Minnitt pioneered gas and air for women in labour.)

Liverpool's first campaign against tuberculosis was in 1901, but the city carried out the first ever mass X-ray campaign in 1959. With the help of 14,000 voluntary workers over a long month, doctors examined 80% of the population over the age of 15; they found 2,776 tuberculosis cases, and 161 people with lung cancer.

1997 saw the opening of the world's first lung cancer research centre in Liverpool, named after Roy Castle. The much-loved entertainer, who was dying of lung cancer from passive smoking, spent his last nine months in 1994 working heroically to raise money for the centre, with his wife Fiona.

Public health is, however, not just about disease and death. It is about the quality of the environment, air pollution, nutrition – mental and physical fitness right into old age. Liverpool has made pioneering strides in all these areas: the Granby Care Home, the Active Age Centre, Greenbank Sporting Academy (designed for the disabled, in and out of wheelchairs), the Merseyside Drugs Council, the GP sports referral scheme and much more. The city still has enormous health issues to solve, like every city, but compared to conditions in 1851 Liverpudlians are a happy, healthy lot.

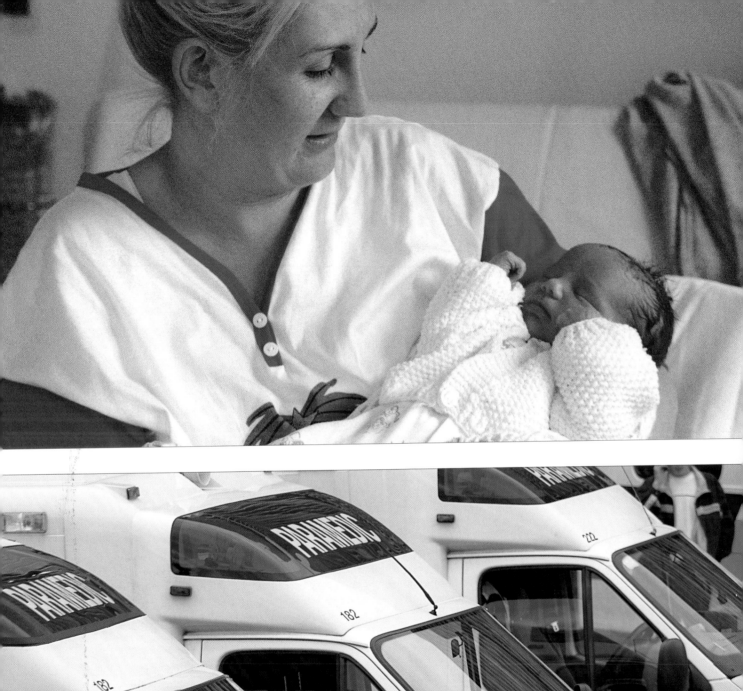

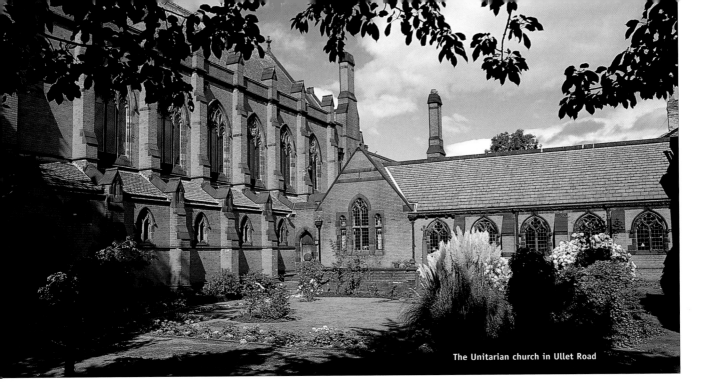

The Unitarian church in Ullet Road

Benedictine monks founded an Abbey at Walton on the Hill after the Norman Conquest.

As well as a sermon from St Patrick, on his way to Ireland, St Germanus is said to have preached here in the 5th century.

In 1872 Catholics in Vauxhall were living in appalling conditions; one woman was found sharing her bed with the corpse of her husband for some days for lack of anywhere else to lay the body out. A group of local Unitarians, appalled by this, raised £5,000 to build them a mortuary chapel in Vauxhall. At the opening of the chapel (which later became All Souls Church) in Collingwood Street, Liverpool's Catholic Vicar General called it 'a monument which shall publicise the alms-deeds of the merchant princes of Liverpool till the last stones shall crumble into dust'.

Until Henry VIII fell in love with Anne Boleyn and fell out with the Pope in 1533, there was only the Roman Catholic church in this neck of the woods. Protestantism had begun to make its presence felt in England through the influence of John Calvin a few years earlier but, despite Henry's dissolution of monasteries, Edward VI's Book of Common Prayer, and years of persecution of Catholics, it wasn't until the reign of Elizabeth I (after five bloody years of heresy trials and burnings at the stake under Catholic Mary I) that the Church of England became the establishment.

In Liverpool, the earliest churches were simple buildings put up by Saxons and Vikings on sites such as St Chad's in Kirkby, and St Mary's in Walton (which has a Saxon font). The earliest church in Liverpool city centre was the Chapel of St Mary of the Quay. This was replaced in the 14th century by a church dedicated to Our Lady and St Nicholas with St Anne – now known locally as St Nick's (the patron saint of seafarers).

For 200 years after the Reformation, Catholics met in secret; the Molyneux family (the Earls of Sefton) at Croxteth Hall gave local Catholics a safe meeting place. Bryan Blundell, slave trader and philanthropist, noted in his diary for 1707 that the first modern Catholic chapel met secretly in North John Street. The first chapel to be built openly (and only the second in England) was in Lumber Street, opened in 1736 by Jesuit priest Father John Hardesty; but this was destroyed in a vicious religious riot 23 years later.

When the town's population grew so fast in the mid 19th century with the influx of Irish migrants, the conflicts between 'Cogger' and 'Proddy-dog' began; confrontations between Catholics and Orangemen were near-riots and in 1856 one Anglican vicar angrily declared that 'the persecution of Protestants was enjoined upon all Catholics as a sacred duty'; two years later Cardinal Wiseman's carriage was stoned and almost overturned. Liverpool's long-fostered sectarian tolerance was swallowed up in religious animosity for the next century, until ecumenism took a firm hold again under the Dynamic Duo in the 1970s.

Bishop David Sheppard and Archbishop Derek Worlock forged a remarkable, even unique partnership and personal friendship, and dragged together Liverpool's Anglican and Catholic communities by sheer force of personality and hands-on involvement in the city's daily life. But before the Dynamic Duo arrived and rolled up their sleeves, Liverpool was home to individuals and groups whose beliefs led to aggression, discrimination and fanaticism, and woe betide any who got in the way.

The first dissenters' meeting place in Liverpool built after the Reformation was an unconsecrated chapel of ease, built on land belonging to the Catholic Earl of Sefton. The Chapel of Toxteth (now known as the Ancient Chapel) was built in 1618 as an extension to the tiny school built in 1611. Toxteth Park had been under forest law since King John's day, and being outside the control of the parish or the bishop, was a natural home for dissenters. The first minister was the young Puritan firebrand Richard Mather (1596-1699), who was not content with preaching to his own flock but strayed outside the Toxteth Park boundaries on to diocesan land, resulting in Mather being silenced by the Archbishop of York.

Other dissenters settled in Liverpool over the years. In the 18th century Liverpool's dissenting churches included Quaker (built 1706), Baptist, Methodist (at which Wesley preached), and two Unitarian. The first Welsh chapel was built in 1787 after years of worshipping in a merchant's warehouse; in 1793 the Scots built their first kirk and by 1837 had enough people to fill six Church of Scotland congregations.

Liverpool became a parish in its own right in 1699, having been within St Mary's Walton till then; St Peter's was Liverpool's first parish church (now St Nick's on the Strand). St Peter's in Church Street was demolished in 1923 to make way for Woolworth's (now Next); at the top of the shop building are the Crossed Keys of St Peter, and on the pavement in front is a granite slab. Inlaid with a brass cross, this marks the site of the door to the old church. Another of Liverpool's lost churches is St George's, built in 1734 on the site of the old castle where the Victoria Monument now stands, and demolished in 1900.

Although one of the world's great 19th century cities, it was only in the 20th century that Liverpool built its Anglican Cathedral (1904-1978), and later the Catholic Cathedral (1962-67).

In 1976 came David Sheppard – a former England cricketer – as Anglican Bishop of Liverpool, and a few months later Derek Worlock as Catholic Archbishop. On Worlock's appointment to Britain's biggest diocese (half a million Catholics), Pope Paul VI told him: 'Make sure Liverpool doesn't become another Belfast,' and gave Liverpool's new archbishop a double task: social justice and ecumenism.

Worlock didn't fail, and is now said to have been one of the greatest Catholic English bishops of the 20th century. He was no hermit – like Bishop Sheppard, he demonstrated the Christian message in action, doing battle with politicians in court, down on the street with black leaders trying to stop the Granby riots, mixing it in Westminster with their controversial document *Faith in the City*, shepherding the grieving city after Hillsborough, visiting local people at home. So close were these two priests in their working lives that they were dubbed Fish and Chips: always together and never out of the newspapers.

The pair's ecumenical approach to life is only fitting for Liverpool, where the first ecumenical conference was held in 1860 (not in Edinburgh in 1910, as is generally thought).

Since Derek Worlock's death and David Sheppard's retirement, Patrick Kelly has taken on the Archbishop's mantle, and James Jones stepped into the Anglican Bishop's robes. They have a tough act to follow.

John Newton (1725-1807) was born in London and went to sea as a boy. At 24 he became captain of a Liverpool slave ship, African, for four years. He then lived in Liverpool, working as a customs officer, before being ordained. While vicar of Olney (a village in Buckinghamshire), Newton wrote the hymns How Sweet the Name of Jesus Sounds *and* Amazing Grace.

Greek Orthodox church

Perhaps Liverpool's most bizarre church was the Mariners' Church, George's Dock. Originally the *Tees* – the Government guard ship of St Helena, which brought Princess Caroline to England for her marriage to George IV – it was converted to a church in 1826 and could hold 1,000 worshippers. It sank on 7th June 1872.

The Greek Orthodox church in Princes Road was built in 1865 by Liverpool's Greek community, which at the time was about 300 strong – and wealthy. Consecrated by the Archbishop of Syra & Tinos in 1870, the splendid Byzantine church lost most of its congregation at the turn of the century, but is now open again to serve the 3,000-strong community of Greeks – mostly Cypriots who came to England in the 1960s and 1970s.

Away from the Christian tradition, Liverpool has a lively mix of cultures and religions, from Buddhist and Jewish to Hindu and Muslim.

The Muslim community in the city, now 20,000-strong, covers up to 45 different nationalities living in Liverpool, including Somali, Sudanese, Malaysian, Bangladeshi, Palestinian, Turkish, Kosovan, Trinidadian, Yemeni, Pakistani, and English. The first mosque in Britain was in Liverpool, opened by a local solicitor William Henry Quilliam in 1889. Quilliam became a Muslim (changing his name from William to Abdullah) after a journey to Morocco, and set up the mosque and a school for Muslim children at 8 Brougham Terrace, as well as an orphanage in Sheil Road. Today the Mosque Al-Rahma is in Hatherley Street, but with such a big community there are plans to build another.

The 3,000 Jews now living in Liverpool have a community dating back to 1740; at one time Liverpool had the largest Jewish community in Britain outside London but, said Jewish community archivist J Wolfman, Jews in the mid-18th century 'are like Yetis: reports of sightings are few; many of these reports are questionable, and the inferences to be drawn from them owe much to the imagination'.

The first Jew known to be in Liverpool was the Portuguese merchant Leon Villareal from Demerara in Guyana. Another name in Liverpool from around that time is that of Aaron Baruch Lousada, who died in Jamaica in 1768: these two Sephardic names (Sephardic Jews are Mediterranean and Moorish, while Ashkenazi Jews came from Northern and Eastern Europe) are rare in Liverpool's records, but Wolfman reckons that it was the arrival of these West Indian Jewish merchants and their agents that resulted in Liverpool having a synagogue as early as 1753. However, the earliest synagogal rule book in Liverpool, from 1799, was in Yiddish, so the majority of the community even then must have been Ashkenazi.

One of the first mentions of a rabbi (unnamed) is in 1776; in the 1790s the 'Jews High Priest' Benjamin Yates is listed in Gore's Directories of Liverpool; the Yates name would originally have been Goetz. (Trying to trace the early community is made next to impossible partly because of Jews who anglicised their names.)

The first synagogue was a small house in a court off Stanley Street, leased in 1753 from a Gentile, Peter Ferguson. In 1772 the synagogue moved to Turton Court, then a few years later to Frederick Street, bought again by Peter Ferguson in trust for Simon and Elias Joseph, Ralph Samuel, Michael Levy, Henry Solomon, Simon Nathan, Isaac Davis and Lemon Nathan. It was in 1804 that the community commissioned architect Thomas Harrison to build a synagogue in Seel Street; 70 years later, the Scottish presbyterian architects William and George Audsley built one of the most remarkable synagogues in Europe (*pictured left*), on Princes Road. In some circles the Princes Road synagogue was referred to as the reform shul, and it was considered rather daring to go there too often.

Tolerance for other ways of life can only be healthy. Liverpool's Town Hall is a venue for civil weddings, and may in the future hold ceremonies for gay and lesbian couples. The 'celebrations of partnership' are not legally binding but may give the couples some recognition in law.

The Hindu Temple in Edge Lane has a number of murals painted by a team of Indian artists led by NB Soni, invited to the city by the Hindu Cultural Organisation.

The Olive Tree in Renshaw Street is Liverpool's only Islamic shop, selling books, textiles, ceramics and glass from the East, and crafts from local Muslim groups; the shop acts as a focal point for local Muslims and anyone interested in Islam.
The olive tree was chosen as the shop's sign as it grows in countries that lie between the East and the West – a peaceful and simple symbol of Islam bringing the whole world together.

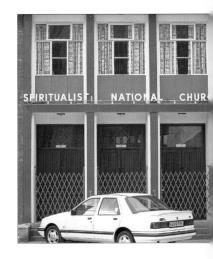

T Major Lester (born 1829) became vicar of St Mary's Kirkdale in 1855; the following year he founded the Kirkdale Ragged Schools, and a few years later the Kirkdale Child Charity, where poor children were fed, clothed, taught trades and crafts. In his lifetime Lester raised more than £1 million for his charities.

William Roscoe was one of the founders of the Society to Supersede the Use of Boys in Sweeping Chimneys.

A marine society for seamen's widows and orphans in the 1750s lapsed for lack of support, but 100 years later a group of shipowners raised money to open the Royal Liverpool Seamen's Orphan Institute in Duke Street.

In 1975 the 15 year old Stephen Yip founded the charity KIND: Kids in Need and Distress. Now 40, with KIND going strong, Yip says: 'There is an old scouting adage that says it is easier to help build the child than repair the adult. If we want decent, caring adults we must provide the environment, opportunities and funding for our children.'

C hildren are always at risk, equally vulnerable to adults' abuse and indifference. It would be good to say that today things are different to life in the 17th century, but in some ways they are worse – because society is more regulated and standards of living so much higher. Human nature hasn't changed, however, and the predatory 21st century adult has even greater scope for abuse. The indifferent plead compassion fatigue – too many starving and miserable children in the world to cope with.

Life in earlier centuries, though, was grim for those not privileged with education and a safe home – and children often got the worst of it. Seafaring was a dangerous way of life; making a living is fine if you actually live to spend your money – too many sailors died, and left widows (if they survived childbirth) and orphans with no welfare state to support them. Children had to work, as childminders, scavengers, or market runners if they were lucky; as chimney sweeps, thieves or prostitutes if they weren't.

Street children who survived on their wits had no hope of education, but even in the late 19th century there were those who thought that educating the poor was a danger to society.

In 1883 Liverpool's Bank of England agent, Thomas F Agnew, founded (with Samuel Smith) the Society for the Prevention of Cruelty to Children, inspired by the New York society; he and Smith later took the idea to London, and this became the NSPCC.

Father James Nugent (1822-1905) was a charitable man who was an advocate of compulsory education and fought for control to be enforced over juvenile street-trading. He founded a Catholic school in Hope Street, opened a Refuge for Homeless Boys in 1865, and set up night shelters for street children, whatever their religion. From 1870 he began to take poor children to America and Canada to find new homes, some of whom thrived and prospered – but not all. Some were placed with families who used them as cheap labour – or worse; Nugent's kind intentions turned to ash in a different sort of hell for some of Liverpool's neglected children.

Beechley Stables is a Riding for the Disabled centre, run by Lynne Williams (right)

Poverty could strike suddenly, as English women discovered when their Chinese husbands were forcibly repatriated after the First and Second World Wars: if they weren't British nationals, many Chinese seamen were deported, regardless of how long they had served in the Navy, and whether or not they had family here. Many families, despite help from a generous community, were left destitute.

Since the end of the 18th century when Liverpool's population began to overwhelm the town's infrastructure, the poor had to rely on the social or religious conscience of individuals like Margaret Beavan, Josephine Butler and Anne Clough. Beavan, the city's first female Lord Mayor, was dubbed the 'little mother of Liverpool'. Secretary of the Invalid Children's Association, she also founded the Royal Liverpool Babies' Hospital in Woolton. Anne Clough (sister of poet Arthur Hugh Clough) and Ellen Gonner were two of Margaret Beavan's contemporaries; Anne Clough became the first principal of Newnham College, Cambridge.

Josephine Butler – who came to Liverpool in 1866 – was a remarkable and courageous woman, working with waifs, strays, prostitutes and the poor sick. She set up a night shelter in Lime Street for women and established refuges for the destitute and for sick prostitutes, opening a training centre to help them get out of prostitution. She was also a tireless campaigner for women's education and suffrage.

One of Liverpool's unrecognised saints was John Jones, a Unitarian minister who in 1836 lived in Greenland Street. The Unitarian philanthropic principle was to do good rather than convert – practical help for the poor such as opening savings banks, providing allotments, supplying sheets and blankets. Jones gave what he had, doled out vouchers for coal, bread and potatoes, set up elementary schools and cared for the sick. He died in 1847 of typhus, caught from a victim that only he and a Catholic priest were prepared to touch.

Liverpool led the way in educating the disabled: Rushton's school for the blind opened in 1791 and William Cowie founded the world's first school for the deaf and dumb in 1825. Not in Liverpool, but over the water in New Brighton, Muriel Crooke began the British guide dogs' kennels and training centre in 1931, which was to become a national organisation. Many of Liverpool's advances in public health were led by philanthropists – pioneering work leading to national or international recognition, despite public or political opposition.

Gladys Aylward (1902-1970) – the 'small woman' played by the tall Ingrid Bergman in the film The Inn of the Sixth Happiness – was a parlour maid before going as a missionary to China, with only £5 and no knowledge of any Chinese language. On her return to Liverpool, she founded a Chinese Gospel Mission in 1953, at 20 Nelson Street. (The film was shot in North Wales, and starred a number of Liverpool Chinese children.)

The Personal Services Society (PSS) was founded here in 1919 in the face of dire social need after the 1914-18 war. The focus on local communities, and on the causes as well as the effects of social distress, has made PSS a charitable pioneer in the UK, with several UK firsts. In 1927 PSS set up an Old People's Welfare Committee – now Age Concern. Its Marriage Guidance Scheme (1936) became Relate; in 1938 it set up the UK's first Citizen's Advice Bureau; in 1948 came the Poor Man's Lawyer (the precursor of Legal Aid).

161

Andrew Carnegie, the Scot who made his fortune in the United States steel industry, paid for four libraries to be built in Liverpool. Carnegie himself came to Liverpool to open Toxteth Library in 1902.

The Liverpool Philomathic Society was founded in 1825 'for the attainment of knowledge by discussion'. Its founders included William Brown, Joseph Shipley and shipbroker James Aikin who founded the Royal Institution with William Roscoe. In 1907 one member complained that: 'A blow has fallen on the prestige of the Philomathic Society – the overwhelming grandeur of the University seems likely to wipe us out. We gave £100 to the Univ. Coll. ... which snuffs us out!'

The RSPCA was born in Liverpool: its fore-runner, the Society for the Suppression of Wanton Cruelty to Brute Animals, was founded here in 1809. It met with violent opposition: those involved with cock-fighting, bear-baiting, those who sold whips, goads and muzzles, those who bred or used pit ponies in mines, and some carters.

Philanthropy is not only about social exclusion and people in distress. Education, the arts and humanities, widening access to what some would term the finer things of life – there is always a need for gifts from generous patrons. These days the gifts more often come from corporate sponsors than individuals, but in the 19th century there were some remarkably generous benefactors.

William Brown, for instance, William Roscoe and Andrew Walker – all names now part of the fabric of Liverpool with buildings and streets named after them.

William Brown was born in Ireland; when he was 16 his family went to New York where his father set up in business with his partner Harrison. When he was 25 William was sent with his colleague Joseph Shipley to Liverpool, to set up a branch of the firm. (The two men later formed their own bank – Brown Shipley & Co – which is still strongly represented in the North West.) Brown, having made his fortune, gave a chunk of it to Liverpool for the central library, laying the foundation stone on the 650th anniversary of Liverpool's royal charter (1857); not only did his gift win him recognition around the world, it got the street named after him.

Other worthies remembered in William Brown Street include Sir James Picton, the architect (the Picton Reading Room), and the brewer Andrew Walker, who paid for the entire cost of the Walker Art Gallery, but for its extension a few years after its opening.

In the same street is the Liverpool Museum which holds the collection of Joseph Mayer, a local jeweller and antique collector who died, aged only 56, in 1886.

The Walker holds the art collection of William Roscoe; mostly Italian, Roscoe's paintings were so renowned that when he went bankrupt, his friends clubbed together and bought the paintings which formed the basis of the Walker's collection.

William Roscoe is usually referred to as 'Liverpool's greatest citizen', and looking at his track record it is hard to imagine how he stuffed so much into one life. Born in 1753, his father was a publican in Mount Pleasant (the Roscoe Head pub is on the site of the old inn); after a spell working for a bookseller, Roscoe became a lawyer, joining Aspinwall in practice in Lord Street; Roscoe's book on jurisprudence won him international recognition.

He then became a banker, and got dragged into the slave trade, which he loathed and campaigned against vociferously as a leading Abolitionist. He was a poet of note, spoke Italian well enough to translate Italian poetry, was an acknowledged historian, an outstanding botanist, an excellent illustrator (his book *Monandrian Plants* is probably the finest book published locally).

Roscoe was a founder of the Liverpool Royal Institution, the Athenaeum and the Lyceum; he set up the first provincial art society in 1773 and founded the Liverpool Academy of Arts in 1810. He became friends with American president Thomas Jefferson – in a letter to Roscoe of 27th December 1820, Jefferson writes, on Roscoe's treatise on penal jurisprudence: 'The great light you have thrown on the subject will, I am sure, be useful to our experiment,' and later in the letter writes: 'Your Liverpool Institution will also aid us in the organisation of our new University, an establishment now in progress in this state, and to which my remaining days and faculties will be devoted.'

The Athenaeum, founded as a newsroom and library in 1797, was the first in Britain (London's did not open for another 27 years), and members included Roscoe, Currie the surgeon, Lace the solicitor and Heywood the banker; the Athenaeum now has a library of over 70,000 books and is recognised as a literary and scientific institution.

Stephen Yip

The United Voluntary Organisation (Liverpool's was the first of its kind in Britain) was set up in 1953. A consortium of local societies raising money for charity, the UVO was a brilliantly simple idea – a forerunner of Give As You Earn – employees of local firms could choose to give a set amount of their weekly wage or salary to be deducted at source and given direct to the UVO, which would then distribute the funds to local charities. In its first year the UVO raised £25,000 for more than 40 charities.

Liverpool held Britain's first Flag Day in 1913 (organised by trade union officer and local politician Alderman Walker) to raise money for the Council of Social Service.

The Marie Curie Foundation, although not with its HQ in Liverpool, was started by a Liverpudlian, Bernard Robinson. Its first-ever Field of Hope – a carpet of more than five million daffodils grown from a million bulbs planted in 1990 to raise money for cancer care – is in Liverpool's Sefton Park.

W hile every town and city can boast a list of patrons and philanthropists, Liverpool's combination of extreme wealth and dire poverty produced an exceptional collection of individuals prepared to give to others. From the almost unbelievable efforts of Kitty Wilkinson, saint of the streets in the cholera epidemics of the 1830s, to businessmen such as John Rankin (1845-1928), chairman of the Bank of Liverpool, of Royal Insurance and of the Pacific Steam Navigation Company, who gave in excess of £1 million to charity during his lifetime.

Many of Liverpool's nonconformist merchants and scholars were generous and benevolent to the needy – names such as Rathbone, Roscoe, Holt, Durning and Booth.

The Jews and the Chinese have strong philanthropic traditions and a powerful sense of community – as, in fact, do all of Liverpool's ethnic groups, from the Welsh to the Somalis. Outside the Christian church groups, the white Saxon/Viking/Irish community is much less cohesive and more dependent on external social structures than their own neighbours. (The League of Welldoers, for instance: Lee Jones, son of a wealthy Alabama cotton planter, was just 23 when in 1893 he started a soup kitchen in Limekiln Lane and went on to start an early form of meals on wheels, taking food to invalids in their homes. Jones died in 1923.)

Little wonder, then, that Liverpool has been in the vanguard of social science and social service. A century before the 1909 Poor Law Commission recommended that voluntary charitable bodies in cities should be co-ordinated, the Liverpool Charitable Institute was doing just that. The natural progression, in 1910, was the establishment of Liverpool's Council of Social Service, chaired by the Lord Mayor Chaloner Dowdall and led by its secretary, Frederic D'Aeth.

In the 1920s Liverpool University pioneered social science as an academic subject; Eleanor Rathbone was one of its first lecturers, and Margaret Simey the first student: she became the first person in the world to get a social science degree.

Still, even in the relative affluence of 2001, Liverpool needs its philanthropists, its campaigners and those prepared to give time and energy to helping others.

No better example than Simon Weston, the Welsh Guardsman whose life was drastically changed in 1982 when an Argentinian bomb hit the ship *Sir Galahad* moored off the Falkland Islands. In 1988 Weston chose Liverpool to launch his charity Weston Spirit, which helps socially excluded youths (21,000 from 1988 to 2001, in six UK towns and cities). Simon Weston was awarded the OBE in 1992, and is a Freeman of the City of Liverpool.

The word indomitable was coined for Margaret Simey; although she is the most civilised, courteous and gentle of women, she is untamed. Attempts to domesticate her failed in her early days as a university wife and they have failed ever since. Many have tried, including several chief constables and government ministers. There is less of the formidable energy evident these days – Mrs Simey no longer leaps up the stairs two at a time as she did aged 89 – but the wildcat spirit is undiminished.

Such zeal could grate after a while, if it weren't for the sparkle of humour and the great warmth she shows for the people she has worked for all her adult life.

A fierce social reformer and local politician, Margaret Simey has been the great champion for Liverpool 8 and Granby, chair of the Police Authority and thorn in the side of the establishment.

Margaret Todd was born in Glasgow in 1906 – there is still a tint of Scots in the voice – but has lived in Liverpool since she was 14. Her father was a lawyer who, unable to make a living in Glasgow, went to teach law in Cairo until the First World War began to loom, when the family came back to Britain. In 1920 he applied for a teaching post at the College of Commerce (one of the constituent parts of the embryonic John Moores University), and the family came to Liverpool. Margaret was expected to go to Oxford University, 'but to my father's horror I wouldn't go. I was offered a place at Somerville, but I said no. New women – horrid lot.'

The new Liverpool University had decided to upgrade social work to a science, to study how a big city manages its affairs, study social groups rather than individual cases. Margaret Todd became the first student of the world's first social science degree course, was taught by Eleanor Rathbone and in return helped Rathbone campaign. 'They despaired of me at the University – I never did any work because I was too busy campaigning.'

She married an academic, Thomas Simey, and when he was appointed a lecturer Mrs Simey was expected to join university wifedom and be good. 'It was such a bore – no nice middle class married women worked – they just sat around. I was a kept woman,' she says.

So she poured her energy, her expertise and her passion into writing, and has never stopped. The latest book, on

social pioneer Frederick D'Aeth, is awaiting publication.

In 1963 Margaret Simey was elected to the city council to represent Granby Ward, which she did for more than 20 years; in 1974 she was appointed chair of the Police Authority, and proceeded to give them hell. Mrs Simey (formally she is Lady Simey, as her husband took a life peerage, but she detests the title) fought bitterly and very publicly with the Chief Constable Kenneth Oxford over the Granby riots in 1981, and tangled with Michael Heseltine afterwards. 'He was misguided. He thought the answer was big business. No – these people long for respect. Who decides how these grants are spent? We should hand the local people the money and say "You choose – we'll help with the business side of things, but it's your responsibility"'.

Margaret Simey is tremendously optimistic about Liverpool, believing it to be a remarkably moral and tolerant city in spite of everything – although there is a desperate need for greater social justice, and she warns of a split society, ignorance on both sides, and complacency.

chapter 11
learning

Too busy making money, Liverpool didn't get round to building itself a university until the end of the 19th century, when a group of enlightened and wealthy merchants proposed a college of higher learning, at a special town's meeting in 1878. On 11th May 1880 the royal charter was sealed, creating Liverpool a city, and on 18th October 1881, Queen Victoria granted a charter to the new University College. For the first 22 years, most University College degrees were awarded by the Federal Victoria University (which also incorporated university colleges in Leeds and Manchester), but on 15th July 1903, the city got its charter 'constituting Liverpool the seat of a separate university to be known as the University of Liverpool' able to award its own degrees; on 4th August the Council held its first meeting in the presence of the Chancellor, the Earl of Derby.

The Council had commissioned local architect, Alfred Waterhouse, to build the Victoria Building, which was completed in 1892; the trademark blood-coloured pressed brick used by 'Slaughterhouse' Waterhouse passed into the language as the 'red-brick university', a term coined by one of the university's own professors, E Allison Peers, professor of Spanish.

New it may have been, but even before it had its university charter, Liverpool had its first Nobel laureate: Sir Ronald Ross, awarded the prize for medicine in recognition of his work on malaria for the School of Tropical Medicine. There have been another seven since: Charles Barkla (1917 physics), Sir Charles Sherrington (1932 medicine), Sir James Chadwick (1935 physics), Sir Robert Robinson (1947 chemistry), HG Khorana (1968 medicine), Rodney Porter (1972 medicine) and Sir Joseph Rotblat (1995 peace).

Since Waterhouse's first university building, the campus has grown and spread to cover 100 acres of the city, within walking distance of the Pier Head – plus another few acres of student halls to the south of the city, on the leafy slopes of Mossley Hill.

With a bit of luck the newest addition to the campus will be ready for the university's centenary, if the builders stick to schedule. Work began in September 2001 on the £23 million Biosciences Centre; it was formally kicked off by the vice chancellor Philip Love, but unlike his predecessors who would have laid a foundation stone, Love shovelled a batch of concrete into the ground floor slab of the new buildings. Not quite as romantic, somehow, but probably more fun than a genteel tapping at a block of sandstone with a trowel.

The University is rare in Britain in having schools of medicine, dentistry, biological sciences, tropical medicine and veterinary science – one of the largest life sciences communities in the country with 450 academic staff, 170 postgrads and 1,000 undergraduates.

> ❛ *At an early age I decided that my main business was with the imponderables, the things that work secretly and have to be apprehended mentally.* ❜
>
> **Sir Oliver Lodge, Professor of Physics 1881-1900**

While Liverpool has been strong on life sciences from its very beginnings, this field is growing at an unprecedented rate worldwide, driven by developments such as the human genome project. The School of Biosciences was formed in 1996 through the merger of three departments: biochemistry, genetics and microbiology, and environmental and evolutionary biology; this is life science across the board, from whole populations down to the building blocks – genomics and proteomics.

Liverpool University had the first department of biochemistry in 1902, the first full-time chair of dentistry in the UK, the first vet school and the first university veterinary hospital in the country, the first honours course in geography, the first department of oceanography, the first institute of coastal oceanography and tides, and was the first university to have a marine biological station (Liverpool's is in Port Erin on the Isle of Man). Liverpool led the way both in social science – offering the first degree course in the 1920s (the very first student was Margaret Simey), and in social anthropology.

But science is not the whole story. Liverpool had the first professorship in Russian and the first British chair of Spanish, both in 1908, the first school of architecture (1895) and the first department of civic design. The University is renowned for its Iberian and Latin American studies, and for Irish studies; it has the largest science fiction collection in Europe.

In a city known as the world capital of pop, it is only right that its University should have the first academic centre devoted to its study. The Institute of Popular Music (part of the 5* rated Department of Music) is becoming an international focus for scholarly activity around this massive industry; it is one of two centres compiling the *Encyclopaedia of Popular Music of the World*. It may seem an unlikely area of intellectual activity, given that bands tend to start with spotty teenagers playing in someone's garage, but the enormous amounts of money to be made, and the fantastically high level of public and media attention it commands, do justify an academic interest. Quite what Chuck Berry or Bill Haley would make of a recent thesis – *Voice & sound recording technology in popular music: towards a semiotics of vocal stream signature* – is hard to imagine.

Sheridan Muspratt (1821-1871), son of the great chemist James Muspratt, was the first British citizen to be awarded an honorary MD by Harvard University, and set up the Liverpool College of Practical Chemistry in 1848. He died at 50, 15 years before his father.

Dr Dora Yates was the world's greatest authority on gypsy lore, and the curator of the Scott Macfie Gypsy Collection.

Sir James Frazer, author of The Golden Bough, *came to Liverpool in 1907 as the first Professor of Social Anthropology, but hated the noise and bustle of the big city. He yearned for the tranquillity of Cambridge and returned there after only a year in Liverpool. He was also said to have been 'disgruntled by the lack of emolument', presumably feeling that if he was to suffer the privations of urban life he should be better paid for it.*

The University Library houses the Science Fiction Foundation collection – the largest of its kind in Europe. SF has only recently begun to get serious critical attention in Britain; the MA in Science Fiction Studies takes in the limits of the genre, its links with political ideologies, the exploration of gender and speculations on the nature of time.

Tung Chee Hwa, chief executive of Hong Kong, was a Liverpool engineering graduate.

Liverpool has the only 5*-rated department of physiology in the country, and is rated eighth in the UK for teaching the classics, ahead of Edinburgh, Durham and King's College London.

Liverpool is one of the major centres in Britain for the study of archaeology, classics and oriental studies; student studies of ancient civilisations cross over with earth sciences, human anatomy and cell biology, geography, evolutionary biology.

Medicine was at the root of Liverpool University – the Medical School's beginnings track back to the founding by Dr Richard Formby of a School of Anatomy in 1818 – and as can be seen from the list of Nobel laureates, medicine and public health have always been world-class disciplines here. In a 2001 league table of medical teaching establishments, Liverpool University overtook Oxford, Cambridge and Imperial College and sits in second place with a teaching score of 92%, a single point behind St George's Hospital medical school in London.

Medicine – albeit a fast-moving science – is a traditional discipline; so, apparently, is business and management. But Liverpool looks at business a little differently. It already offers MBAs in music industries and in football industries, and is now taking students for the UK's first degree in e-business. A study of internet technologies, e-commerce, IT systems, e-business and management studies should equip the next generation of managers and business leaders for an online commercial environment. Despite the reversal of sentiment in the world's stock markets against dotcoms, telecoms and computer-related technologies, and the slower-than-expected growth of online business activity, it is but a blip in the upward graph; a reaction against the febrile excitement of the first dotcom phase. Within the next couple of years the level of online trading should top the trillion dollar mark.

Two of Liverpool's graduates are in the top tier of global business – Robin Saxby, chief executive of ARM Holdings (the world's leading designer of RISC microprocessor chips) and Paul Roy, senior vice president of Merrill Lynch. Both came back to Liverpool to launch the University's new management school (due to open in 2002) that will pull together existing departments of economics and accounting and public administration and add in three key themes: e-business, online learning and entrepreneurship. The new MBA in Entrepreneurship (one of ten available) is the School's flagship programme, recruiting students on the strength of their business ideas as well as on their academic record. The point of this course is that students will apply academic discipline to their own commercial ideas, with mentoring from senior business figures. The dissertation will be a business plan, to be pitched to financiers for start-up funding. It will be fascinating to see how the programme develops, as entrepreneurship is notoriously hard to teach – in fact there are those who say that true entrepreneurs are born, not made.

Robin Saxby, who graduated with an engineering degree in 1968, discovered by chance that he could sell when he joined Motorola, so from being 'a very poor engineer', as he put it, to becoming the boss of a billion-pound business was down to Saxby's innate talents and an element of luck. In 1990 he started ARM with $1.5 million from Apple, and made a personal fortune in the process of taking ARM to the top of the world. A fair old chunk of his fortune he has now given to Liverpool University – some $1.5 million.

The days of flying a business by the seat of one's pants are, by and large, over. There is too much legislation from Europe, too fast-moving a market, and too technical an environment. Let's hope that the good MBA graduates stay in Liverpool to build their businesses rather than taking all that knowledge somewhere else.

As in any good university, Liverpool's range of study is enormous, across the spectra of time, distance, scale and discipline. Even in the general field of 'science' the choice is vast, from forensic pathology (not for the squeamish) to the beautiful and sweet-smelling Botanic Gardens at Ness (gardens given to the University in 1948) where students research plant and environment science, including big projects on recycling and global warming.

Over 76% of the first graduates from LIPA got jobs in their specialist sector.

When Liverpool Polytechnic was established in 1970, it brought together four colleges: art, design & building, commerce, and technology. Later additions included City College of Higher Education, the IM Marsh College of Physical Education, the FL Calder College of Home Economics and the Liverpool College of Nursing & Midwifery. The Polytechnic became Liverpool John Moores University in 1992.

Liverpool Hope University College has a long reach, with international links to Akure in Nigeria, Bucharest, and Ladakh in the Indian Himalayas.

JMU's European Institute of Urban Affairs is a dedicated team of consultant researchers in areas of crucial concern to urban policy makers throughout the world.

Ambitious screenwriters can apply for the Linda la Plante scholarship at JMU's School of Media, Critical & Creative Arts.

Just as Liverpool has two cathedrals and two football teams, the city has two universities – and a university college. There are over 60,000 higher education students in Liverpool overall, 20,000 of them from outside the region.

The three HE institutions alone employ more than 8,000 people, and the local economy benefits from education and training by over £1 billion a year.

Liverpool John Moores University (JMU), established in 1992 from the old polytechnic, is now one of the largest in the country with 20,000 students. JMU made giant strides in the last decade under the energetic and entrepreneurial leadership of vice chancellor Peter Toyne, building its reputation, its numbers and its infrastructure to make a serious impact on the city. Toyne's successor is the American physicist Professor Michael Brown, while the chancellor is Cherie Booth QC.

JMU encompasses the Liverpool Art School (alma mater of John Lennon), LIPA (the Liverpool Institute of Performing Arts) and now the International Centre for Digital Content, backed by Phil Redmond, creator of *Brookside* and head of Mersey Television. ICDC will explore the impact of the digital revolution on business behaviour and society in general.

Taking a new approach to a traditional industry is JMU's Centre for Automotive Studies, which runs the Merseyside Automotive Group, which has a series of manufacturing improvement programmes and has set up an automotive e-community. The blueprint for other groups around the country, MAG is another first for Liverpool.

So is the Foundation for Citizenship – the brainchild of former Mossley Hill MP David Alton, now Lord Alton of Liverpool – which was set up at JMU to promote the ethos of citizenship in the community, and particularly to develop an ethical culture amongst schoolchildren. Awards for good citizenship, and a stunning series of prestigious Roscoe Lectures (recent speakers include Lord Robertson, head of NATO, Greg Dyke, director general of the BBC, Don McKinnon, Commonwealth Secretary General, and Lord Howe.

What spurred Lord Alton to establish the Foundation were the concerns about the increasing isolation of the individual in the modern city and the fracturing of communities; the low levels of participation in local and national elections and the lack of understanding about each person's duties in a democratic society; and the lack of any teaching of citizenship at school. Said Professor Alton: 'All 600 schools on Merseyside are part of our award scheme; the initiative is now being used as a national blueprint and citizenship is being taught on the national curriculum. I passionately believe that it's a subject which should also be experienced. Real-life stories of courage and devotion help to inspire others and underline that the region's finest resource is its people.'

Aldham Robarts building

LIPA

Hope (Liverpool Hope University College) is a church foundation, and unique as an ecumenical university college; its council is chaired in rotation by the Archbishop and Bishop of Liverpool, and it has the only Professor of Theology & Public Life (Ian Markham), neatly bridging the gap between church and commerce. As well as the main campus at Hope Park, the college has invested millions in Hope in Everton, Hope on the Waterfront and even Hope at Liverpool Airport. In Everton, the old St Francis Xavier school has been redeveloped as Hope's arts faculty, injecting some vibrancy into an area long dormant. Under the inspiring direction of chief executive Simon Lee, Hope's ethos of regeneration through education extends far beyond Liverpool boundaries, through its links in Africa, Eastern Europe and India.

Paul McCartney, the Beatle who has maintained the strongest links with Liverpool, weighed in to the city's education sector with huge financial backing to turn his old school into the Liverpool Institute of Performing Arts (LIPA), and persuaded some of the world's top performers to kick in as well. The result is the country's focal point for training in the entertainment industry, with a degree course validated by JMU offering six specialisms from acting, dance and music to enterprise management, performance design and technology.

Liverpool Community College is one of the largest FE colleges in the UK with more than 20,000 students taking over 600 academic and vocational courses; its new £8.5 million Arts Centre is the largest in the country. The College gives access to people who have been excluded from education before, with a fee waiver budget, free nurseries, English language support, even a fund to help students buy or borrow essential materials and equipment.

The Women's Technology Centre at Blackburne House was highlighted as a model of good practice in the Kennedy report on widening participation in further education. Blackburne House, in Liverpool 8, encourages all local women to explore their potential through courses from basic skills to advanced electronic engineering, computing and telematics. Driven forward by director Claire Dove, Blackburne House is a keystone of Liverpool's innovative education sector.

Adult education is thriving in Liverpool: the city council offers some 600 courses; the Workers' Educational Association runs another 150, and Liverpool University 500 more.

Bluecoat School in Church Road, near Penny Lane; the
original 1700s building is in School Lane

Education was a patchy process before the 20th century: there was high quality private education for the children – or rather the sons – of the wealthy; their daughters were mostly taught at home, and taught just enough to catch a good husband and run a home. From about 1750 there were some charitable schools of varying quality for the deserving poor, but a huge proportion of Liverpool's children remained unburdened with book learning, and mostly condemned to a battle for survival at the bottom of the economic and social heap.

As an example of the arbitrary nature of education in past times, John Crosse, patrician owner of Crosse Hall, founded the town's first grammar school in 1515 and allowed any poor boy called Crosse to attend for free. Everyone else paid up or didn't get in.

In 1709 the Bluecoat Charity School was founded by slaver Bryan Blundell at the instigation of Robert Stithe, vicar of St Nicholas church. The children were fed as well as taught: breakfast was bread and cocoa, but boys' education ended when they were 12 and girls' learning was focused on getting a place in domestic service. Later in the 1700s churches began to set up charity schools; the first Unitarian free school was opened in 1790, the first Catholic school opened in 1792 on Copperas Hill, followed over the next decade or so by Welsh Chapel, Anglican and Scots Presbyterian schools.

The first girls' high school in the country was founded at Blackburne House in 1844; John Blackburne's country house was bought by George Holt, who had also had a hand in the foundation of the Liverpool Institute for Boys. The Institute, which began life as the Mechanics' Institute in 1835, is where Paul McCartney went to school; it has now reached its third incarnation as the Liverpool Institute of Performing Arts.

Catholic priest Father James Nugent spent much of his life trying to help poor children, and in 1855 opened two Catholic schools to take children from the streets. Around the same time the Anglican priest Major Lester established a Ragged School in Kirkdale where poor children were fed, clothed and taught crafts and trades.

The Liverpool Collegiate Institution, founded in 1839, was the first public school in the country (it was followed by Cheltenham, Marlborough, Rossall, Lancing and Wellington over the next 20 years); the school building in Shaw Street has a magnificent Gothic facade.

At the beginning of the 21st century, when education is a right for all, there is still an appalling percentage of children being failed by the system, emerging after more than a decade of schooling illiterate, innumerate – but in Liverpool very rarely inarticulate. These are not stupid children – they need something the system isn't offering. One school set up to provide what these kids need is the Elimu Academy, in Dove Street, Granby. So-called 'problem' children are proving to be successes after graduating; these were mainly black teenagers who had been excluded from other schools. Mixed in with their academic subjects are fun lessons such as circus skills – designed to motivate them and raise their self-esteem. Some of the graduates want to stay on at school, then go on to college or university.

For some reason education has never been celebrated in England as it is elsewhere. Most children drag themselves into school in the morning, have to be cajoled and entertained in the classroom, and can't wait for release. Talk to families from other cultures, though, and get a different perspective. Talk to Kosovans, or Chinese, or Nigerians living in the city, and discover that for these children school is a privilege, it is exciting, and stimulating, and very, very important. They need no encouraging to study and on average do better than white English children – despite, in some cases, having to cope first with a new language.

1809: the first female school of industry instituted.
1876: first school for cookery & domestic science.

Jessie Crosbie MBE was the headmistress of St Augustine's Church of England school in Vauxhall. In the 1920s, Vauxhall was the poorest ward in the country, and her pupils had a tough time of it. Since Crosbie believed children could learn better in decent conditions (ie food, safety and hygiene) Crosbie started the first school meals service: she found food (often paying for it herself), cooked and served it to hungry children. She set up the first evening play scheme, to keep latchkey kids off the streets. She set up the first school washrooms and baths for children to help get rid of nits and fleas.

The Women's Hospital

Since a group of enlightened doctors in Liverpool formed the Medical Library in 1779, medicine in this city started to see remarkable progress. Among that group was Dr Matthew Dobson, who in 1776 discovered diabetes melitus by testing the urine of his patients for sugar; he defined this as 'the failure of the body to assimilate sugar'. Dobson also discovered that the human body's temperature stays virtually constant at 98.6°, unaffected by the environment (barring extreme conditions).

John Bostock, a local doctor, discovered in 1804 that the digestive process creates carbon dioxide; two years later he identified the three principal constituents of bodily fluids, and in 1819 was the first to describe hayfever and its symptoms. The same year, one of Bostock's colleagues, James Carson, developed the artificial pneumothorax (injection of gas or air into the pleural cavity) to help tuberculosis patients.

The Liverpool Medical Society was formed in 1833 'for the promotion of medical research and knowledge'; medicine had, until the 18th century, been a matter of quacks, leeches and haphazard surgery. One quack, however, paved the way for a branch of medicine that would acquire the label orthopaedics. Evan Thomas, living in Crosshall Street at the beginning of the 19th century, had a reputation as a clever bonesetter despite having no medical training. He was sued three times by the medical profession but vindicated each time, to popular acclaim. But his enemies did not give up, and when he retired his cottage was burned down.

Evan Thomas's son Hugh Owen (born in 1834) qualified as a doctor and had a free clinic in Chinatown at 11 Nelson Street; he developed a way of re-breaking bones that had set badly so they could heal properly. His book *Knee, Hip and Ankle* was dismissed in Britain, but regarded as a masterpiece in America. Hugh Owen Thomas's nephew, Sir Robert Jones confirmed Liverpool as the cradle of orthopaedics, founding the world's first orthopaedic hospital. He was once visited by Buffalo Bill Cody, who presented him with a pistol.

Sailors coming home to Liverpool with tropical diseases were bad for Liverpool's maritime trade (not to mention the well-being of the sailors), so Joseph Chamberlain, secretary of state for the colonies, asked for help to research tropical disease and train doctors in their treatment. The result was the School of Tropical Medicine, founded in Liverpool in 1898 – the first in the world. Driving force behind its foundation was Sir Alfred Lewis Jones, head of the Elder Dempster shipping line, which virtually monopolised trade with West Africa.

It was the first British medical institution to gain a Nobel prize for medicine. In 1902 Sir Ronald Ross, the School's first lecturer, won the prize for his discovery that malaria was transmitted by a mosquito. Even today up to two million children a year die from malaria; it is one of the School's most high-profile programmes, both here and in the Third World.

Two other discoveries to note are the identification by Everett Dutton of the tsetse fly carrying sleeping sickness (1901), and in 1905 the cause of tick-born relapsing fever of which he was to become infected and die. The School's reputation has been built on its work on malaria, tuberculosis and HIV/Aids, but there is other world-leading research going on. Dr Alistair Reid, for instance, was one of the world's top toxicologists; the venom research unit is a world reference centre for snake bites, recognised by the World Health Organisation.

Professor Alexander Trees has discovered a cure for onchocerciasis – river blindness – which affects more than 17 million people. Trees discovered that the parasite causing the disease (discovered by Professor Blacklock) can be killed by antibiotics.

Exactly 100 years after scientists at the School identified the parasite that causes elephantiasis, Professor David Molyneux and his team have been invited to join an international network of scientists dedicated to finding a cure by the end of the decade. Elephantiasis is a hideous, disfiguring disease that affects 120 million people in 80 countries; it is a mosquito-borne infection that makes limbs, breasts and genitals swell causing great pain and anguish – sufferers are often ostracised because of their disfigurement.

Public health and tropical paediatrics are priorities for the School, which runs the only diploma course in reproductive health.

Now the School has its first female boss: Professor Janet Hemingway, aged 44, joined the School in September 2001 from Cardiff University, where she was head of entomology. Her team of 29 researchers has also joined the School to boost work into insect-born diseases.

Professor Brian Maegraith, former dean of the School of Tropical Medicine, helped establish the Faculty of Tropical Medicine in Bangkok in 1959. It is the biggest and most active school in South East Asia, and 80% of its senior staff have graduated from the Liverpool School.

One of the most famous pedlars of patent medicines was Dr Samuel Solomon MD, a member of one of the leading Jewish families in Liverpool at the start of the 1800s. Almost certainly unqualified as a doctor, he made his fortune from his Balm of Gilead, a cure for almost everything. He is remembered in Liverpool by three streets in Kensington: Gilead Street, Balm Street and Solomon Street.

Professor Roderick Gregory spent months at the Stanley Abattoir grinding down the intestines of 18,500 cattle to isolate a microgram of the digestive hormone gastrin.

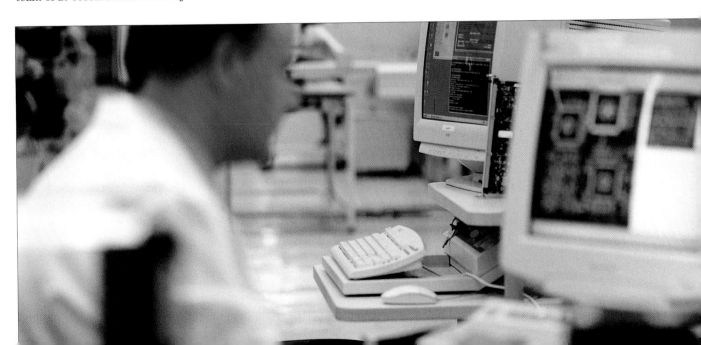

In 1944 Dr Cecil Gray and Dr John Halton pioneered the use of South American poison curare as a muscle relaxant in conjunction with an anaesthetic. Gray became Professor of Anaesthesia at Liverpool University.

Professor William Blair-Bell was a great pioneer of chemotherapy in the treatment of cancer in the first half of the 20th century.

Frederick Donnan held the Brunner Chair of Physical Chemistry in Liverpool (1903-1913) – the first in the UK. His work on semi-permeable membranes was an important stepping stone in the search for a treatment for diabetes.

Richard Caton, Liverpool University College's professor of physiology from 1882 to 1891, was the first to detect electrical activity in the brain (he must have had a brainwave ...), which led to the invention of the electroencephalograph (EEG). Another forerunner in the field of neuroscience was William Alexander, a surgeon at the Royal Southern Hospital and consulting surgeon at the Epileptic Institution in Maghull. Alexander published a work on the treatment of epilepsy in 1889, which included a chapter on brain surgery – almost unheard of in his day.

Another Nobel prizewinner for Liverpool was Sir Charles Sherrington, president of the Royal Society. His pioneering work at Liverpool University (where he built a physiology department of world renown) included discovering the synapse (connections between brain cells) and describing the motor functions of the spinal chord – an unconscious reaction to a close external stimulus. He won the Nobel prize in 1932 for his work on motor behaviour.

Liverpool has a remarkable record in the field of radiology. Oliver Lodge, Liverpool University's first professor of physics, worked (among a long list of other projects) on medical X-rays with Dr Robert Jones and Thurstan Holland. They installed an X-ray machine in the Royal Southern Hospital in 1896 (the first hospital to have a radiology department). Asked to look for a bullet in a child's wrist, Holland made the first X-ray plate, and Lodge found the bullet. Further work on X-rays was done by Professor Charles Barkla who came to Liverpool in 1902 as holder of the Oliver Lodge Fellowship; his work included the polarisation of X-rays (1904) and the description of their characteristics (1906).

One of the most outstanding physicians of the 20th century was Sir Cyril Clarke, Emeritus Professor of Medicine at Liverpool University. Born in 1907, Clarke came to Liverpool after the war as consultant at the Northern Hospital. He switched to an academic career, soon being appointed as professor, and honorary consultant physician at the Royal Infirmary and Broadgreen Hospital.

Clarke was a popular teacher, and many of his students were outstanding; David Price Evans did ground-breaking work in pharmacogenetics and his most successful house physician, David Weatherall, became Regius Professor of Medicine at Oxford and founded the Institute of Molecular Medicine.

Clarke's passion for butterflies led to his most important research; he perfected a technique of hand-mating butterflies and produced some rare hybrids. He began to research into butterfly genetics with Professor Philip Sheppard, and later extended the genetic research into medicine. Working first on the relationship between ABO blood groups and peptic ulcers, Clarke then turned his attention to the Rhesus factor.

The group of genes that controls the colour of butterflies' coats are called polygenes: similar genetic groups control inheritance in Rhesus blood groups. Working with Richard McConnell, Clarke researched the potentially fatal condition that can occur when a Rhesus negative mother has a Rhesus positive spouse, producing a baby with Rh Haemolytic Disease. Clarke's team developed a method in 1966 to prevent RHD which has been in use since 1975, saving several hundred thousand lives.

Professor Ronald Finn – part of that team – said of Clarke: 'He was rather shy, with a total lack of pomposity. He was a great team leader – charisma and boundless energy were clearly evident.' But for all his academic success (even after becoming president of the Royal College of Physicians), Clarke was a doctor first, said Finn: 'For Cyril Clarke, patient care came first, and all other aspects of medicine, however important, came second.'

Professor Ole Petersen

Liverpool John Moores University is the first in the world to have a validated MSc in homeopathic medicine. JMU also offers a BSc degree course in science and football, looking at the psychology, biomechanics and physiology of the world's most high profile sport.

Between 1998 and 2003 the annual intake of undergraduates to Liverpool Medical School will have risen by 50%, with 308 students starting their degree course in September 2003.

Work continues at both of Liverpool's universities on ground-breaking medical innovations as well as in battering against the diseases, stresses and physical abnormalities that afflict humanity. As the cradle of orthopaedics, it is maybe not surprising that Liverpool is a world centre of excellence in the repair and replacement of elbow and shoulder joints.

Pancreatitis affects more than 10,000 people in the UK each year; at the moment there is no known cure, and one in 10 dies from complications brought on by the disease. A group of researchers at Liverpool University, led by Professors Ole Petersen and John Neoptolemos, has made a breakthrough in understanding what causes pancreatitis, and might have pointed the way to a cure. The group found that sudden rises in levels of calcium in the body can trigger enzymes which, instead of digesting food in the gut, start to digest the pancreas, causing serious damage. Trials are now planned to see if drugs to stop the rise in calcium in the pancreas can stop the disease in its tracks.

In a joint venture with Manchester University, a national centre for tissue engineering is being set up by Liverpool University's department of clinical engineering, led by Professor David Williams. With a research grant of £9.7 million, the Interdisciplinary Research Collaboration (IRCol) will research ways of producing connective tissue to repair the human body inside and out. The two world-class teams will look at putting cells in place and giving the body the right chemical signals to persuade it to heal itself.

In the heart and blood system, for instance, this research could lead to the body regrowing damaged arteries. Blocked and furred-up arteries are the most common cause of heart attacks, but grafting in new ones or bypassing them means open-heart surgery and long-term treatment. The north-west team beat off competition from 19 other university groups.

Professor David Williams

The three higher education institutions in Liverpool, as well as a strong group of life science and technology companies, are continually pushing at the constraining boundaries of scientific thinking – as Liverpool's bright and curious minds have been doing for centuries. There is pure research, done for its own sake, and there is research done with a view to commercial, medical or humanitarian use.

Liverpool University's Lairdside Laser Centre, for instance, offers designers and manufacturers laser processing and a rapid prototyping service that speeds innovation to market and cuts development costs: it is one of only two centres of its kind in Europe.

At JMU, the Research Institute for Sport & Exercise Sciences has developed a revolutionary new football boot for sports equipment makers Umbro. The boot uses a new material which promotes maximum friction on the ball without loss of touch or feel; a new stud configuration improves the player's ability to turn on soft ground. The new boot – the XA1, made its debut in the FA Cup Final on the feet of Liverpool star Michael Owen.

The two universities are collaborating on a £3 million research project to explore both the fundamental nature of matter and energy, and the structure of the universe: the Liverpool Semiconductor Detector Centre. LU's high energy physics group and nuclear structure group will use the Centre to design and build detectors for leading experiments around the world; JMU's astrophysics team will use the facility for the Liverpool Telescope.

Funded by the European Objective One programme for Merseyside, MerseyBIO has been set up to build a thriving bioscience business community. Within the universities, the NHS Trusts and the private sector are bits of science that could have lucrative commercial potential, if only they can be recognised, exploited and brought to market effectively.

Heading the MerseyBIO team is John McQuilliam, a Liverpool graduate who has already taken a biotech idea through commercial development and sold it to a major British plc. 'We are not only looking for world-class science but for entrepreneurial scientists with the vision and determination to build an enterprise potentially worth millions, if not billions of pounds and employing significant numbers of local people.' There are already six serious ideas being developed; each proto-business will make use of MerseyBIO's incubation centre and the access to venture capital and development funding for the long-term innovation process. Pure research delves into improbable possibilities, but applied research finds a use for the results, and innovation can turn science into jobs and better lives.

In the late 1870s the geologist Thomas Reade discovered through his work on the sedimentation of rocks that the Earth is many times older than previously thought. Reade proposed that the Earth was around 1,000 million years old, 10 times older than the thinking at the time.

Another of Liverpool's Nobel laureates was Sir Robert Robinson, professor of chemistry at the University from 1915 to 1919. He won his prize for work on alkaloid biosynthesis.

To give schoolchildren a chance to take part in the astrotelescope project at JMU, Dr Martin Faulkes has commissioned two more from Telescope Technology (JMU's spin-off company) donating £4 million to build two identical robotic telescopes in Hawaii and Australia. Faulkes, a cosmologist, made millions by investing in the computer software industry here and in the USA. School children will have access to the telescope images via the JMU website.

The start of the nuclear weapons industry is linked to Liverpool – and maybe one day the end of it – through two of the University's most famous scientists, Sir James Chadwick and Sir Joseph Rotblat. While Chadwick won his Nobel Prize for physics in 1935 for discovering the neutron before leading the development of the atom bomb, Rotblat was awarded the Nobel Peace Prize in 1995 for his work with Pugwash, the extraordinary international group of scientists bent on ending war and ridding the world of nuclear weapons. Rotblat worked alongside Chadwick at Liverpool and on the Manhattan Project in the USA to develop the atom bomb – and has spent much of the rest his life campaigning against it.

Chadwick's story is remarkable, not least for its beginning. Born in Cheshire in 1891, James Chadwick went to enrol at Manchester University in 1907 for a mathematics course, but found himself in a queue of hopeful physics students. Chadwick, too embarrassed to say anything, ended up doing physics by mistake. After working for two years under Ernest Rutherford on radioactivity and getting his MSc in 1913, Chadwick went to Germany to work for Hans Geiger and, trapped by the outbreak of war in 1914, spent four years interned in a stable at a racetrack which had been hastily pressed into service as a prison camp.

Returning to England, Chadwick went to Rutherford's laboratory in Cambridge in 1919; in 1932 Chadwick proved the existence of neutrons (atomic particles with no electrical charge), which could split the nuclei of the heaviest elements. This, then, was the path towards the fission of the Uranium 235 isotope, and the creation of the atom bomb. It was for this work that Chadwick was given the Nobel Prize in 1935, by which time he had moved to Liverpool to take the Lyon Jones Chair of Physics.

With Rotblat on his team, Chadwick went to the United States in 1943 as head of the British mission on the Manhattan Project to build the bomb. After the war Chadwick – now Sir James – came back to Liverpool for another two years before returning to Cambridge as Master of Gonville and Caius in 1948; he died in 1974.

Joseph Rotblat was born in Warsaw in 1908, got his doctorate there in 1938 and came to Liverpool the following year on the Oliver Lodge Fellowship. After the Manhattan Project, Rotblat stayed in Liverpool as senior lecturer, then director of research in nuclear physics. In 1950 he went to London as Professor of Physics at St Bartholomew's Hospital College. To say Rotblat's CV is distinguished is an understatement; but throughout his post-war career, he has been a driving force behind Pugwash.

Ten years after the bomb destroyed Hiroshima and Nagasaki, Joseph Rotblat chaired a press conference to launch the Russell-Einstein Manifesto – a powerful declaration by 11 of the world's top scientists and scholars, every one of them Nobel laureates, against armed conflict and nuclear weapons. The Manifesto called on scientists of all political persuasions to come together to discuss the nuclear threat posed to civilisation. To the first meeting, in Pugwash, Nova Scotia, came 22 scientists from the US, Russia, Canada, the UK, Australia, Austria, China, France and Poland. To the end of 1999 there have been more than 250 Pugwash conferences, and there are now over 3,500 Pugwashites around the world, exerting influence – purely as private individuals – upon governments, organisations and public opinion. Said Rotblat in 1995: 'We are gradually coming to appreciate the futility of war; we are slowly learning how to resolve conflicts without resorting to military confrontation. We are not there yet. But, in the meantime, the human species may be brought to an end by the use of the tools of destruction, themselves the products of science and technology.'

Star-gazing has been a passion of Liverpool scientists for almost 400 years. The first and greatest of them – the father of English astronomy – was Jeremiah Horrox, born in Toxteth Park in 1619. An undoubted genius, he died at the tragically early age of 23, but even in that short life he made his mark on science. He went up to Cambridge at 14 to learn the secrets of the universe, but frustrated by the hidebound thinking of the establishment, came back to Toxteth after graduating and started to construct his own theories about the motions of celestial bodies.

Horrox realised, from close observations of the stars, moon and planets, that what he saw did not fit the map based on the *Almagest* – the masterpiece of 2nd-century Alexandrian mathematician Claudius Ptolemaeus (Ptolemy) – which had been the bible of astronomers for more than 1,000 years. Horrox was excited by the controversial work of Polish astronomer Copernicus (who in about 1530 discovered that the planets revolved around the sun) and his follower Keppler (who discovered that planets had an elliptical orbit). Horrox produced a model of planetary motion, based on experiments with a conical pendulum, that was almost heretical in its challenge to orthodox thinking.

The first person to predict the transit of Venus across the face of the sun, Horrox also calculated the distance of the Earth from the sun by observing the solar parallax. He worked out a detailed theory of the moon's motion, realised that planets exerted forces on each other (Newton was not to publish his theory of gravitational attraction for more than 40 years), and discovered irregularities in the motions of Jupiter and Saturn.

Horrox died in 1641 and is buried at the Ancient Chapel of Toxteth.

Isaac Roberts was a pioneer in astrophotography, the first to make long exposures of nebulae and star clusters, in 1886. His photograph of the Pleiades (the Seven Sisters) showed previously unsuspected nebulosity; he exposed Andromeda as a spiral nebula and the nearest to Earth.

The Liverpool Astronomical Society was founded by the Reverend TE Espin in 1881 (nine years before the British society was set up almost as a splinter group from the LAS). Within five years, the LAS had branches in Brazil and Australia and counted Dom Pedro III, Emperor of Brazil, amongst its members. Despite a turbulent history, the LAS is still going strong 120 years later.

Comets like Hale-Bopp would have been much easier to see over the dark 17th century city

Lassell's reflecting telescopes had mirrors made of speculum, an alloy of tin and copper, which keeps its polish for a long time. The mirror for his 24-inch telescope weighed 370 lbs (168 kg); the whole telescope on its stone supports weighed over five tons.

James Nasmyth, the foundryman who invented the steam hammer, built the machine that Lassell invented to grind and polish his speculum mirrors.

What a shame that the word 'amateur' has come to mean someone bumbling or inept. The word, literally, means a person who does something for the love of it rather than for money – and there is no better example of a grand amateur than William Lassell, one of Britain's greatest astronomers in the 19th century. Lassell was not a trained scientist but a brewer who made his fortune from the thirsty Scousers who built and operated the great seaport in the early 1800s.

His parents were of good Toxteth Park nonconformist stock, although William was born in Bolton in 1799. The family moved back to Liverpool in 1815, William got himself apprenticed to a wine merchant, then, at the age of 25 set up in business for himself, as a brewer. Within five years he had made his pile and could concentrate on his great passion for astronomy.

It was not the distant stars that drew Lassell, but the planets in our own solar system.

The great thing about the grand amateur is that he is not reliant on research grants or sponsorship; he is not constrained by academic protocol and politics. Lassell had been building telescopes since he was 21, but it was in 1840 that he designed and built his first revolutionary instrument – a nine-inch telescope that was immediately recognised by the Royal Astronomical Society as a brilliant piece of engineering.

For Lassell to observe his first and enduring fascination – Saturn – he needed a telescope that was not only optically excellent, but rock-steady and able to produce a continuous image as the heavens moved around the Earth. Lassell, in his observatory at Starfield, his house in West Derby, built first the nine-inch, then set about his great masterpiece, the 24-inch reflecting telescope which is the direct ancestor of the world's largest robotic telescope being built by astronomers at Liverpool John Moores University and installed in the Canary Islands in the autumn of 2001.

assell's brilliance as an engineer earned him an international reputation; not only his superb mirror, but his solution to mounting the heavy telescope on a smooth roller-bearing controlled, iron equatorial mount. Until then astronomers such as Rosse and the Herschels had been tugging their great wooden tubes about with ropes and could never get the smooth tracking required for good observation.

Already having earned his place in history, Lassell then made great discoveries. When Neptune was discovered in Berlin in September 1846, Lassell was told of it within days and immediately trained his 24-inch on the 'new' planet and saw that Neptune had a satellite, which was later named Triton. In 1848 Lassell found Saturn's eighth satellite, Hyperion, at the same time (within a day) as American astronomer Bond. Two years later, Lassell noted Saturn's innermost ring; the following year he found two moons around Uranus: Ariel and Umbriel. In 1858 Lassell built his monster 48-inch telescope and took it to Malta where he had clearer skies than in cloudy, smoky Liverpool, and continued making discoveries and deepening understanding about the planets and star clusters such the Orion Nebula.

Lassell's standing within the international scientific community was of the highest, and when Queen Victoria came to Liverpool in 1851, Lassell was the only local figure she specifically asked to see. It is said that the Queen rose and went to meet Lassell as he entered the room – a thing almost unheard of, and a clear indication of how highly he was regarded. Quite a celebrity for the time.

It is probable that, but for an unhappy accident, Liverpool could have claimed the discovery of Neptune. In October 1845 an astronomer called Dawes wrote to Lassell about the computations of a Cambridge undergraduate, John Couch Adams, of the location of Neptune. Lassell was laid up with a sprained ankle and couldn't get to his telescope; Dawes' letter was lost by a housemaid, and Liverpool lost the chance of the planet's discovery.

Lassell claimed that his speculum mirror was as close to optically perfect as it could get. In 1995 the original mirror, still in Liverpool, was tested and found to be accurate to within a fraction of a wavelength of light.

The 24 inch telescope was about 30 feet high and weighed about two tons (with its stone supports the total weight was more than five tons); the main tube was 20 feet long (the 24 inches refers to the size of the aperture).

185

O liver Lodge, aged 30, was the first Professor of Physics at Liverpool's new University College, and spent a remarkably productive 19 years here from 1881 to 1900. Arguably his greatest contribution to modern life was his development of radio, beating Marconi to the first radio transmission and patenting radio tuning. Why Lodge never won a Nobel prize is utterly perplexing – although some say it is because of his high-profile involvement in spiritualism and psychical research.

Declared one of the top brains in Britain in 1930, along with George Bernard Shaw, Churchill and Lord Birkenhead, Lodge was not only a brilliant physicist but could explain his ideas clearly to the layman and inspire the raw science undergraduate.

Born in 1851 near Stoke, Lodge left school at 14 and worked for his father selling glazes and clays to potteries until he went to stay with his aunt in London, heard some lectures at the Royal Institution and 'got impregnated with physics', as he put it. Fired up, he went back to education and got his doctorate. In his autobiography he wrote: 'At an early age I decided that my main business was with the imponderables, the things that work secretly and have to be apprehended mentally.'

Lodge's genius led him to all sorts of different fields of thought and experiment, from spark plugs and electrolysis to thought transference. He investigated lightning, the voltaic cell and electrolysis; he worked on electromagnetic waves and studied the nature of the ether. His electric spark ignition system for the internal combustion engine led to his sons forming the Lodge Plug Company; he and Thurstan Holland were early pioneers of medical X-rays in 1896, and the following year Lodge calculated the size of the electron.

Academically regarded as his greatest piece of research, Lodge's experiments with ether drag were an important step towards Einstein's theory of relativity. Ether – the vacuum or void between particles of matter in which energy moves – was a hot topic in the 1890s; American scientists Michelson and Morley had shown that there was no detectable 'ether wind', and Lodge took the next step in 1891. He set up two steel discs a metre in diameter, revolving at 4,000 rpms, and measured the velocity of light close to the discs and again away from them. Had there been any difference in the two measurements, then it would have been possible that moving bodies do drag the ether along. Lodge's results were negative – no ether drag.

Lodge could be said to have 'invented' radio – in that he sent the world's first radio message in 1894 (Marconi didn't make his breakthrough until 1895) although with such a huge invention no one person can really claim the credit.

Such a milestone as radio is reached by a long process of development, and Lodge's friend Heinrich Hertz had proved the existence of electromagnetic radio waves in free space in 1888. It was Lodge who developed the coherer, a sensitive detector – what we know as a radio receiver; in 1894 he was asked to demonstrate his apparatus to members of the British Association. The first radio message was transmitted, on 14th August, from the Clarendon Laboratory through two stone walls and across a distance of 180 feet to the lecture theatre in the Oxford Museum.

In 1897 Lodge set up a transmitter at the top of the Victoria clock tower on Brownlow Hill, and a receiver on the roof of Lewis's store in Ranelagh Place, about half a mile away at the bottom of the hill. His long-distance wireless messages began to have a very practical use for Lodge – he would send messages to his wife to let her know he was on his way home.

Lodge was the first to apply for a patent for the wireless and patented his radio tuning apparatus; he later applied successfully for an extension to his patent, effectively invalidating the Marconi patents, so the Marconi company agreed to buy Lodge out and appointed him scientific advisor to the company. But it is Marconi (whose work was first announced in Liverpool) who achieved so much in the commercial development of the wireless, and who is now thought of as Mr Radio, and not Oliver Lodge.

It isn't hard to see why Lodge was so fascinated by psychic phenomena; he had started investigating in 1883, alongside his academic work on ether, energy and matter, when Malcolm Guthrie asked him to join his experiments in thought transference. Lodge, who saw no end to the possibilities of physics, joined the Society of Psychical Research with the likes of John Ruskin, Lord Tennyson, Lewis Carroll and Arthur Conan Doyle. 'There is no further room in my mind for doubt ... that things hitherto held impossible do actually occur,' said Lodge.

The modern links between new physics and spirituality is something that Oliver Lodge would heartily applaud.

chapter 12
living

David's Throne was a tree-covered headland separating the two glens through which the Dingle stream ran into the Mersey between sandstone cliffs in beautifully eroded formations.

In 1874 Liverpool had the first Parks Police in the country.

In the early 1800s, Liverpool was the most popular bathing resort in Lancashire, with a line of bathing machines stretching for a full mile along the North Shore, to the sandhills of Seaforth. A little further north, the rural area around Bootle was renowned for golden sandhills, 'where genteel company resort for sea-bathing and sea air in the summer months', according to Moss's guide in 1799. South of the city, Mather's Dam – a reservoir formed from a stream at the top of Upper Warwick Street – was a favourite swimming place for local youngsters.

Birkenhead Park, landscaped by Joseph Paxton, was the model for New York's Central Park.

The eyebrows of first-time visitors to the city, expecting only urban grunge and industrial sprawl, usually climb to the hairline at the sight of the city's modern and ancient greenery. The racket of 21st century life is inaudible in the rustling, leafy heart of the parks and woodlands of Liverpool. The Victorians weren't slow. It didn't take them too long to work out that an obscenely overcrowded city led to disease and crime. When Liverpool's population increased logarithmically in the 18th and early 19th centuries, disease inevitably followed as the streets were crammed with immigrant families wanting work, and those longing to escape Britain's shores for the New World. Liverpool was one of the world's richest cities, but had an average life expectancy of just 32.

The extreme conditions led to medical, social and charitable innovation and reform; including the great parks laid out around the city – in the eight years from 1864 the Corporation created nearly 500 acres of parkland.

In Liverpool alone there are now a million trees in over 2,500 acres of parks and open spaces, making this one of the greenest cities in Britain. It is perfectly possible in Liverpool to plan long walks through parks and woodlands with hardly a sniff of a car. And given that Liverpool has lower pollution levels and cleaner air than some rural areas, let alone other cities, it is perfectly possible to escape the metropolis for a while without leaving the city boundaries. Sit in the delightful little park around Sudley House on the top of Mossley Hill, and stare out over the Mersey to the Welsh mountains; on a clear day you can see Snowdon. Walk through the woods of Woolton and Childwall, the ancient Black Wood, or the little Priory Wood at St Michaels in the Hamlet and forget about tarmac for a bit.

One of the most beautiful golf courses on Merseyside (or anywhere, come to that) is the municipal course at Allerton, where you can walk for hours in peace, albeit with the risk of having to duck a whizzing golf ball from a sliced tee shot.

The creation of parks didn't start – or stop – with the Victorians. Over 100 years earlier, in 1726, the burgesses of Liverpool bought a spent sandstone quarry and landscaped it for the pleasure of the people. Mount Zion – close to where the Anglican Cathedral is now.

And even earlier, in 1722, the Ranelagh tea gardens opened (where the Adelphi Hotel is now), offering refreshment and entertainments; they finally closed in 1830.

❛ *...where the most obdurate heart may be softened and gently led to pursuits which refine, purify and alleviate the humblest of the toilworn ...* **❜**

A good deal of open space now in public ownership was for centuries private estate land. Walton Hall Park dates back to 1199, when Henry de Walton was steward of the West Derby Hundred; in 1934 the 130 acre park was opened to the public by King George. Croxteth Hall – home of the Molyneux family – and its 500 acre park dates from 1575 and was given to the public by the last Countess of Sefton in 1973. As well as the splendid Queen Anne hall and the park, Croxteth's home farm has a collection of traditional breeds of farm animals and birds.

Now outside the city boundaries, Knowsley is the ancestral home of the Stanleys, Earls of Derby. Today a five-mile Safari Park trail, the 2,000 acre park was for centuries used by local people for scoring (the practice of putting farm stock out to good pasture to finish off before going to market). Tenants were allowed to graze animals in the park for a charge; by the 19th century, the score for the season (13th May to 11th October) was 12 shillings for a sheep, sixpence for a lamb, £2 for a heifer and three guineas for a colt. The huge park, enclosed by a 12 mile stone wall with 11 lodges, included the Earl's private racecourse.

Otterspool Promenade, on the bank of the Mersey, was created in the 1940s (opened in July 1950) from 30 million tons of city rubbish and diggings from the Queensway Tunnel; originally proposed by city engineer John Brodie in 1919, it was approved by the Council in 1928. It was extended in 1984 by the 250-acre International Garden Festival site, and is now one of Liverpool's linear parks (along with the Sustrans Loopline, a green cycleway created from a series of disused railway lines circling the city).

Otterspool was mentioned in records of 1228, and in the 17th century was a Puritan settlement based around the stream which was dubbed Little Jordan. Back in the time of King John, the stream was called the Osklebrok and was formed by two streams – the Upper and Lower Brooks – both rising from springs in Wavertree and in the 19th century widened to form the lakes in Greenbank Park and Sefton Park. The joined stream now runs under Aigburth Road at the Vale and can be seen by the main gates in Otterspool Park.

Calderstones (the park and house were owned by the Perceval family and later the Bibbys) now incorporates the Botanical Gardens, which were founded in 1802 by William Roscoe, originally on a ten acre site to the south of Mount Pleasant. Almost 4,000 species of plants brought from all over the world by ships' masters (ship's ballast was pressed into service as rock gardens). The gardens moved to Edge Hill in 1836 and moved again in 1951 to Harthill; but although the cactus house is still open to the public, along with the stunning English and Japanese gardens, much of Liverpool's valuable botanical collection has been removed from public access in recent years.

An ancient living gem is the Allerton Oak, under which the Hundred Court sat 1,000 years ago; the sap still rises in the venerable tree, which has been alive longer than Liverpool.

The Neolithic Calder Stones carry extremely rare markings of six kinds: spirals, concentric circles, arcs, cups and rings; even rarer is the carving of a footprint with an extra toe and finger.

Two large stones worth seeing are the great boulder discarded in the Ice Age, now in the grounds of Wavertree library, and the Robin Hood's Stone in Booker Avenue, thought to be where archers sharpened their arrows before going off to the Crusades.

International Garden Festival Hall

When looking for green and leafy spaces, don't overlook Liverpool's cemeteries, which have the added bonus of hunting out interesting gravestones and memorials. St James's cemetery, by the Anglican Cathedral, was once a quarry, then a pleasure garden; William Huskisson is buried there, as is artist Sarah Biffen. In the sandstone cliff of the cemetery is a chalybeate spring, mineral water full of iron salts.

Grant's Gardens in Everton was an old cemetery, the Necropolis.

There was an attempt at a zoo in Liverpool, built in 1832 on nine acres in Derby Road by Thomas Atkins. The novelty of the menagerie soon wore off, and though Atkins tried fireworks, theatricals and exhibitions, it didn't last. According to James Picton: 'By degrees it fell lower and lower on the social scale till the gardens became notorious for the low, dissolute company which resorted thither.' Exactly a century after the first, in 1932, there was another zoo opened on Mossley Hill (opposite the church) on the 12 acre Rosemont Estate, but it lasted only six years before being closed.

Princes Park – the first of the great Victorian parks in Liverpool – is another remnant of the great medieval hunting forest of Toxteth. Princes Park was built not by the city council but as a private venture by Richard Vaughan Yates, a property developer in the city. Yates bought 100 acres from Lord Sefton in 1842 and gave Joseph Paxton (architect of the Crystal Palace) his first independent commission, to landscape the park. To pay for this venture (it cost him £70,000) Yates built elegant houses which he thought would provide the income to pay for the laying out and upkeep of the park. It didn't work very well for him, but the idea was highly popular. Having cost Yates £70,000 to build, Princes Park was snapped up by the council in 1918 for a bargain £11,000. The lake in Princes Park, incidentally, is supposed to be bottomless, but as it was an old quarry, that legend is a little hard to credit.

Over the next 25 years, the council created a ring of parks around Liverpool, with Stanley Park to the north, Sheil and Newsham Parks to the east – and the great Sefton Park to the south. The council bought 200 acres of Toxteth Park from Lord Sefton in 1866; local architect Lewis Hornblower (who also designed the main entrance to Birkenhead Park) and his partner Edouard André won the competition – and a prize of 300 guineas – to landscape the park, at a cost of £146,000. André was head gardener to the city of Paris (he later created the Citadel of Luxembourg gardens, and the public garden of Monte Carlo) and his rather exotic tastes were not wholly restrained by Hornblower's more conservative ideas. The prize-winning plan included a cricket pavilion, restaurant, aviary, apiary, summer house, aquarium, grand cascade, swan hut, cast iron fountains, sheep pen and shepherd's hut, arbours and hidden rustic seats.

Gog and Magog, the giants at the gate of Calderstones Park

Another of Liverpool's rare trees is the flowering thorn tree in the churchyard of All Hallows in Allerton. Planted in January 1958, it is an offshoot of the Thorn of Glastonbury. Joseph of Arimathea is said to have struck his staff in the ground at Glastonbury on Christmas Eve and it flowered on Christmas Day.

In 1895, 10,000 children came to the opening of the Wavertree playground (now used for the Liverpool Show each May bank holiday). Probably donated by a member of the Holt family, at the time the generous philanthropist insisted that he remain anonymous – hence the 108-acre park's local nickname: the Mystery.

The obelisk erected by the Hardman family on land that now forms part of Allerton golf course is exactly five miles from Liverpool Town Hall. The obelisk's four faces point north, south, east and west.

Sefton Park is one of the greatest examples of its era, and is one of the least overtly man-made parks in the country. From the ground, the stands of beech and other indigenous British trees, carpeted with bluebells and millions of daffodils (the Field of Hope, planted in 1990 to raise money for the Marie Curie cancer fund) around the five-acre lake, gives an excellent impression of rural permanence, but an aerial view shows the manufactured shapes of the park with its distinctive curved paths and driveways. The Hyde Park of Liverpool, Sefton boasts a statue of Eros (cast at the same time as the one in Piccadilly Circus), a twin to the Peter Pan statue in Kensington Gardens (both Eros and Peter Pan were in 2001 undergoing restoration at the Conservation Centre), an obelisk, and the glorious Palm House, opened by Queen Victoria in 1896.

Donated to the city by Henry Yates, the Palm House is second only to that at Kew Gardens, 100ft in diameter, three glazed tiers rising 70ft from the octagonal red granite base to the lantern. The humid interior of this breast-shaped fantasy land, full of tropical plants and an exotic haven for local people, was a much-loved asset until the glass was shattered in the May Blitz of 1941. It took ten years to reglaze the Palm House; its glazed glory was revived and well-used until the political nonsense of the 1970s and 1980s, when upkeep was stopped and vandals allowed to smash the glass and wreck the ironwork.

A fierce band of volunteers has fought valiantly for the restoration of the Palm House, and after many years of fundraising and campaigning, the Palm House has been wonderfully restored, and reopened with a great flourish in September 2001, complete with its statues of explorers and discoverers around its circumference (including the only statue of Christopher Columbus in the country).

Also being funded by lottery money is a hydrological study to see how best to get Sefton Park's lake and streams flowing again.

Land on the park's perimeter was eagerly snatched up by the affluent keen to show off their wealth. Sour commentators of the time remarked that 'the *nouveaux riches* exhibited low taste with their love of the ornate and debased classical and Gothic styles'. Typically brash Victorian piles they may be, and nothing like the elegant houses around Princes Park, but Sefton Park's monsters have earned their place.

Now a multimillion pound programme of refurbishment for Liverpool's great parks is underway, so that Scouse flora and fauna thrive and prosper for following generations.

Liverpool's only remaining 17th century dwelling is Tuebrook House in West Derby Road. A small Jacobean house, with the initials of John Mercer and the date (1615). It has a secret room with walls three feet thick.

Queen's Drive ring road was laid out by the brilliant city engineer JA Brodie, who in the 1930s was at the forefront of building wide tree-lined avenues radiating out from the city centre.

Home, for the 400,000 people living in Liverpool, might be a small Victorian terrace, a flat in a dockland warehouse, a Georgian villa or a new housing association semi. Or anything between. Great swathes of terraced housing were built first by the Georgians, then further out from the centre in a great sweep in the 19th century, and on into the 20th. Post-war slum clearances of anything the German bombers had missed meant huge estates being built in Norris Green and Kirkby, as well as tower blocks.

These were not an unqualified success, and solutions to housing needs in the 1990s and afterwards have taken into account what the inhabitants might want out of them, not just what planners and architects might think a good idea at the time. Still, despite some clunking mistakes over the years, Liverpool has a better track record in providing decent social housing than any other city. From 1925 to 1948 city architect Sir Lancelot Keay built more than 35,000 houses and flats – such as Speke, a vast scape of Neo-Georgian estates on the edges of Queens Drive.

One of the worst experiments in social housing, by contrast, was the rurally-labelled Cantril Farm – an estate built in Kirkby to replace the slums of Vauxhall. Cantril Farm got such an appalling reputation that its name was changed to Stockbridge Village, in a feeble attempt to change its image. In the end it was the residents who made the area viable as a place to live.

Another Keay scheme was the 1935 Bullring, otherwise known as St Andrew's Gardens, designed with John Hughes. Five floors of high-density flats – 316 in all – surrounding a large circular courtyard; although architecturally important, the Bullring became a notorious inner city estate before it was refurbished as student accommodation and reopened by the Queen in the mid-1990s.

Liverpool's population is choosing from an increasingly eclectic range of buildings to live in, and house prices rocketed over the turn of the 20th century; while there are still run-down terraces to be had for under £30,000, small flats in converted city centre warehouses and commercial buildings are going for £100,000 or more.

Most of Liverpool's old houses have been lost – there is very little left that was built before the 1800s, and even less before 1700. For at least 300 years there were fishermen's cottages on the shores of the Mersey, which disappeared only when industry, commercial shipping and housing developments finished them off. Heritage – a reverence for the old – is largely a recent phenomenon. Our forefathers' thinking of old = bad, new = good meant that all the sway-backed old cottages and wonky timber-framed houses (which would today sell for a king's ransom) in Liverpool's old streets are long gone. The oldest building in Liverpool today is a 13th century farmhouse in Aigburth: Stanlaw Grange is a red sandstone cruck building dating back to 1291, with changes and extra bits added over the years; in the 1960s architect David Brock converted the Grange into two houses.

Unlike the unobtrusive Stanlaw Grange, the spectacular half-timbered Speke Hall – completed in 1598 – would be hard to ignore. Now a National Trust property too close to Liverpool Airport for comfort, Speke Hall was built by Sir Edward Norris on the site of the Norris family home since the 14th century; an inscription on the house reads: 'This work, twenty yards long, was wholly built by EN 1598'. The panelling in the baronial great hall is said to have been brought by Norris from the palace of the King of Scotland after the battle of Flodden Field, but a lot of the interior is Victorian.

Once into the 1800s, Liverpool can show some stunning Georgian terraces on the edge of the city centre. Rodney Street – birthplace of prime minister William Gladstone (at No62) and poet Arthur Hugh Clough – became the Harley Street of Liverpool, and still boasts a number of GP and dental surgeries amongst the architects' and advertising agencies' offices. Although giving an impression of Georgian uniformity, the houses here and in adjoining streets are not to any unified design – each has its own distinctive detailing from fan lights to classical porticoes. These were streets built for the middle classes – merchants, professionals and academics who a century earlier would have lived down the hill, closer to the river and the docks.

At the north end of the city there survives a Georgian terrace in Shaw Street, and some elegant buildings in Islington Square, dwarfed by the Collegiate Building – once one of the city's most important schools and now stylishly converted by Urban Splash into flats.

Rodney Street may largely be the professionals' domain, but the streets east and west of Catherine Street – Huskisson, Canning, Percy, Falkner and so on – are very much a residential area, much of it run by housing associations – there's nothing like living in 1830s architectural splendour. Falkner Square – white stucco terraces around a garden square lined with plane trees – is often used for period TV and film productions, as is Falkner Street, one of the few streets left in the city with its original cobbles. If something looks like Victorian London on screen, it's more than likely Liverpool.

In contrast with the brick or stucco facades of most of Liverpool 8, Percy Street is a charming stone terrace, reminiscent of the most elegant of Edinburgh's New Town. Parallel, one row further west, is Gambier Terrace, a splendid 1836 terrace running the length of St James's cemetery; in the grand Classical manner for most of its length, it was later extended in a yellow brick French style. One Gambier Terrace resident complains bitterly about the Anglican Cathedral, which blocks her view of Snowdon and the sunset.

n Aigburth, to the south of the city centre, are Fulwood, Cressington and Grassendale Parks – three delightful private estates built in the 1840s with later additions; villas and smaller houses set in spacious gardens surrounded by forest trees – beech, oak, chestnut and all kinds of blossom trees. Each of the parks has an entrance on Aigburth Road and runs down to the Mersey (Fulwood now runs down to Otterspool Promenade). The original houses were Regency buildings; later additions have been made in subsequent decades, some prettier than others; Cressington has its own delightful railway station on the Northern Line.

There is also Hadassah Grove, a charming, winding cul-de-sac just off Lark Lane; the road is unadopted, and full of horrendous potholes – lethal for cars. Another half-hidden treasure is Windermere Terrace, which overlooks Princes Park. These houses have joined the list of TV locations, used by Granada TV for the 2001 production of the *Forsyte Saga*.

From the elegant, detailed Regency style to the astonishing clean lines of Jesse Hartley's dockland warehouses – the stark box of the 1850s Wapping Warehouse, even more brutally modern than his Albert Dock, which was shocking enough in 1845. The first of the dockland buildings to be converted into flats, in 1989 they were selling for £27,000; a year later their value had more than trebled. To the north, the Waterloo Grain Warehouse was built in 1867 by George Fosbery Lyster – a six story building sitting on massive granite arches. In the mid 1990s the block was converted into flats, and the dock is home to flocks of seagulls, swans, mallard, the occasional cormorant and cloudy jellyfish.

Regrettably, Liverpool is not noted for late 20th century housing design. In his delicious book *Liverpool: city of architecture* Quentin Hughes has picked out two houses for praise. The first, a stable block conversion by Robin Clayton in 1966, is a quirky two-bedroom brick house in Cressington Park. The other is in Grassendale Park, designed in 1991 by Irena Bauman and Maggie Pickles; the house is designed round a courtyard that contains an ancient wisteria. Says Hughes: 'The result is magical. The design deservedly won the Daily Telegraph Homes Award.'

To house the enormous increase in student numbers, both the University of Liverpool and JMU have been building or converting with zeal. The old and long-disused North Western Hotel is now student flats, as are some of the Cathedral Close buildings (those not occupied by the Chapter); student villages have sprung up between Oxford Road and Myrtle Street, and off Tithebarn Street.

Many Liverpool alumni look back fondly at their time in the Carnatic Halls of Residence on Mossley Hill, but most of them probably don't know the origin of the name. The site was that of Mossley Hall, once the home of the tobacco family Ogdens, but built by shipwright Peter Baker in about 1779. Baker had built a privateer ship, the *Mentor*, but failing to sell her, Baker went into the privateering game himself. The *Mentor*, under Captain Dawson, captured the French East Indiaman *Carnatic* which proved to be a very rich prize worth £114,000. Baker built his house with part of the profits, but the local wags dubbed the building Carnatic Hall and the nickname stuck.

Around the Millennium, the emphasis for private housing has been on inner city apartments. The trend started with Wapping Dock, then new developments around the Marina, spreading along the waterside down to Armstrong Quay near Dingle Point, and up to Waterloo Warehouse. Then developers began looking into the city for redundant commercial buildings, such as the Plessey building on Tithebarn Street, and the hideous 1960s blot, Wilberforce House, on the east side of the Strand, right opposite the Port of Liverpool Building. Both of these buildings have been converted by Beetham Developments, which is also bringing back to life the narrow streets at the bottom of Duke Street. Wilberforce House has been clad in green glass and given two extra floors on the top. The smart Heathcotes restaurant is on the ground floor, there is parking space for residents in the basement, and a revitalised piazza with its entertaining fountain restored to splashing life.

The innovators in the refurbishment of 'difficult' buildings in the heart of the city were Urban Splash; their first major development – Concert Square – became a model for other chic urban professional enclaves in the tight back streets, and as a result the population of L1, L2 and L3 has leapt from 2,340 in 1991 to almost 10,000 by the turn of the century.

The Leeds-Liverpool canal is still neglected. How long before the developers move in?

Clockwise, from top right: Beetham Plaza, student accommodation at North Western Hall, Dingle streets above Herculaneum, Princes Park and Cressington Park

Trials hotel (pictured above) was built in 1868 as the Bank of North Wales, on the corner of Castle Street and Derby Square. Standing outside, look up to the second floor and spot the prow of a ship projecting outwards, supported by reclining figures. The main bar is in the splendid old banking hall.

The Eagle pub in Paradise Street has been a pawnshop, coffee house, boarding house and beer house. Over 100 years ago it was called the American Eagle and has now one of the only old pub signs left in the city.

A poet who visited Liverpool in 1760 had this to say about the town's hospitality: 'For ten pence a man dines elegantly at an ordinary, consisting of ten or a dozen dishes. Indeed it must be said that in Lancashire and Cheshire they have plenty of the best and most luxurious food at a cheap rate. The great increase of their commerce is owing to the spirit and indefatigable industry of their inhabitants .... The merchants are hospitable, nay friendly, to strangers even to those of whom they have the least knowledge, their tables are well furnished and their viands well served.' Apart from the idea of getting a dozen dishes for 10p, the rest of the poet's description would probably stand scrutiny today. In 1760 there were only four inns in Liverpool: the Golden Lion and the Fleece in Dale Street, the Millstone in Castle Street, and the Talbot in Water Street. Today there are hundreds of pubs, not to mention bars, cafes and restaurants, dozens of which have sprung up in the last ten years. There is, surely, a drinking hole or an eaterie to suit every temperament, whether in raucous or reflective mood.

If you want to hear a good story, there's no better place in the world to go than a Liverpool pub – and Liverpool has some astonishing pubs. 'No other city has such beauties. I think the Liverpool man drinks in the best surroundings in the world,' frothed a visiting artist. What about Liverpool women?

Well – many years ago, in The Vines on Lime Street, a lady was escorted in by a gentleman friend (ladies in those days were only admitted by invitation); the lovely chap sank a few pints and promptly fell asleep in his chair. While the gent was snoring peacefully, the lady was asked to dance by a tall, dark, strangely compelling stranger – an invitation she accepted with alacrity. When the stranger had returned the lady to her chair, however, he disappeared, and she was found to be dead as a doornail. 'That's what you get when you sell your soul to the Devil for a dance,' said the landlord in sepulchral tones.

Liverpool city centre boasts a collection of public house jewels from the turn of the last century; art nouveau gin palaces in which you could believe the most extraordinary events might take place. Half a dozen of these extravaganzas are the Philharmonic, the Crown, the Vines, the Midland, the Central and the Railway. Even for the teetotal visitor to Liverpool, these establishments are worth a pub crawl.

The Vines – aka the Big House – was originally built by wine merchants Richmond & Son, then some years later it was bought by Mr AB Vines and built up into a favourite snuggery for Liverpool lawyers and merchants. A bunch of dipsomaniacs, apparently, for Mr Vines would order 100 hogsheads – 5,400 gallons – of Allsopps bitter on a single day, according to local journalist at the time, C Millward: 'Truly, we are a thirsty race!'

Vines himself was a notable greyhound racer, the owner of 'two clinking good hounds', and Millward remembered dog *Markham*'s win in 1883 when his jubilant owner filled the prized Gosforth Cup with 14 bottles of champagne which was immediately 'poured out again by his admirers'.

❛ *Oh yes, Adolf Hitler drank here while he was a student at Liverpool Art School.* ❜

The Vines was rebuilt in 1907 in an extravagant baroque style. The architecture is credited to Walter Thomas, but the brewery is said to have 'improved upon his vision'. It is certainly hard to miss on its Lime Street corner site next to the Adelphi Hotel. The facade of carved stone and marble, with its outrageous cupola, hides an expansive interior. Travel writer Ian Nairn was obviously bowled over. He just loved the vast room at the back, variously described as a cocktail bar, ballroom and now the 'heritage' room. Any description, Nairn felt, is 'a misnomer for a Great Hall or Throne Room, tall and luminous with brown and gold giant pilasters combining elegance and immense force. Sitting in it you feel ten feet tall – you realise London has nothing like this.'

The Vines' open secret was the presence of two mammoth paintings by George Earl, commissioned by brewer Andrew Barclay Walker (patron of the Walker Art Gallery) and built into the walls of the ballroom. Titled *Going North* (1893) and *Going South* (1895), the paintings show a crowd of huntin', shootin', fishin' types at King's Cross station on the way up to Scotland to lay waste to the moors and rivers, and the same crowd on the railway platform at Perth, bags and boxes stuffed with game, dogs smug and ghillies exhausted. The paintings, leant on and brushed past by generations of Scouse drinkers, were hoicked out of the wall in 1990 and sold to the British Rail Museum in York for vast sums.

In 1905, architect Walter Thomas had had fun building the Crown at the other end of the block from the Vines. The Crown Hotel, its name splashed in archetypal art nouveau typeface all over the facade of the building, is a glorious example of its time. The picture postcard facades are upstaged by the interior with more glass, mahogany, colourful plasterwork, polished brass and beaten copper than you can shake a stick at. Curiously, architectural pundit Nikolaus Pevsner is not impressed: 'a pleasant start to the street proper, though the decoration is conservative for its date'.

The Slaughterhouse pub, in Fenwick Street, was built during the reign of George III by wine merchants importing from France, Spain and Portugal. Close by, on the corner of James Street, were the old Fish Stones, or fish market.

Dicky Sam's was either named after a tobacco ship, Dicky Sam, which was wrecked on Bootle shore in 1848 and looted of its cargo; or named after one of its licensees, Richard Samuel. The inn was so famous world-wide that Liverpool sailors were known as Dicky Sams.

If architecture is what you look for in a pub, rather than the beer, atmosphere or entertainment, then look out for the Crown Hotel in Norris Green, or the Mere in Heyworth Street, Everton. For something a little older, head down Lark Lane to the Albert, built around 1840 when Victoria had not long been married to him. If you've had enough architecture by then, head over to the road to Keith's, Lark Lane's legendary wine bar.

Why can't breweries and pub companies leave well alone? The Grapes in Mathew Street – where the Beatles used to drink between sessions at the Cavern – has been renamed The Famous Grapes and given a facelift, effectively destroying the original pub that fans want to experience.

For a quiet breather, head down Ranelagh Street to the Central Commercial Hotel. The smallest of the famous gin palaces, the Central is still a riot of curlicues and glinting facets, green ceramic panels vying with ornate mirrors, the richly decorated dome topping the whole thing off with panache. The Midland, right next door, is pretty spectacular too.

A pub which attracts little or no attention from the gin-palace aficionados, but which deserves a leisurely look is the Lion Tavern. On the corner of Tithebarn Street and Moorfields, the Lion faces the old Exchange Station (now Mercury Court), and is named after one of the first locomotives to haul trains between Liverpool and Manchester.

Stuffed with carved woodwork, ceramic tiles, mirror and cut glass panels, high ceilings, fine fireplaces and the rest, the Lion boasts a reading room with a pretty stained glass dome.

Sensation-seekers who enjoy a decent pint are in for a treat, for this is another pub with a story – this time both recent (in the mid 1990s) and real.

Joe Riley, the current arts editor of the Liverpool Echo, was dallying over a pint or three with a fellow scribe when the landlady's gentleman friend came downstairs. 'Would you drink up, gentleman, please – we have a very sick child upstairs and we want to close up.' Full of sympathy, the journalists went on supping, albeit a mite faster. Minutes later the chap made another appearance and demanded that they make a swift exit, which they did.

'It wasn't till I read the paper the next day,' said Riley, 'that I realised that far from having a sick infant upstairs, this fellow had just murdered the landlady and was a bit concerned to find witnesses downstairs.' The Lion Tavern Strangler is now doing life.

What with the Lion's landlady and the Devil's dancing partner, women haven't always had an easy time of it in Liverpool's pubs. They weren't even allowed inside Ye Hole in Ye Wall – Liverpool's oldest surviving pub in Hackins Hey – until 1975.

Close by in Dale Street is Rigby's, where Admiral Nelson is said to have drunk. It is perfectly possible; the date on Rigby's facade is 1726, and Nelson did come to Liverpool; for one thing the Navy bought ropes and other equipment from Liverpool yards, and Nelson liked to buy Marsala from wine merchants here.

Another celebrity pub is the Grapes in Mathew Street: the Cavern, just up the road, didn't have a licence, so the Beatles (and presumably every other musician) piled down to the Grapes when not on stage in the 1960s. The Grapes was another venerable Liverpool pub (until an unwelcome makeover in 2000), with a flagstone floor, wooden settles, a roaring fire and, blessedly, no canned music.

The cancer of themed pubs has got into the bones of the licensed trade now, so there is no escaping them. Some, however, are better than others. The art of dusty decor has lent a certain patina to Flanagan's Apple, the thoroughly Irish pub with bare floorboards, bicycles hanging from the ceiling and live music upstairs and in the basement. Flanagans may be manufactured Irish, but it has a good deal of blasé charm about it.

Dr Duncan's is more recent addition to the scene, named after the first-ever officer of health, and housed in the old Pearl Assurance HQ (built by Waterhouse). Queen Square, reinvented for the Millennium, is stuffed with bars and restaurants so that even on imperfect summer evenings the whole place is leaping with sociable Liverpudlians and tourists.

Anyone wanting a quieter, more civilised establishment might go to the Brewery Tap which, being attached to Cain's Brewery in Stanhope Street, is for serious beer fans. Cain's is a real ale brewery awash with awards; formerly it was Higsons , which had been brewing in Liverpool since 1780 until it was bought by Boddington's in the 1990s.

Another pub beloved of beer experts is the Roscoe Head, a tiny but excellent pub in Roscoe Street, not far from the Dispensary. For good craic, try Ye Cracke in Rice Street – elbow your way between policemen and artists in this least themed of all Liverpool pubs (from which John Lennon was banned in the 1950s when he was at art school round the corner). Or head for Little Egerton Street and squeeze into Peter Kavanagh's – a real Irish pub now run by the formidable Rita Smith; look out for the radios on the ceiling.

Back in the commercial hub of the city, the Poste House in Cumberland Street boasted Prince Louis Napoleon and William Thackeray amongst its patrons; in 2001 it was saved from demolition to make way for wholesale redevelopment of the block. An oddity is the Nook in Nelson Street – the only Chinese pub in the country; another is the Childwall Abbey; the guest book includes Henry Irving, Herbert Terry and JM Barrie, and part of the hotel is said to be the Chapel of St Thomas the Martyr, dating back to the 15th century.

To the east, the Old Swan pub has lent its name to the whole area; there were three inns at one time – the Lower Swan, Middle Swan and Old Swan. The name refers to the swans on the coat of arms of the Walton family, who used to own the land.

To stick to writing about pubs cuts out all the bars, cafes, hotels and restaurants in the city, which hardly seems fair. The best solution, however, is to conduct personal investigations. It may take some years, and require a strictly disciplined gym programme to undo the effects, but like so much of Liverpool, it is worth the effort.

LIVERPOOL PLACES – THE PHILHARMONIC DINING ROOMS

Up the hill on Hope Street, close to the Philharmonic Hall and halfway between the two cathedrals, is undoubtedly one of Britain's most extraordinary pubs – no accusations of conservatism here.

The Philharmonic Dining Rooms, known as the Phil, is a monument to *fin de siècle* exuberance. Built by brewer Robert Cain between 1898-1900 there is no connection between the pub and the concert hall beyond the name, but the Phil has been a haven for thirsty musicians and concert-goers for a century.

Walter Thomas, brilliant architect of the Vines, the Crown – and the Liver Building – was responsible for the gabled exterior. The gloriously flamboyant bronze wrought iron gates, incorporating the singularly inappropriate motto *Pacem amo* (*I love peace*), were designed with abandon by H Blomfield Barr, a staff member of the University College's school of architecture. Since these wonderful gates are without equal in British pub architecture, it would be nice if the publican could arrange for them to be polished once in a while.

For the outrageous interior, architects Stretton & Hall Neave raided the Cunard White Star shipyards for the city's finest craftsmen, and had a bottomless brewery budget.

The jaws of first-time visitors, then, drop satisfyingly to their chests when they walk inside and set disbelieving eyes on an interior in which every square inch is ruthlessly decorated – even the two tiny wood-panelled snugs which are boldly labelled *Brahms* and *Liszt*. Crystal chandeliers, plaster friezes, beaten copper panels, carved mahogany, intricate mosaic ceramics and engraved mirrors are relentless. In the Grand Lounge, wild-haired plaster caryatids (designed by Charles Allen) hold up a splendidly ornate ceiling.

The Phil is a favourite drinking hole for students; when Bill Clinton was at Oxford he had a Scouse girlfriend, and on visits to Liverpool with her they would drink at the Phil.

Maybe Hitler felt at home in the Germanic-sounding snugs – for here it was, indeed, that Adolf is said to have wet his whistle. The story of Hitler's visit to Liverpool may be true: certainly some of his relatives lived here, although he was never a student at Liverpool Art School.

John Lennon was, though, and often came to the Phil for a pie and pint at lunchtime. The gents' loos even made a guest appearance in Lennon lyrics, somewhere.

The gents' loos are everyone's favourite bit of the pub, and the room which gets all the headlines. Probably the only men's loo in the world that women want to visit, the Phil's flamboyant Victorian urinals are carved out of unashamedly pink marble, and the basins have marble tops and copper taps. The Philharmonic's gents' loo is on the Blue Badge guided tour of the city – surely unique.

chapter 13
renewal

From the Merseyside Development Corporation's initial development strategy in 1981: 'Most of the area is severely degraded, being non-operational docks and back-up land, demolished goods yards and sidings, part-cleared tank farms and petroleum stores, or is land in the process of reclamation by landfill using commercial and domestic waste. The overall impression is of severe degradation, inaccessibility, danger to the public and much vandalism.'

ould we draw aside the thick veil that hides the future from us, we might perhaps behold our great seaport swelling into a metropolis, in size and importance; or we might behold Liverpool, by some concatenation of calamities, dwindled down to its former insignificance: its docks shipless, its warehouses in ruins, its streets in decay. Under which of these fates will Liverpool find its lot some centuries hence? Which of these pictures will it then present?' James Stonehouse, writing his *Recollections of a Nonagenarian* in 1863, presents us with a remarkably clear picture of his city as it would look 100-odd years later. A concatenation of calamities indeed. War, politicians, economists, the free market and world events happened to Liverpool, as they did to every city – but the cocktail of circumstances was particularly lethal for this city and, for whatever reason, Liverpool's decision-makers couldn't find the answers to stop the terrifying speed of decline.

No sooner had Liverpool recovered from the war than its heart – the docks – began to falter as the world shifted on its axis. Post-war life was very different; attitudes and ambitions had changed, people were more mobile, society had made a quantum shift. Television opened up the world, computers were born, a youth culture grew all over the established order of things. Change destroyed the old Liverpool; the great seaport, at the height of its power and wealth in the 1920s, was no more. By the end of the 1970s Liverpool was a drifting hulk; given the depths of despair, anger and bitterness in the city at the time, it's a miracle that the Granby riots of 1981 weren't much, much worse.

The spirit of Liverpool's people – despite the pitiful lack of effective, positive leadership in the 1970s and 1980s – dragged the city back from the brink and 20 years after the riots the city has changed enormously for the better. But the investment and uplift has been patchy; chunks of the city are still in a dreadful state with high unemployment and low morale, high crime and low educational achievement.

But what do you expect? After such a shattering turn of fortune Liverpool is, in fact, picking itself up and recovering remarkably fast. It seems a long, slow, painful process to those who have lived through it, but in the context of 1,000 years, Liverpool's decline and regeneration is a mere blip in the city's lifeline.

Quite why the city's image became and remained so negative is material for a doctoral thesis; overcoming the short-term and long-redundant model of Liverpool as a strife-torn dump is taking millions of pounds and many years, to the frustration of the locals.

Of course there have been bad decisions – or no decisions at all; of course there are tantrums and furious rows. The problems are complex and there are serious conflicts of interest that slow the process of positive change. The private sector want one thing, the public sector another; the unemployed and those in the poverty trap have to sit and wait while the political, economic and bureaucratic games go on – but it's the same in every city.

So where do we look for answers? Not very far. We only have to look to the people of the city. All the ideas, the talent and the energy are there, if only they can be given the leeway to come through, and a bit of wind in their sails. Look at the Eldonians, who started with nothing but determination and strength of community. Look at all the individuals who have succeeded without the benefit of privileged education or contacts. And look at the resources in the city, the bright minds, the drive, the goodwill and the money. Then look to the future.

From a point in the early 20th century when Liverpool had a staggering share of the world's trade, to the end of the century when the city was so poor that it qualified for European Objective One status – Liverpool had a long way to fall, and it hit hard. But if Liverpool did it once, it can do it again. If the city can capitalise on its greatest talents – communication and ideas – there is no limit to its long term potential.

When Merseyside won Objective One status (a funny prize to want – confirmation that this is among the poorest regions in Europe) the county was promised around £3 billion in public and private sector investment by 2007, which is not to be sneezed at. There was fierce criticism of the way the first wedge of European cash was handled, with years of delay, cack-handed bureaucracy and little enthusiasm from the small and medium business sector or the general public.

But to go back to the 1980s – after the Granby riots in 1981, Michael Heseltine (dubbed Minister for Merseyside) swung in on a liana and whipped up some enthusiasm here and in Westminster; whether or not his strategies were right or wrong, he helped changed attitudes and mobilise the forces of regeneration. The Merseyside Development Corporation was parachuted in with an enormous plateful of objectives to lift the docklands out of the sludge, create new jobs, new houses, new businesses and new investors. Bitterly resented at first by the city, the MDC busied itself on the water side of the dock road without having to go through normal local authority planning procedures.

It worked. Doubtless there are those who say it could have been done better, but drive along the river from Otterspool right through the city centre to Waterloo Dock and the achievement is unmissable: a marina full of sailing boats, thousands of new houses, hundreds of business premises, a cleaned-up river full of frolicking wildlife, young trees and wildflowers, all the signs of renewed affluence.

The most important remaining waterfront site – King's Dock, right next to the now famous Albert Dock – is causing some public debate (for which read stand-up rows) with plans for Everton's new football stadium likely to win a lacklustre competition to develop one of the most stunning sites in the country.

Merseyside has one of the fastest growing economies in the country, according to a government report in 2001. Wages are rising higher than anywhere else in England, by an average of 9.6% over the past three years. The average hourly wage is still just under the national average (£10.30 compared to £10.80) but at least the gap has closed.

Liverpool held the most popular Millennium party in the country after London.

In 1996 each employee on Merseyside produced 26% more than the average worker in the UK, and generated 37% more sales than the average Greater Manchester worker.

Spending on vital research and development is higher on Merseyside, at 6.1% of overall manufacturing output, than the rest of the North West (4.5%).

Derrick Walters, Dean of the Anglican Cathedral (who died in 1999), was quite an entrepreneur; seeing the need of the area around the cathedral, he didn't bother waiting for someone else to solve the problem but dived in himself. In the great tradition of Liverpool entrepreneurs, the 'developing dean' headed up Project Rosemary which included the building of the splendid new Women's Hospital, the new Cathedral Close to house the Chapter and some very lucky students, and JMU's media and arts department.

It is so easy to forget how things looked even ten years ago: glancing through old brochures and reports from City Challenge and the MDC it is quite shocking to see photographs from the 1980s and early 1990s: shocking because the shape of the city today seems to have been that way for ever. But before the start of City Challenge in 1992, there was no LIPA, no Blackburne House, no Queen Square, no Conservation Centre; areas like London Road, Chinatown, St Andrew's Gardens, Hardman Street, Seymour Street and Canning were desperately run down. The Pier Head, now a World Heritage site, was then a dull bus terminus.

City Challenge was the first regeneration programme outside the MDC's dockland area; the Tory government put in £39 million over five years, which levered in over £200 million from public and private sector investors. Much of the programme was driven by established property developers, but not all. The narrow streets squeezed between the commercial district and the main shopping drag – including Mathew Street, where the famous Cavern Club is – were dingy and underused. Thanks to the energy and commitment of a group of local business people such as solicitor Gregory Abrams, and with the financial backing of agencies including the city council and the Police, the Cavern Quarter was invented; buildings were cleaned up and redeveloped, street furniture, lighting and signage were put in, shops, bars and restaurants opened, and the whole place brought to life.

After London developers Charterhouse Estates made an abortive attempt in the late 1980s at the wholesale redevelopment of what they dubbed the creative industries quarter, the Ropewalks area is rapidly being gentrified (or rather trendified), kicked off by the award-winning development of Concert Square by the innovative Urban Splash.

After the 1930s depression, when unemployment in Liverpool was running at 25%, Liverpool was the first municipality in Britain to try to bring jobs to those without them. Speke was the chosen site; amongst employers who moved in were Dunlop, Bryant & May and Evans Medical; the 'village' housing estate – part of the plan – was another first for the city.

Sixty years later, Speke has undergone another transformation. Dunlop and Bryant & May have gone; Evans Medical is going strong, albeit afer several changes of ownership. Speke is now pushing itself as a centre for pharmaceuticals and automotive companies.

The biggest coup for the city in years was getting Ford's bosses in Detroit to sign a company cheque for £400 million – the investment needed to turn Ford Halewood into Jaguar, ready to produce thousands of the new X-type (the so-called Baby Jag) to compete with the BMW 3 series. Ford's faith in Halewood lit the green light for other manufacturers to come to Speke, so on the Boulevard industrial park are several shiny new factories, mostly making shiny bits for the shiny Jaguar. On a very much smaller scale, but causing great excitement, is the new Jensen factory, producing a few hundred two-seater S-V8 convertible sports saloons each year. Reviving the famous marque, and choosing to do so in Liverpool, was another boost to local confidence. No company board – let alone its financiers – will invest millions in a poor workforce or an unstable economic environment.

Bryant & May's rather scrumptious 1930s match factory has been revamped as a 'business village', as part of the long-term plans by the Speke-Garston Development Company to revive the fortunes of the area. Plans were boosted enormously by the sizable investment by Peel Holdings in Liverpool Airport (or Liverpool John Lennon Airport, as we must all get used to calling it). Good to see the old Speke air terminal and splendid hangars smartened up by Neptune Developments and put back to good use, albeit as something rather different than their original purpose.

In 1936 Liverpool was the first local authority to get the power to buy and sell land for industrial purposes and to build factories. This was well before the Hunt Report which led to statutory powers for the whole of the UK. Speke's first industrial estate was 340 acres, and Aintree (north of the city) was 300 acres.

The 1930s Speke air terminal transformed into the four star Marriott Hotel

The Palm House in Sefton Park
– on the day of its reopening
in September 2001

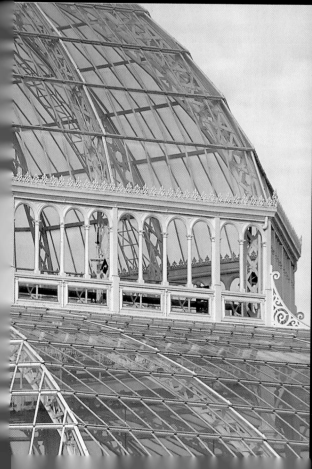

The woods at Formby, just up the coast from Liverpool, are one of the last English refuges for the harassed red squirrel.

William Roscoe's Botanic Garden just off Mount Pleasant was the model for botanic gardens in Philadelphia and India.

Liverpool may not exactly be able to claim status as a health spa, but it does have its own mineral water spring – the chalybeate spring in St James's cemetery is full of health-giving iron salts. If the Romans had bothered to conquer Liverpool properly, the city might have become a magnet for hypochondriacs coming to the baths to take the famous Liverpool waters.

Leafy is probably not the first adjective that a stranger would attach to Liverpool, but there were over a million trees in the city in 1990, and with extensive landscaping on the garden festival site as well as the smartening up of Speke Boulevard there are now quite a few more. Some 250,000 trees, shrubs and plants have put down roots in and around Speke Boulevard, including horse chestnuts, limes, poplars, pear and cherry trees, roses, ivies, crocuses and daffodils, water plants and wildflower meadows.

The city has 2,500 acres of parks and open spaces and there are more than 2,000 allotments. Acres of former industrial grot in Vauxhall have been magicked into green lawns and herbaceous borders; from the top of the Anglican Cathedral the view across to Everton is of green parkland acres where once there were grey tower blocks.

Where there's no space for a garden, there are hanging baskets and window boxes. The balconies of city centre flats and dockland apartments brim over with flowers and foliage, and the council tenants' garden competition is energetically contested each summer.

The investment in greening the city pays off, as the Victorians discovered. Not only do plants gobble up tons of pollutants and spit out oxygen for us, but they are much prettier than tarmac and concrete and bring the inner city to life.

First time visitors are usually astonished by the grassy landscapes, dense woodlands and stunning wide avenues of copper beech, oak, chestnut, plane and blossom trees underplanted with spring bulbs. It rather destroys their preconceptions of an urban wasteland – where is the run-down, strife-torn Liverpool they were expecting?

Newcomers are usually a bit stunned by the views, too. They have forgotten that Liverpool is on the west coast between Wales and Cumbria; the Welsh mountains are just across the water; from high buildings or hills on a clear day you can see Snowdon. Drive for 60 minutes and reach the Lakes or the Peaks.

Palm fronds against brilliant white ironwork and sparkling glass set against a blue sky: Sefton Park's glorious palm house finally re-opened in September 2001 after a £2.5 million restoration – a potent symbol of Liverpool's resurgence. Closed in the early 1980s and left to rot for over a decade, the Palm House's near-destruction and salvation mirrors the city's journey through bad times and back out.

New palm trees were driven overland from Italy – the largest weighs over two tons – and planted with Olive, a 100 year old Canadian date palm that stayed in place throughout the restoration. The main collection of exotic plants, housed for several years at Greenhill Nurseries, were returned, as were the statues to their plinths outside; the enormous white marble bench has been restored and put back in place. More than 3,700 panes of glass had to be individually cut and fitted to the curving three-tiered dome.

But while the echo of champagne corks popping has barely died away, other parts of Sefton Park are in desperate need of attention: the boat house, the pretty band stand, and the aviary, not to mention the streams and lakes. Two of Sefton Park's most famous statues, Eros and Peter Pan, are in the Conservation Centre for restoration.

It's the same story in the other parks around the city – and all over the country (nationally about £3.5 billion is needed to restore Britain's parks). Liverpool spends £3 million a year on parks maintenance, and has set aside £17 million to restore the city's 37 parks and gardens over the next five years, to repair the neglect caused by underfunding over the last two decades. Walton Hall Park is a dumping ground for stolen cars; the lovely glass house in Stanley Park is a wreck and the whole park a sad, worn out space.

The thinking, presumably, was that there were other priorities for council spending – but there's little point in arguing about it now. It's time to follow the example of the Palm House.

Liverpool's Park Rangers take people on guided walks throughout the year, from four-hour treks through the city's green spaces to shorter walks studying plants from China and the Himalayas; from birdwatching trips to sketching afternoons.

A huge multi-million pound sewage plant might not sound like a boon to the city environment, but the Sandon Dock plant and the vast 27-mile long interceptor sewer have turned the Mersey back into a waterway rather than a big and dirty ditch. People living within sniffing distance of Sandon Dock, however, do have to put up with a nasty pong on very hot summer days (luckily the UK doesn't get too many of those any more).

Apart from the sort of creatures you'd expect to find in a river, like octopus and porpoises (both seen in the Mersey since the big clean up), sea trout, squid, cormorants and kingfishers, there are some wartime aircraft buried in the river bed – at least one Spitfire, an American Thunderbolt, a Heinkell HE111 bomber and three Hurricanes.

A north-south divide exists in Liverpool; to the south of the city centre much of the housing and the environment is lush and prosperous. To the north and east it is a different story. In contrast to the gleaming new apartment buildings in the city centre, where two- or three-bedroom flats can sell for £200,000 or more, almost 70% of Liverpool's houses are in Band A, the lowest council tax band. It is easy to find houses for sale under £20,000. Over half of the city's council houses need renovating (which would cost almost £500 million) and a third are classified as difficult to let.

The problem has become bad enough in Kensington – the area immediately to the east of the city centre – that one proposal was to demolish 2,000 homes and start again. But the slum clearances of the 1960s and 1970s left painful scars in Liverpool, and Kensington residents didn't much care for the idea that wholesale 'solutions' might be imposed on them.

Acknowledging that the plan was 'badly handled from the delivery of information aspect', Kensington's regeneration manager Stephen Boyle said that there needed to be much more involvement from local residents in the whole process.

The New Deal for Communities programme in Kensington is something of a coup for the area, with funding of £250 million over ten years and another £31 million to improve the housing stock. Plans for the second year of the New Deal include reducing prostitution in the area, backing a local credit union to help local people get affordable house contents insurance and other financial services, and working with schools to improve children's results and reduce truancy.

There is a great deal of money to be spent – or wasted; as has been proved many times over in Liverpool, if local people are drawn in and injected with enthusiasm for the plans, they will make it work. If their imaginations are not engaged, if they are not convinced that all this money will have a tangible effect on their lives, then it will be a long uphill battle.

Whether as a backlash against the tribulations of Militant, or just out of political fatigue, participation in local politics is woeful in a city with a strong political tradition. Concerned about the apathy in the city, Radio Merseyside and the Liverpool Echo commissioned a debate on local democracy in January 2000, which resulted in the setting up of the independent Liverpool Democracy Commission. Its task was to find out how people wanted their city governed.

The answers weren't very comfortable; few people in the city believed that voting was worthwhile because they felt that however they voted, the council would go its own sweet way regardless. A member of the Granby Residents' Association said: 'I have just come from a meeting with 150 people who were really angry about housing in their area. When I told them I was going to a meeting about democracy they all burst out laughing.'

Roger Phillips, the Radio Merseyside presenter who was one of the driving forces behind the democracy commission, is convinced that the important issue is getting back to genuinely local government: 'We have to get back to grassroots power – get people involved in deciding their own futures.'

This is a national problem, of course, not just a local one. But if Liverpool is to regenerate itself, it must not fail to involve every part of society. Unless those who now feel excluded are drawn into the circle and respected for their ability to make a difference, the change will not be sustainable. People whose lives are bound up with Liverpool's future must be excited about it – or angry about it – whatever gets them involved and active.

Liverpool Democracy Commission chairman James Ross said: 'Liverpool's people are its greatest resource. If we can tap their energy and creativity and devise a way of governing the city that can excite public interest and confidence, then Liverpool can look to the next millennium with real optimism.'

The city council's willingness not just to listen to criticism but to invite it, in its efforts to improve local government, is a healthy and welcome sign. There is also evidence that the current council is making far greater efforts than ever before to consult local people on matters that affect them – a far cry from the 1980s.

Tony McGann

There are usually two options when you're in trouble: wait to be rescued, or get yourself out of it. When your rescuers turn out to be planning not a rescue mission but a different sort of trouble, the options shrink to the only answer: do it yourself. In the 1970s, when jobs were disappearing like the ebb tide in Morecambe Bay with no prospect of the tide ever turning, the city council of the day thought the solution was to move people out of the worst areas to nice shiny new estates outside the city. Bad mistake. Ripping communities up by their roots did not work.

'Don't want to go to Kirkby, to Skelmersdale or Speke, Don't want to go from all we know in Back Buchanan Street' went the song. And came the day in 1978 when the council wanted to clear out the area around Eldon Street in Vauxhall, it came up against a wall of resistance. At a meeting at which councillors and officers explained to local residents about the move, a man stood up and said: 'No, we're not going.' He was Tony McGann, and that was the start of the Eldonians.

A tight-knit community descended from the Irish immigrants who made their homes in Vauxhall in the 1840s, these people wanted to stay in Vauxhall and bring the area back to life rather than have their community scattered. The area had been one of the most deprived in the country, with atrocious housing conditions, overcrowding, poverty and bad health. The Blitz flattened much of Vauxhall in the 1940s and the city council flattened more of it in the 1960s, demolishing new houses to make way for the second Mersey Tunnel.

This time the Eldonians were determined to win – and their plans began well with the Eldonian Community Association, refurbishing the 1920s walk-up tenements blocks and building new houses in Portland Gardens.

Vauxhall was dealt a major blow when Tate & Lyle's sugar refinery in Love Lane closed in 1981, throwing hundreds of local people out of jobs.

The Eldonians turned the disaster to some good and built 145 new houses on the old Love Lane site.

In 1983 Militant took control of the city council. Tony McGann was summoned by Derek Hatton, who told him that the co-operative project could go ahead, but only under council control – there was no compromise.

Militant ambushed every scheme the Eldonians proposed, but the Eldonians persisted, and with the help of the whole community, local priests, local councillors, and Liverpool's public sector regeneration machine, they achieved a remarkable transformation. Prince Charles was an early supporter, and a fair amount of business backing came, too. Eventually even the Tory government acknowledged the Eldonians' fantastic success.

Over the 1980s the Eldonians built scheme after scheme – sheltered housing, shared ownership houses, a residential care home, hundreds of new houses, a day nursery and leisure facilities. The Leeds-Liverpool Canal has been brought back to life after years of stagnation and neglect. Jobs, though, were still desperately needed; the Eldonians' first business start-up – the Garden Market – didn't survive, but businesses are moving into the Vauxhall area and creating jobs.

Tony McGann and his ever-growing team asked businesses to come and see them, look at the area, meet their potential workforce and think about the opportunities. The Eldonians have had no shortage of visitors over the years: planners, politicians, government groups and journalists came from all over the world. In one year alone they welcomed people from France, Germany, Hungary, Italy, Paraguay, Netherlands, USA and Australia.

Said McGann: 'It's all down to ordinary people. If you invest in people, if you get people to work on their own ideas, share the power, you can get things done.

'It's no good sitting back and crying. If you want something just get on and do it.'

chapter 14
language

The first reference to a noticeable Liverpool accent was in a study by Alexander Ellis in 1880.

The accent is always developing; influences inflicted by film and television are shifting sounds and dialect. Instead of hearing the Irish influence in words like tick *for* thick, *these days young Scousers are more likely to say* fick, *after too much time spent watching* Eastenders. *While an identifiable Scouse accent is unlikely to vanish entirely, it will almost certainly sound very different in 50 years. Before radio, television and the talkies, accents were slow to develop; the globalisation of life has speeded up change enormously.*

Given that some Scousers pronounce hair *as* hur, *there were some misunderstandings in the late 1990s when a pop band called Blur were making headlines at the same time as the newly-elected prime minister Tony Blair (who is, incidentally, married to a Scouser).*

S couse – not so much an accent as a way of life. Until the 19th century Liverpool voices were, by and large, Lancastrian (the county borders only changed in 1974 to create Merseyside), so the accent wouldn't have been so different to Manchester's – which sounds like heresy these days. But the Scouse sound is a fairly new phenomenon, created over centuries of maritime comings and goings, with little bits of words and sounds rolling off the tongues of foreign sailors and falling into the linguistic soup of Liverpool's language. *Bushwa*, for instance, means nonsense or gossip, from the Australian 'bush-wire'; a bit of shipping slang for boss or foreman is *the head serang* – a linguistic gift from Lascar seamen.

It was in the mid-19th century, though, that Scouse really swerved away from Lancashire to become a linguistic planet all of its own, with precious little connection to Lancashire or Cheshire – its immediate neighbours. The Welsh had been streaming into Liverpool for ages, then the Scots started to arrive – and then the Irish, in droves. It was this serendipitous recipe that created the bubble and squeak of Liverpudlian.

Scouse is spoken in a fairly small area. It doesn't reach the outer corners of Merseyside: Southport and St Helens have remained Lancastrian; Birkenhead and Wallasey are definitely Scouse, while a more refined Cheshire sound is heard in the posh bits of the Wirral.

‘ *O for a cob of chuck beneat de boughs*
The Football Echo and a pan of scouse;
A Black and Tan, and Maggie sweatin bricks
In Sevvy's rough, dat's Paradise enough. ’

from The Rubaiyat of Omar Khayyam, translated into Scouse by Stan Kelly
(*Lern Yerself Scouse*)

omplicating matters further, there are several distinct kinds of Liverpool voice; from the nasal drone of John Lennon and the throaty mutter of Ringo to the posh Scouse of Paul and George. Then there's the catarrhal sound that is almost impossible for an outsider to understand; a recent visitor from Sussex overheard two young men debating something, but the visitor has no clue what the topic was: 'They might have been talking Martian,' she said, bemused.

There are academic studies of Liverpool's accent being carried out at Liverpool University, but one of the experts on the subject is Liverpool's Viennese treasure, Fritz Spiegl, whose books on Scouse language have been best-sellers around the world since the 1960s. Spiegl – who came to Liverpool for a visit in 1948 and hasn't left yet – is a world-class musician, which is perhaps why he has such an ear for accent. He explains some of the vagaries of the Liverpudlian sound: 'Where one Liverpudlian will tear his hair, another will tur his 'ur. The *-ur* sound is made through forward lips, the *-air* sounded with a reedy, back-of-the-throat squeeze, lips drawn back and the teeth exposed. In other words, the sound is velarised, the tongue being shifted upwards and backwards toward the velum, or soft palate, which constricts the throat in the way an oboist squeezes his reed.'

Spiegl explains with great clarity the fricative Scouse 'k' and the affricated 't', but his books are funnier than this one, so his linguistic tutorials are better read in context.

Suffice to say that an impressionist, or a new arrival bent on sounding like a local, has a number of tricky verbal contortions to master, not to mention keeping up with the evolutionary shifts made by the language and its expression by the banks of the Mersey. Even the definite article is no such thing in Scouse. In standard English, 'the' is pronounced either *thuh beer* or *thee ale*. In Scouse, 'the' can sound like *thuh, thee, der, duh, dee, deh*.

A man from Blackburn was in a Liverpool pub one New Year's Eve, having a bevvy before going to a party at a friend's house. A happy Scouser accosted the stranger in a friendly fashion and asked him what he was doing there. 'Ah'm gwin to a porrteh,' said the Lancastrian. 'Arr-ey,' said the Scouser. 'I don' go t'them. I go to paaaaaahties, me.'

Listen for the 's' that Scousers tuck inside a 't' – as in tsable, ts'raa and tsarts (only one tart, that is). It's subtle, but distinct.

Fritz Spiegl (pictured below) has a keen ear for local accents and several recipes for Scouse

Liverpudlians love shortening words and names: Pivvy for Pavilion, Lanny for landing stage, thisavvy for this afternoon. Names get diminutives, too: James is Jazzer, Norrie is Nozzer, Currie is Cuzzer, Barry is Bazzer and Michael Heseltine (the 'minister for Merseyside') became Hezza. This is nothing new: the 18th century diarist Thomas Creevey gave nicknames to the great and good of his era: Lord Liverpool (Robert Jenkinson) was Jenky, and Fergy was General Ferguson.

Moggy is now a slang word for cat, used all over the country. It originated in Liverpool and means mouse, but over the years got transferred to the mouse-catcher. A jigger-rabbit, by the way, is an alley cat; and the birds they catch are mickeys (pigeons) and snadgers (sparrows).

Where Londoners dispense with the letter 't' wherever possible, replacing it with a glottal stop (*Tha'll be a bi' o' bu'er*), Scousers replace it with an 'r' or two. So 'that'll be a bit of butter' becomes *darrel be a birra burra*. Liverpudlians appear not to like certain letters: 'h' at the beginning of words tends to vanish; the 'g' at the end of *-ing* goes missing, along with the 'i', so that 'having' becomes *'av'n*. But 'av'n also translates as 'have not', as in the denial of ownership: *I avn gorri*.

Conversely, Scousers will find wonderfully lyrical ways of expressing the least poetic of thoughts; the Scouse use of imagery is worth studying by any student of creative writing. 'Teaching these kids is like shovelling smoke with a billiard cue' is clear enough; more lyrical is the husband's plea to a talkative wife: 'Stop rattlin' like a fart round a curtain pole, woman.' There are numerous powerful images deployed to illustrate stupidity and other undesirable personal qualities: 'He sounds like a pig in pain'; 'That smell's enough to knock a buzzard off a bin lorry'; 'If it was raining soup, he'd be standing with a fork in his hand'; and the delightful: 'He's so low 'e could walk under a snake with a top 'at on.'

There is the purely surreal: 'Yer all me arse and that's bum' and the perplexing: 'Got a gob on it like a farmer's arse on a frosty morning.'

Descriptions of faces and expressions can be charming: 'He's got a face like split welly ... like a ruptured custard ... like a burst boot ... like a robber's dog ... like a wet Echo ... like a slapped arse ... like a dollop of mortal sins ... like an old man's knee ... like a bulldog chewin' a wasp.'

Parental guidance for children comes in colourful chunks: 'Go and clean yerself up – yer look like nobody owns yer'; 'Don't come runnin' to me when you break both yer legs'; 'If you get yerself killed, I'll bloody murder yer!'. And the answers to a child's enquiry about the menu for that evening's repast: 'What's for tea?' 'Iffit .' 'Wass da?' 'Iffit goes around you'll get a bit.' 'What's for tea? Three runs round the table and a kick at the table leg.'

Spud, a true Scouse moggy

Local references in insults are only really effective if the target understands them. Telling a woman she's 'all done up like a May horse' only makes sense if she knows about the horse parade through Liverpool on the May bank holiday. To say of a man that 'he's standing there like one of Lewis's' indicates that he's as stiff as a dummy in a shop window – Lewis's being one of Liverpool's big department stores. Moaning that a tobacco addict 'smokes like a Vauxhall Road chimney' is now well out of date, but originally referred to Muspratt's evil-smelling chemical works in the early 19th century. A tall man is said to be able to 'wind the Liver clock'. To be told you 'talk Blendalsahnds' suggests an over-refined accent, and refers to Blundellsands, a wealthy suburb north of Liverpool.

There must be easier ways to say it, but Liverpudlians enjoy taking the linguistic scenic route: 'He causes more trouble than a pack of camels in a sweet shop'; 'He's that tight, that when his little boy was constipated, he took 'im down the dark cellar and told 'im ghost stories'; and 'The beer's so flat it should be sold in envelopes.'

Sporting passions produce small masterpieces of literary economy. 'He's got both legs in one knicker!' or 'I've seen milk turn faster', and 'He couldn't stop a pig in a jigger!' all suggest incompetence on the football field. Advice to the referee about a breach of the rules might include: 'He 'ad the lace out twice!' (he handled the ball for a long time) or 'He was from 'ere to the Pier Head off!' (he was slightly offside).

Pubs in Liverpool are important cultural centres, of course, where not only can one enjoy a well-informed debate on the topic of the day, but is given little choice, dragged into the conversation willy nilly. In between philosophical bouts, there might be comment about fellow drinkers. One might have been allowed out by his wife only 'for a sniff of the barmaid's apron', while another might be so eager for a drink that 'he'd drink out of a sweaty clog.' And if a chap is delaying buying his round, he might be told: 'Eh, mate, there's a cactus in the bottom of my glass', or 'You waiting for the Queen to buy yer a drink, or wha?'

Scouse is more than a dialect, more than a language: it's a sociolinguistic marvel.

Personal pronouns in Liverpudlian are a little different to the standard: uzz = me; dem = them; yews, yer, yiz = you; yizzl = yourself; me = my; im = him; ar = our; er, air = her.

Jobs, professions and vocations can be intriguing in Liverpool. Dentists are fang farriers or molar maulers; a cardiologist is a ticker quack; piano players are jangler wranglers, and coffin makers are boxers. The rent collector is Satan 'imself. Customs & Excise officials are cuzzies, and the police are scuffers, rozzers, mingies, muskers, or bizzies.

A visitor wanting the train from Birkenhead into Liverpool asked the ticket collector: 'Does this train go to James Street?' Back came the reply: 'Well if it duzn't, luv, it's goin' to bore its own bluddy 'ole.'

225

As well Liverpudlian or Scouser, the good citizens of Liverpool might be called wack or wacker (a nickname used in The Sailor's Farewell of 1768). A nickname for 19th century Liverpool sailors was Dicky Sam, which probably comes from Richard Samuels, the landlord of a seamen's pub on Mann Island, next to Pier Head.

Leece Street in the city centre was named after a Mr Leece, and is still pronounced Leece's Street.

The various tribes of visitors to the area left their mark on the map. Saxon names include Aintree, Allerton, Bootle, Everton, Fazakerley, Garston, Gateacre, Hale, Knowsley, Netherton, Newsham, Speke, Stanley, Toxteth, Tuebrook, Walton, Wavertree, Woolton. Norse names include Childwall, Crosby, Croxteth, Formby, Ince, Kirkby, Kirkdale, Litherland, Thingwall and West Derby.

Place names in Liverpool come from all kinds of sources: the owners or tenants of that area (Hackins Hey, Hope Street, Manesty's Lane), the business that went on there (Leather Lane, Lime Street, Copperas Hill), a big building (Tithebarn Street, Castle Street), to honour an individual (William Brown Street, Lord Nelson Street, Sir Thomas Street), or a local landmark (Knotty Ash – an ancient tree by the local blacksmith's forge).

There are some in-jokes among the pages of the Liverpool A-Z. Jericho Lane, for instance, was the locals' tag for the Puritan settlement at Otterspool; the stream was dubbed Little Jordan. In the Dingle is Holyland – four streets with biblical names (Moses, Isaac, Jacob and David), right opposite the Ancient Chapel of Toxteth on Park Road.

Little Bongs is one of Liverpool's strangest addresses, in Knotty Ash: a pretty Victorian backwater of small cottages, no-one seems to know where the name came from.

Quite a few streets have had names changed; Frog Lane (once a marshy track) became Whitechapel when the meeting house was built there. Paradise Street was once an open sewer running into the Pool until the street was laid out in 1721. Folly Lane, where the Folly Fair was held, became Islington in 1803; Limekiln Lane became Lime Street, and Byrom Street was once Dog Kennel Lane, where Liverpool's pack of hounds was kept.

Streets near Abercromby Square are named after plants in the old Botanic Gardens near Mount Pleasant: Myrtle, Vine, Mulberry, Walnut and Peach. Parliament Street marks the edge of Toxteth Park – Lord Sefton needed a special Act of Parliament to develop the area.

There are place names going back to the Domesday Book and earlier: Speke (Spec, as it was in those days) meant a swine pasture, Garston is a grazing place, and Grassendale a grassy valley. West Derby is from the Norse *dyr*, wild animals, and *-by* meaning village. Breck Road was a place with lots of bracken, and Aigburth is the Druid name for a grove of oaks. Calderstones refers to the Saxon name for wizard – *galdar*, and Tuebrook is the brook of the Norse god Tiw. Delving back into time for accurate meaning is not always straightforward. Toxteth is in the Domesday Book as *Stochestede* – does that mean a stockaded place, or the homestead of Stoch or Toki?

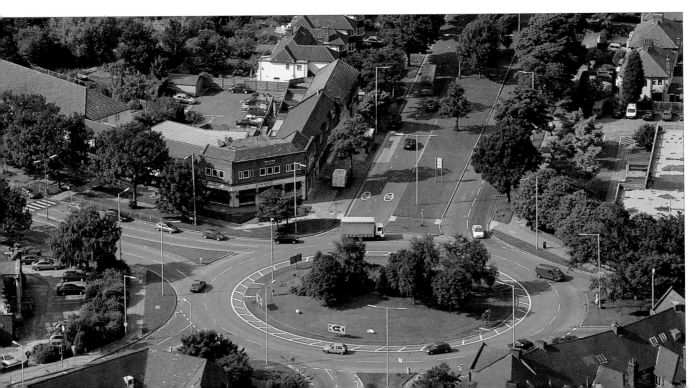

The first and last word: Liverpool. The earliest reference to the name was in 1190, since when the great name has been spelled at least 40 different ways: Lle'rpwll, Lerpwl, Lyrpwl, Lyrpal, Leverpul, Laverpul, Lyfrpwll, Leverpole, Liverpul, Lyrpul, Lytherpul, Lieurpul ... and so on.

What does it mean? The arguments over the meaning of the name continue to rage, with each theory's supporters rubbishing all other theories and casting aspersions on the sanity of anyone believing any theory but theirs.

One theory is that the name derives from the Welsh *Lyfrpwl*, 'the pool of confluence', but another is that the creek that ran from the Moss Lake into the Pool was a red-brown colour from the peat (or the clay, depending who you're listening to), hence 'liver'.

Yet another links Liverpool with the bit of seaweed, or laver, in the beak of the Liver Bird. Laver, an edible seaweed, is also known as sea-liverwort. Obvious! But the problem here is that the Liver Bird looking like a cormorant with seaweed in its beak is a poor reinvention of the original Liver Bird, redrawn when the town's common seal was lost during the siege of 1644. The original Liver Bird is supposed to have been a St John's Eagle, holding a sprig of broom in its beak. The Latin name for broom is *genista*, so it was *planta genista*, the symbol of the Plantagenets, the house of Richard I and King John.

There is extra confusion due to the fact that the *liver* of Liverpool is pronounced to rhyme with *giver*, whereas the *liver* of Liver Bird rhymes with *fiver*.

Then there is the district of Litherland, to the north east of the city centre. What linguistic connection is there between Lither*land* and Liver*pool*?

The name Liverpudlian, incidentally, is someone who lives in Liverpuddle – the nickname given to the city by some cheeky Mancunian, probably. The correct name for a denizen of Liverpool is Liverpolitan.

What about the Mersey? The river, which begins in Cheshire and winds through south Manchester before heading for the sea, is connected to the old kingdom of Mercia which spread over the English Midlands; both names are derived from *maere*, meaning boundary.

As for Scouse and Scousers: it was Tommy Handley, the Liverpool comedian behind the BBC radio show *ITMA* (*It's That Man Again*) during the war, who publicised Scouse.

Scouse is a dish brought over by German, Norwegian or Dutch sailors; properly called Lobscouse or labskaus, this is a flavoursome but rather sloppy stew or hash. The reasonably authentic German recipe calls for salt beef or corned beef, lots of onions, and potatoes; cooked to rags, the meat and onions are turned into the mashed spuds and eaten with pickled cucumber and a glass of beer.

The influence of Lancashire hotpot and Irish stew turned Liverpool Scouse into a cheap stew of mutton, potatoes, onions and whatever other veg came to hand. Eaten with pickled red cabbage or pickled beetroot (and doubtless the glass of beer), this is cheap and cheerful stuff but hardly gourmet nosh. For those who couldn't afford a bit of mutton, it was blind Scouse – just spuds, onions and veg (and a glass of beer).

Not quite salade Niçoise, Wiener schnitzel or even a hamburger, but to a hungry sailor it was ambrosia.

more to read ...

Lern Yerself Scouse
Scouse International
Liverpool packets
all edited by Fritz Spiegl
pub Scouse Press
www.merseyworld.com/scouse_press/

Adrian Henri – paintings
pub National Museums & Galleries on
Merseyside
ISBN 1-902700 07 4

Herdman's Liverpool
Introduction by WCM Jackson
pub The Gallery Press

Well I Never Noticed That!
Statues and monuments in Liverpool
& Bootle
by Andrew F Richardson
pub West Derby Publishing
ISBN 1 871075 01 5

Lost Villages of Liverpool
by Derek Whale
pub 1984
ISBN 0 901314 24 2

Chinese Liverpudlians
The Chinese community in Liverpool
by Maria Lin Wong
pub Liver Press (1989)
ISBN 1 871201 03 9

The American Connection
Liverpool's links with America from
Christopher Columbus to The Beatles
by Ron Jones
pub Ron Jones (1986)
ISBN 0 9511703 2 5

Memories of Liverpool
pub True North Holdings (1998)
ISBN 1 900 463 07 5

Receiving Erin's Children
Philadelphia, Liverpool & the Irish
famine migration 1845-55
by J Matthew Gallman
pub University of Carolina Press
(2000)
ISBN 0-8078-4845-X

The Disinherited Society
A personal view of social
responsibility in Liverpool in the 20th
century
by Margaret Simey
pub Liverpool University Press
ISBN 0-85323-800-6

Charity Rediscovered
A study of philanthropic effort in
19th century Liverpool
by Margaret Simey
pub Liverpool University Press
ISBN 0-85323-078-1

The Life of Riley
25 Years at the Liverpool Echo
by Joe Riley
edited by Gladys Mary Coles
pub Headland (2000)
ISBN 1-902096-62-2

Both Sides of the River
edited by Gladys Mary Coles
pub Headland (1993)
ISBN 0903074656

Liverpolitana
by Peter Howell Williams
pub Merseyside Civic Society (1971)
ISBN 9502018 0 4

Liverpool Heritage Walk
by Philip Browning
pub Bluecoat Press (1990)
ISBN 1 872568 25 4

Novels:

Framed
by Ron Ellis
pub Headline
ISBN 0-7472-6220-9

Suspicious Minds
by Martin Edwards
pub New English Library
ISBN 0-340-73922-3

Past Reason
by Margaret Murphy
pub Pan
ISBN 0-330-38992-0

Poetry:

The Way Things Are
by Roger McGough
pub Penguin (2000)
ISBN 0-140-28632-2

Love Poems
by Brian Patten
pub HarperCollins (1991)
ISBN 0586092056

The Mersey Sound
by Henri, McGough, Patten
pub Penguin
ISBN 0140585346

Down in Liverpool
by Jim Bennett
pub Long Neck Media (CD)

Curse of the Killer Hedge
by David Bateman
pub Iron Press (1996)
ISBN 0906228557

G

H

A selection of Liverpool superlatives: first, best, longest, biggest ...

1648 The first recorded cargo from America lands in Liverpool 1679 Liverpool's mayor founds the first charity for sailors 1715 Steer's Old Dock in Canning Place is the first wet dock to be controlled by floodgates 1758 Building of the Lyceum, the first circulating library 1763 The first lighthouses to use parabolic mirrors are built by Liverpool's dock Master at Hoylake and Bidston 1770 Work begins on the Leeds-Liverpool Canal, the longest and highest in Britain, finished in 1816 1776 Ether is first used as an anaesthetic 1786 Great Howard Street houses the first purpose built prison 1790 World's first American consul, James Maury is posted to Liverpool 1791 The first school for the blind opens at Commutation Row 1793 Liverpool becomes the first and only municipality with the right to issue its own money 1803 Liverpool Underwriter's Association is the world's first 1814 St George's, in Everton, is the first all cast iron church 1822 James Muspratt opens an alkali works in Vauxhall – the origins of ICI 1823 First mechanics lending library 1825 World's first school for deaf people 1830 World's first passenger railway line built by Liverpool & Manchester Railway Company 1830 The world's first train shed and large wooden station roof are built at Crown Street station 1830 MP William Huskisson is the first railway fatality 1835 Lacy's publishes the world's first railway timetable 1838 The first travelling Post Office runs between Liverpool and Birmingham 1840 Cunard's wooden paddle-steamer Britannia is the first scheduled transatlantic passenger service 1840 Liverpool appoints Britain's first borough engineer 1840 World's first photograph developing and printing service 1841 Brunswick Buildings: the first purpose-built office block 1841 The Society for the Prevention of Cruelty to Animals (later RSPCA) is founded 1842 First public baths and wash-houses in Upper Frederick St 1844 Blackburne House is the first girl's day grammar school 1845 Liverpool is the destination of the first package tour 1847 Dr Duncan becomes the world's first Medical Officer 1848 First British trades council 1850 Liverpool is the first borough to start a library committee 1851 The first provincial Children's Hospital opens in the city 1856 The 21 ton Horsfall Gun – the largest in the world – is built at the Mersey Forge in Sefton Street ; it could fire a 300lb cannon ball five miles 1857 Liverpool Rugby Club is the world's first 1857 Liverpool starts Britain's first chess club 1859 The first nurse paid to look after the poor 1860 First purpose built public library 1861 Britain's first ecumenical conference 1861 A Liverpool-made gun fires the first shot of the American Civil War 1862 The first street refuges for pedestrians built 1862 First provincial school of nursing set up in Liverpool 1864 The first slum clearance scheme gives the Medical Officer power to demolish unsafe and unfit buildings 1867 Britain's first steamroller is bought by Liverpool 1865 The last act of the American Civil War was the surrender to the Mayor of Liverpool of the Confederate ship Shenandoah, by her captain James Waddell, at the Town Hall 1867 Liverpool Velocipedes is the country's first cycling club 1868 Liverpool is the first borough to secure an Act of Parliament to establish a tram network 1869 St Martins Cottages are the first municipal housing 1870 Liverpool Society of Accountants is the first 1875 The first disarmament campaign: Liverpool Peace Society 1876 Britain's first gorilla arrives at Liverpool Docks 1877 The Walker Art Gallery is the first UK public art gallery 1880 Liverpool hosts the first Irish Nationalist MP in England – TP O'Connor at the Liverpool Exchange 1883 The Liverpool Society for the Prevention of Cruelty to Children – forerunner of the NSPCC – is founded 1884 Britain's first female doctor opens a practice in Liverpool 1886 The first under-river tunnel is built under the Mersey 1886 Northern Hospital has the first purpose-built ambulance 1889 Britain's first mosque opens on Mount Vernon Street 1889 Liverpool Gas Company installs the first pre-payment gas meters 1889 Liverpool's police force is the first to wear rubber-soled boots for night duty 1892 Liverpool University opens the first Marine Biological Station 1893 The world's first overhead electric railway built in the city 1894 First ever radio broadcast made by Oliver Lodge, Liverpool University professor of physics 1895 First British school of architecture and applied art 1896 The x-ray is used in medical diagnosis for the first time 1897 Liverpool is the first to employ female health visitors 1898 First city to employ a municipal bacteriologist 1898 School of Tropical Medicine is the first founded in the UK 1901 Liverpool runs the first anti-tuberculosis campaign in Britain 1901 Seaforth Sands gets the first escalator in a railway station 1902 The School of Tropical medicine is the first British medical institution to gain the Nobel Prize for Medicine 1902 Hatton Garden fire station has the first motor fire engine 1904 The University of Liverpool founds the first school of veterinary science in the country 1909 Eleanor Rathbone becomes the first woman councillor 1909 Woolworths opens its first British store on Church Street 1912 First automatic telephone exchange 1913 New York World carries the first 'word cross', or crossword, compiled by Scouser Arthur Wynne 1913 Liverpool-born John Archer is elected Britain's first black mayor, in Battersea 1917 First public commercial library in the country 1919 Liverpool's is the first – and only – police force to strike 1919 The first department of oceanography opens at the University 1924 Lister Drive power station has the first hyperbolic cooling tower 1925 Crosshall Street hosts the country's first Juvenile Court 1927 The Bluecoat is the first British Arts centre 1927 West Derby is the site of the first municipal Jewish cemetery 1932 The first purpose-built boxing stadium (Bixteth Street) 1933 Dr Minnitt at Liverpool's maternity hospital uses gas and air in childbirth for the first time 1934 Liverpool Police are the first force to use two-way radios 1934 Tatler, on Church Street, is first provincial news theatre 1936 The Liverpool Corporation Act is the first giving the council the right to buy, sell and develop land 1936 Speke sees the first purpose-built municipal industrial estate 1943 Richard Burton makes his theatrical debut at the Royal Court 1944 Hua Chow Pao is Britain's first Chinese newspaper 1946 Liverpool FC's Jack Chalmer becomes the first player to score three consecutive hat-tricks 1947 World's first radar lighthouse 1948 The Mersey Ferries were the first to have a radar system for safe navigation in fog 1950 The first helicopter service flies from Liverpool to Cardiff 1952 Hospital radio kicks off in Liverpool 1952 First package holiday flight departs from Liverpool airport 1953 Liverpool's Lita Roza is the first woman to top the pop charts 1959 National Westminster opens the first drive-in bank 1959 First mass x-ray campaign 1960 Martin's is the first bank to use a computer 1962 The Mersey Docks and Harbour Company is the first port authority to use a computer 1964 Liverpool's police force is the first to use closed circuit TV 1965 Liverpool FC is the first football club to be televised 1967 First seminar for orchestra conductors 1968 World's best selling poetry book published by Liverpool 8 Poets 1984 Liverpool FC becomes the first club to win three major trophies in one season 1984 The first British International Garden Festival is held in Liverpool 1997 The Roy Castle Foundation for Lung Cancer Research is the world's first dedicated cancer research centre 2001 Liverpool is named World Capital of Pop with 53 No1 chart hits since 1953 2001 Liverpool FC the first club to win three major cups in one season.